PRELUDE TO D-DAY
Devon's Role in the Storming of Hitler's Europe

For Bryan and Maria

PRELUDE TO D-DAY

Devon's Role in the Storming of Hitler's Europe

GERALD WASLEY

HALSGROVE

First published in Great Britain in 2014
Copyright © Gerald Wasley 2014

All rights reserved. No part of this publication may be reproduced,
stored in a retrieval system, or transmitted in any form or by any
means without the prior permission of the copyright holder.
British Library Cataloguing-in-Publication Data

A CIP record for this title is available from the British Library

ISBN 978 0 85704 245 3

HALSGROVE
Halsgrove House,
Ryelands Business Park,
Bagley Road, Wellington, Somerset TA21 9PZ
Tel: 01823 653777   Fax: 01823 216796
email: sales@halsgrove.com

Part of the Halsgrove group of companies.
Information on all Halsgrove titles is available at: www.halsgrove.com

Printed in China by Everbest Printing Co Ltd

Foreword

SEVENTY YEARS AGO an Armada of ships set out from the shores of Britain to land troops on the beaches of Normandy. Success would mark the first stages of the defeat of Nazi Germany and the liberation of Europe. The American force that set out from their ports of departure was part of the greatest Armada of all times. This massive fighting force also comprised the British Second Army made up of British, British Empire, British Commonwealth and Allied forces which were scheduled to assault Gold, Juno and Sword beaches. The American military force was to land further west along the Normandy coast at Omaha beach and Utah beach.

Prior to the D-Day landings a vast amount of planning, building up supplies, training and rehearsals were carried out by all the military forces concerned to meet the vast challenge ahead of them. This book focuses on the American forces that were based in South West England, with emphasis on their presence and activities in Devon. However for purposes of placing the D-Day preparations in context I have also referred to the American forces based in Cornwall. My main themes are the Woolacombe Assault Training Centre, the compulsory evacuation of villagers in the South Hams area to make way for the Slapton Battle Training Area and the major amphibious exercises carried out at Slapton Sands.

I have taken the opportunity to help dispel the myth that still exists, that the E boat attack associated with Exercise Tiger occurred off Slapton Sands and not at Lyme Bay, Dorset. Further evidence is given of the friendly-fire massacre of American troops that took place on Slapton Sands the day before the Lyme Bay disaster. However this major incident confirms the stories that have been circulating for many years that there were graves of American soldiers buried in the Slapton Battle Training Area, albeit in the Blackawton and/or Strete area. This little known tragedy had until recently been suppressed by the American Government.

Dr Gerald Wasley
Molesey, Surrey. 2014.

Acknowledgements

MOST OF MY information is taken from primary American and British sources deposited at various reputable archives and published secondary sources. As the events described happened seventy years ago I have limited the use oral evidence to those people who are still alive and who lived through the war years. I based this decision on the belief held by the distinguished historian, the late Angus Calder, who believed 'memory does not always deliver the truth'. I wish to thank the following people and organisations that have in their various ways helped me in producing this account.

The author has made searches to trace copyright owners of images published in this book, sometimes without success. To these copyright owners the author apologises and asks them through the publisher to contact him so that any future editions will include the proper acknowledgements.

I would like to acknowledge the help or use of their material from the following individuals. The list below has not been prepared in any form of priority: John Anderson, Nevil Shute Norway Foundation; Richard Bass; Arthur Clamp; Dominique François; Jackie Evans Ivybridge; Nigel Lewis; Menor Pipe; Maria Jane Benge; Bryan Benge; David and Muriel Murch; Norman Howard; Gladys Inder, Dartmouth; Gwen Pearce, Ivybridge; Dale Rodman, USA.

I wish to thank the staff of the following organisations that have obtained images, published papers or information that has helped me in my research: The National Archives, Kew, London; The American National Archives, Washington, USA; The Naval Historical Center, Washington, USA; The Dwight D Eisenhower Library, Abilene, USA; Kingston Heritage Centre, Kingston, London; Kingfisher multimedia Braunton, Devon; Dartmouth Museum, Devon; Kingsbridge Heritage Centre, Devon; British Newspaper Library, Colindale, London; Appledore Museum, Devon; The *Western Morning News*, Plymouth; *Dartmouth Chronicle*, Devon; Plymouth Library, Devon; HMS *Britannia*, Royal Naval College Dartmouth, Devon; Ivybridge Library, Devon; Molesey Library, Surrey; Reading Agriculture College, Berks; Imperial War Museum, London; West Devon Record Office, Plymouth; Bloomsbury Publishing Limited, London; Knights Photographer, Barnstaple, Devon; *Life* Magazine, USA; Society of Friends, London; West Country Studies Library, Exeter, Devon.

Contents

1	Devon in the Thirties	9
2	The Home Front: Devon	26
3	Establishing US Naval Bases	42
4	American Troops in Devon	53
5	The Woolacombe Assault Training Centre	69
6	The Evacuation of Villagers in South Hams	88
7	The Major Amphibious Exercises	109
8	Exercise Tiger: 26 April–28April 1944	132
9	Departure for D-Day	148
	Memorials	156
	Bibliography	157

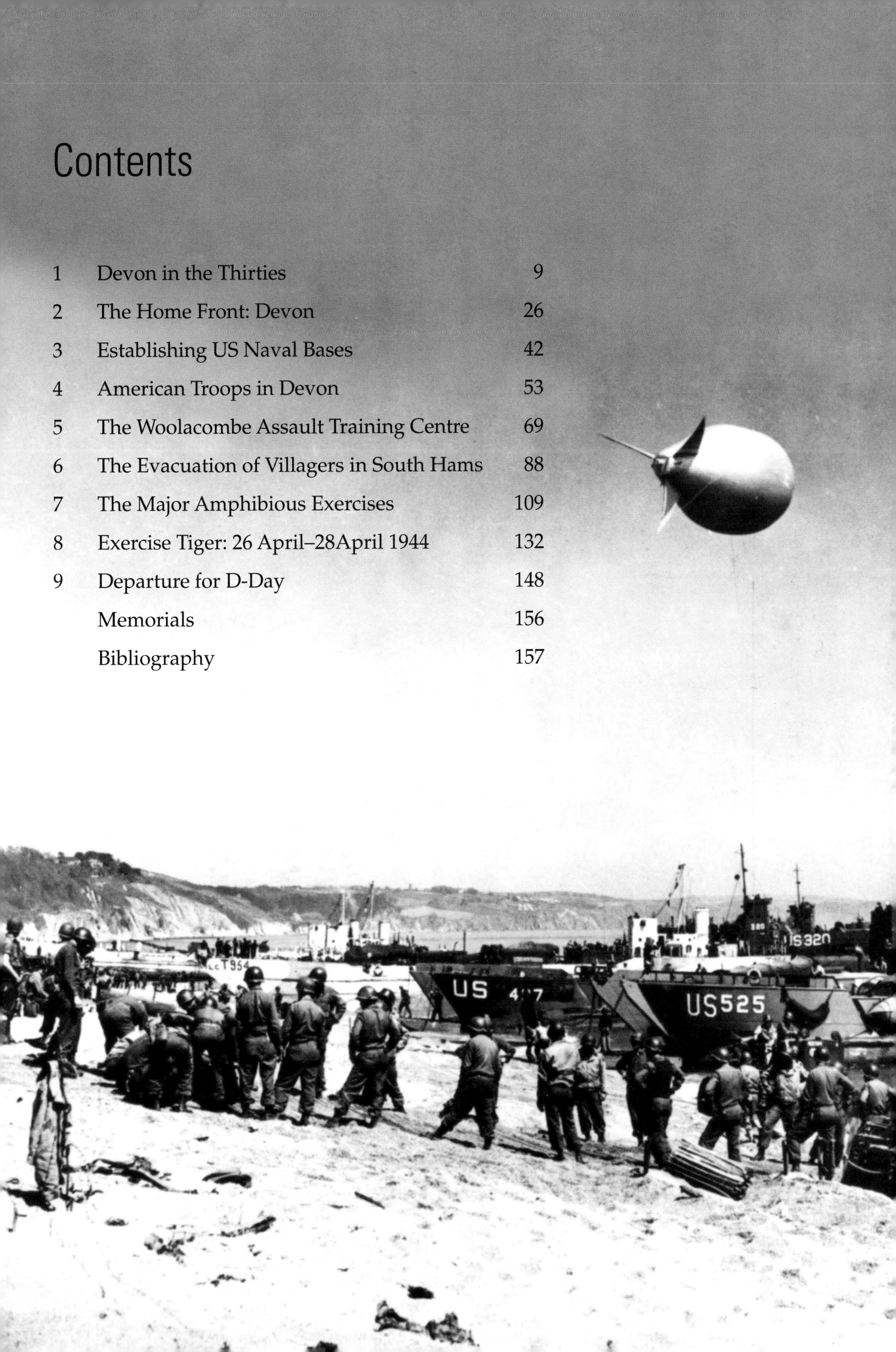

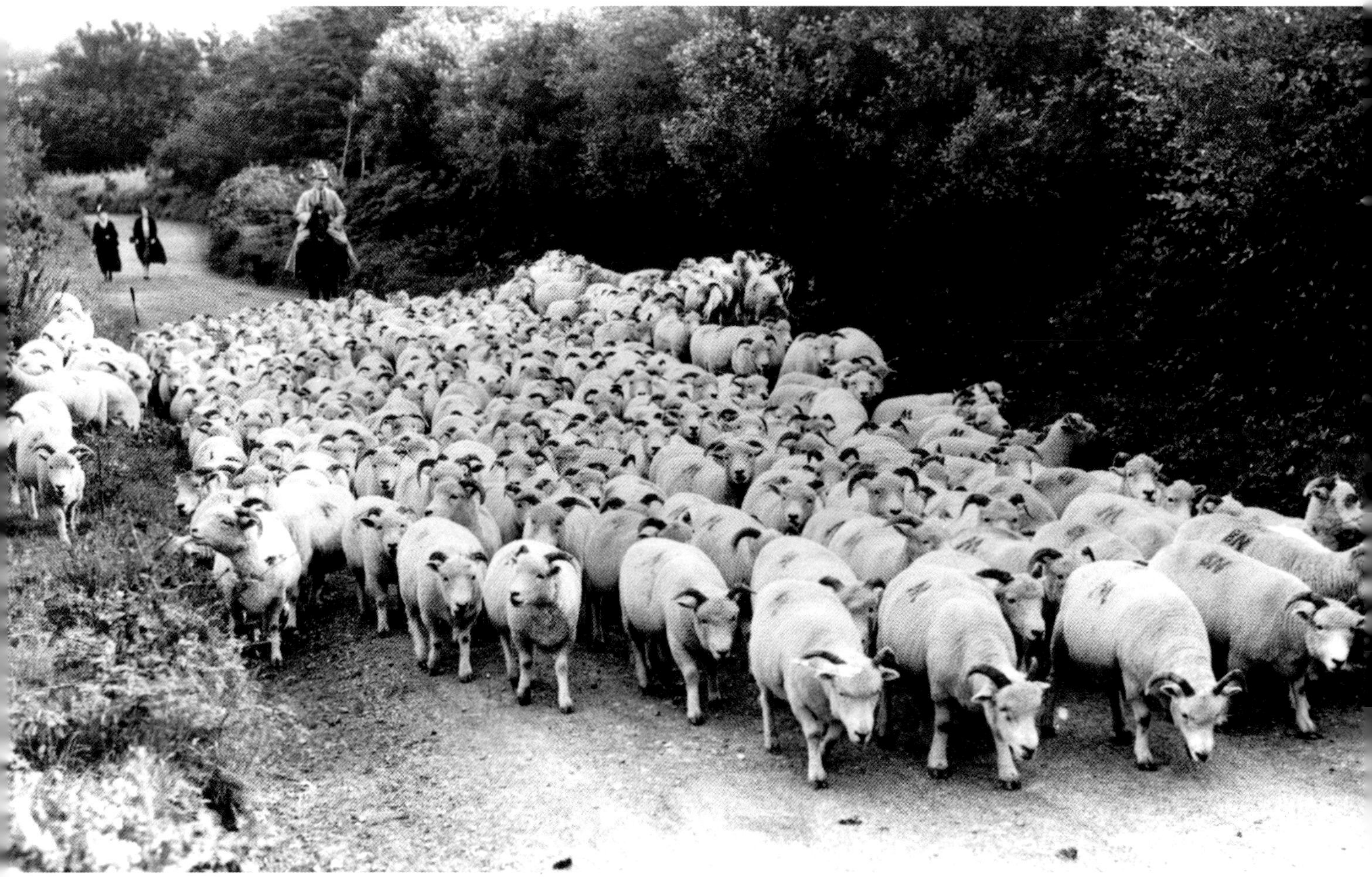

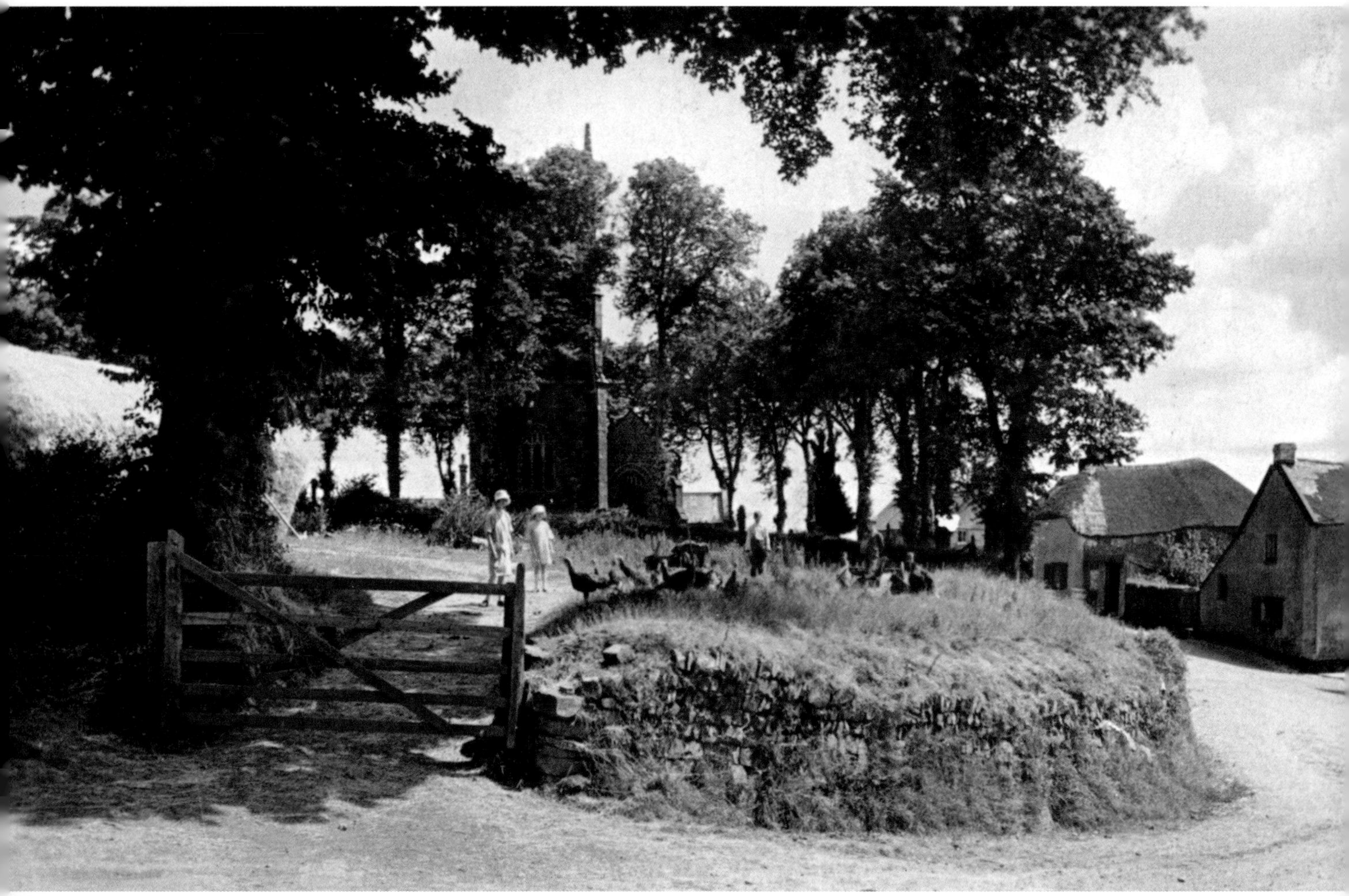

1 Devon in the Thirties

PEACE HAD COME with the signing of the Armistice in November 1918, but at a terrible price for many people. The Great War had taken away a large part of a generation of young men. In Devon there were many widows, hundreds of children were fatherless, parents bereft of son's killed. For many young women who had been betrothed there would be no wedding. The consequences of the First World War had bought about changes in social and patriotic attitudes in British society that were manifest in the post-war years of Britain. The young men recoiled from warfare. The idea of patriotic virtue no longer commanded the general imagination.[1] For many years in post-war Devon the presence of the blind, disfigured and mentally scarred ex-servicemen was to been seen out on the streets. The Prime Minister, Lloyd George replied to his own question, what is our task? He declared: "To make Britain a country fit for heroes to live in." At the 1919 Paris Peace Conference, where there was discord among the victorious Allied nations, Field Marshall Foch prophesied, "This is not peace, it is an Armistice for twenty years." How right he was!

The ending of the war was replaced with severe economic problems that resulted in mass unemployment and severe cuts in Government expenditure, including cuts in unemployment payments by the implementations of the Geddes Axes.[2] Among the people that suffered were the Devon farmers who had been severely affected by the sudden dramatic fall in market prices that during the war had been guaranteed by the Government, but which now rescinded their agreement. Devon agriculture, with a few exceptions, was in a miserable plight. Farm workers left the land for the town with the hope of seeking a better wage; that is, if they could find employment. What were once the farmworkers cottages lay in a state of disrepair and rusting agricultural machinery was abandoned in unkempt fields.

Devon shipyards also suffered in the economic crisis. The decline in orders at Appledore, North Devon resulted in local men moving to Devonport hoping to find employment in the Royal Dockyard, but here men were also being laid off. Devon's unemployment problem was disturbing but it was not so severe as in other parts of Britain, for example, in the great the industrial towns of the north or the coal mining communities of South Wales. However it was difficult for people used to working on the land to find alternative work in Devon, particularly as there was very little industry in the county.

The latter years of the 1920s were marked by a social revolution, with mass entertainment brought about by the introduction of talking pictures. In 1928 Alexander Fleming discovered penicillin, the forerunner of antibiotic therapy that defined the decade.

Opposite, top: A familiar 1930s Devon rural scene; a herd of sheep on the move.

Bottom: A peaceful scene of rural Roborough, showing turkeys wandering in the churchyard. With a population of 252 in 1930, this tiny Devon community is located on the western edge of Dartmoor

This picture was taken around 1930 along the main Princetown to Moretonhampstead road, looking towards Postbridge. This was a time when an increasing number of visitors were coming to Dartmoor, although the moor retained its reputation as a forebidding place.

A snapshot of a middle class Devon family celebrating Christmas Day 1936 in the village of Horrabridge, near Yelverton.

Guide books were becoming popular in the 1930s, as more people took to hiking holidays through Devon's beautiful countryside.

The popular Croyde Bay holiday camp, built in 1930, was located near Georgeham in North Devon. It offered hutted accommodation for campers for £2.25 per week. During the Second World War American soldiers who were attached to the Woolacombe Assault Training Centre used the camp.

The 1930s began with Britain still experiencing severe economic problems that reduced families to penury; the decade ended by sending many menfolk to war. Devon in the thirties was in transition, the main employment during in the 1930s being in the service industries, with personal service providing the most single source of work.[3] Throughout the county there was still plenty of evidence of Old England, of castles, manor houses, thatched cottages and ancient stone bridges set against the glorious countryside and moorland. The industrious Victorians had left a legacy of well-built public buildings, churches, chapels and schools; towns still had their Victorian horse troughs and public drinking water fountains. Travellers on foot met few people walking between the villages and towns as increasing numbers of people travelled by train, bus and motorcar. The horse and cart was still used but was being replaced by motor vehicles. In some areas of the county, the face of the communities had changed with the building of petrol stations and cinemas, and the rhythm of life varied depending if one lived in a town or in a rural part of the county. In some areas Devon was becoming urbanised, yet one could still wander through the streets of some towns that abruptly changed to the countryside. Most people owned a wireless set – a major asset particularly for those people living in rural area for they no longer felt so remote.

The 1931 census revealed that Devon had a population of 732,968 people. It was the second largest county in England and Wales with a population density that was less than

Farmers and their drovers at the street cattle market in Modbury, South Devon.

half that of the rest of the country. Between 1931 and 1938 the county's population increased by 1.2 per cent. Apart from Plymouth the most urbanised region of Devon was in the south-east. The largest communities in Devon were in Plymouth, Exeter, Torquay, Paignton, Newton Abbot, Barnstaple, Exmouth and Teignmouth. According to a social survey there were evident fluctuations of population growth and decrease within the county. For example, there was a decrease in the number of residents during the 1930s in north and west Devon while, in contrast, the south-eastern and western population increased, with the exception of the South Hams where many of the village populations declined. In common with other isolated towns, villages, hamlets and farms throughout the county, Dartmoor remained sparsely inhabited.[4]

In the mid 1930s Devon celebrated a number of events associated with the royal family. This began in 1935 with the Silver Jubilee of King George V and Queen Mary and ended in May 1937 with the Coronation of King George VI and Queen Elizabeth. One person described the delights of living in Devon during the 1930s: "it felt that each day would never end".

During the succeeding years of the 1930s the economy began to improve helped by Britain re-arming. This was also a period of revolutionised high street shopping with many large stores appearing throughout Devon. "New consumerism" had arrived, heralding in a social and economic order based on creating and fostering a desire to purchase goods and services. People with money could spend their time shopping for pleasure, buying fashion clothes, quality furnishing and the newly introduced labour-saving devices. Middle class families that were credit worthy could purchase a refrigerator or vacuum cleaner on weekly instalments.[5]

Local residents throng Okehampton on the occasion of the Coronation of King George VI and Queen Elizabeth. Union flags decorate the buildings and bunting is hung across the Square. Best clothes were worn for such an important event and everyone, with few exceptions, wore a hat.

As with the rest of Britain, class distinction was an integral feature of Devon society during the 1930s. Historians will argue over the difficulties of defining social class, as the boundaries between classes are blurred, but the recording of class structure is important because it contributes evidence for future generations about the type of society that existed at a particular period of time. Before the Second World War in Devon there was a sameness of life for most people, irrespective of an individual's

A busy street scene in the popular market town of Barnstaple where people came from the surrounding villages to purchase household goods in its famous covered market.

High Street Exeter during the 1930s. A time when the horse and cart was still being used for household deliveries, but was being replaced by the motor van.

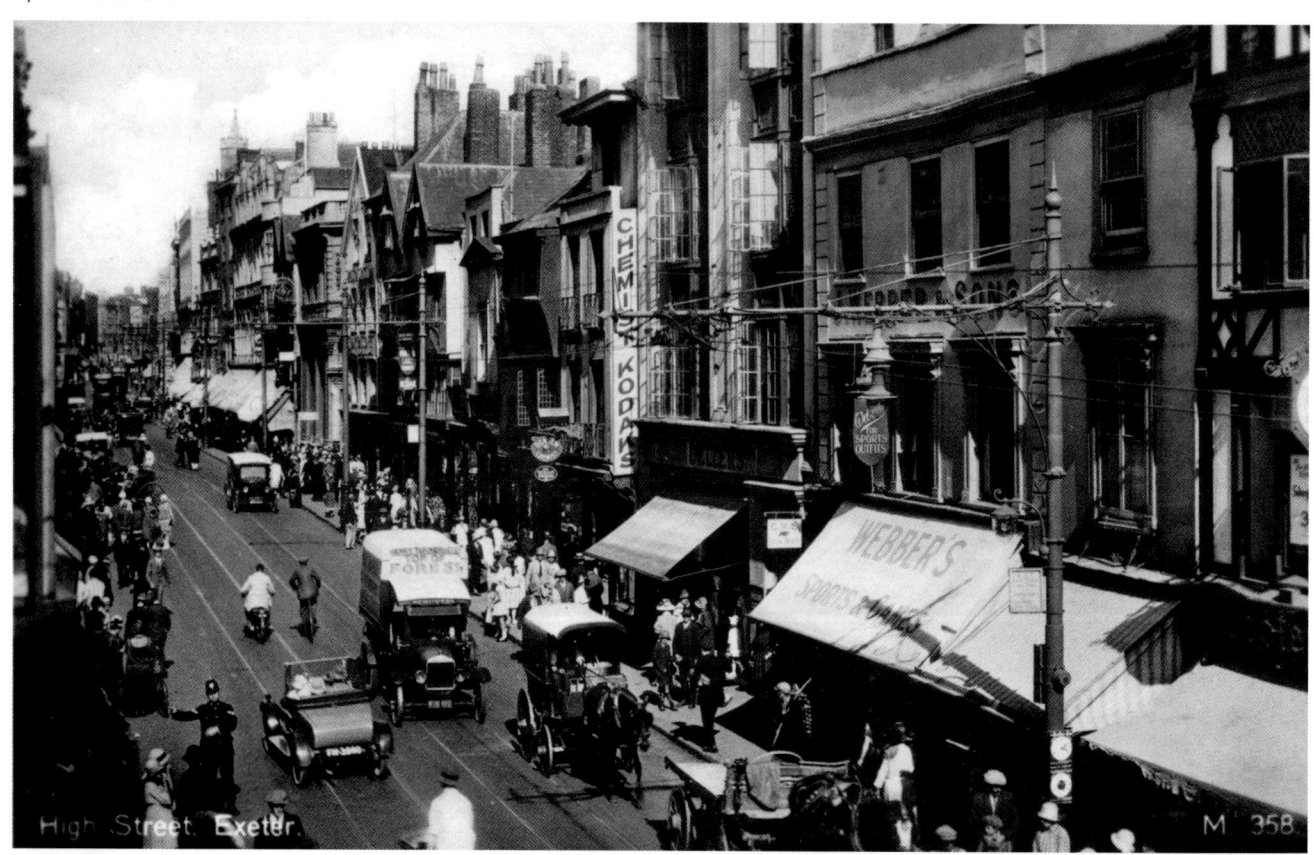

quality of life. Many middle class Devon families employed day servants to help in the household.

Most larger communities had a market day. This for villagers was a day out. They would travel to their nearest market town, not only to visit the market but also to explore other shops and perhaps treat themselves to a meal at one of the cafés or restaurants. The two main regional shopping centres were Exeter and Plymouth, although Barnstaple and other similar towns attracted weekly crowds of people from the outlying areas.

Midweek early closing day provided a chance for shopkeepers and their employees to visit friends or relations or to go somewhere locally for an afternoon tea. Better access by road and rail meant that towns such as Barnstaple and Paignton expanded, at the expense of the rich fertile farmland being taken to build new houses. Exeter in the thirties was also in a state of expansion as new housing estates were creating new suburbs.

Plymouth with its naval base at Devonport was also a garrison town for the Army and Royal Marines. In 1928 it had achieved its status as a City, having been formed in 1914 by the merging of three towns, Devonport, Stonehouse and Plymouth. Whatever the consequences of the merger the city remained socially as three distinct communities.

Suburban Devon was in a state of development. This was partly due to the continuous influx of new residents into the county, mainly retired people or others intent on escaping the industrial centres, settling mainly in north or south-east Devon. However these 'newcomers' were important as they made a significant contribution to the local economy with their shopping and their employment of local tradesmen.

Above left: Bedford Street, the shopping centre of Plymouth, decorated to celebrate the Coronation of King George VI on 12 May 1937. Within four years of this photograph being taken most of the buildings in this picture had been destroyed during the Plymouth Blitz.

Above right: A snapshot taken in the early 1930s of Appledore market, North Devon.

Open-air musical concerts, particularly military bands, were very popular throughout Devon before the Second World War. This picture shows crowds of people at a concert in Barnstaple in the 1930s.

Tea Gardens were very popular in Devon prior to the Second Word War. They were places one could purchase a Devon cream tea or a plate of 'fancies'. This picture shows the Beach Tea Garden, Croyde, North Devon.

Ladies of fashion take the air along the promenade in Torquay during the early 1930s. The town, known as the English Riviera, attracted large numbers of visitors, many of them wealthy, who stayed in the resort's high class hotels.

Contemporary photographs and local newspaper fashion advertisements suggest that the same women's fashion prevailed through out the county. Devon women, when out in the street, tended to wear a soft felt hat, a neatly pressed cotton blouse and a below-knee-length skirt or a tailored woollen suit. In warmer weather the trend for Devon women was to wear a cotton frock and to carry a handbag and summer gloves. For men, the quality and cut of the cloth they wore for their suit indicated their social class. Many had a 'Sunday Best' suit. Shirts were usually white, with a stiff starched detachable collar. Few men went out into the streets without wearing a hat, and this would be removed if they entered a building, or at least touched, if they met a lady. Photographs during the 1930s show most men wearing a trilby hat or flat cap. A man wearing a bowler hat was recognised as a professional person.

The Slapton area of the South Hams

South Hams, with its scenic splendour, is the location concerned in the main theme of this book. The region stretches from the port of Dartmouth to the outer limits of Plymouth. The northern part of the region's hinterland is bounded by the busy A38. It could have been a hand of an ancient god holding a giant compass that reached down from the sky and inscribed a three mile curve that defines Slapton beach. Just as aesthetic is the crescent shape of fine shingle that makes up Blackpool Sands, set against a backcloth of green foliage and elegant pine trees. It is this area that today attracts thousands of tourists, despite its geographical isolation. Many of the small villages and hamlets are hidden from view by the steep undulating hills that appear to sweep down to the water's edge. Narrow sunken lanes, a relic of packhorse days, criss cross each other. In past times many of the fields around the villages of Chillington and Stokenham were fenced with shiners (locally quarried slate) to prevent grazing cattle from straying.[6]

During the decade of the 1930s, most of the South Hams village populations decreased.[7] For example, depopulation became severe in the parish of Blackawton where the number of residents fell significantly. Gone were the days when the village would organise a large agricultural show, second only to Kingsbridge. Yet the small village of East Allington where the local residents say "You only find our village when you are lost" had increased its population in the early 1930s.[8] Farming had always been the main source of employment in this

Blackpool Sands in the 1930s. This was a popular venue for visitors between the two wars. It was also a favourite local venue for Dartmouth people as they had no beach of their own. This peaceful summer scene was transformed during the Second World War when the American forces used the beach for amphibious exercises.

A summertime beach scene at Westward Ho!, North Devon. It was on this beach that some of the experimental trials of the Great Panjandrum were carried out.

The Southern Railway station at Braunton during the 1930s. The area was well known for its daffodils that were taken by train to be sold on the London market. During the Second World War trains of American Soldiers arrived at Braunton Station to participate in the training programs held at the Woolacombe Assault Training Centre.

A popular route in south-west Devon during the 1930s was the scenic coastal journey of the Great Western Railway passenger trains that made their way from Exeter via Torquay and Paignton to Kingswear. Here the train is running between Dawlish and Teignmouth.

part of the region. Most of the farms were small, worked by the family assisted by one or two farm labourers. Up to the outbreak of war the horse had been the beast of burden used for ploughing and hauling the carts, perhaps loaded with swedes. Few farmers at that time owned a tractor. In the barley belt around Blackawton there were 64 registered holdings that employed 62 farmworkers. The South Hams was renowned for its South Devons, a breed of cattle reared in the area capable of producing large quantities of milk with a high butterfat content.

Many of the properties here were traditional cob-built, but there were buildings, for example at the village of Strete, where there were substantially built stone and brick houses. The roofs of the thatched cottages in the area were often made from the reeds harvested from the freshwater lake at Slapton Ley, a stretch of water separated from the sea by the raised beach road that runs from Strete Gate to Torcross village. The Ley during the 1930s could be fished by obtaining a permit from the Royal Sands Hotel. Despite all the fresh water that fed into the Ley there were no municipal piped domestic water supplies. A hot dry summer would turn a season into a drought. Villagers in the area would have to obtain their water from the shallow wells, the water having to be boiled before drinking.

The market town of Kingsbridge in the 1930s. Although most of the shops have changed ownerships over the years, the town has not significantly altered in appearance.

Nor were many local households connected to mains electricity. Homes were lit by candle or oil lamps; a kitchen grate was used for cooking.

Market Day was something special for the local farmers. Cattle markets in the area were at Dartmouth, Kingsbridge and Modbury. Farmers attending a market would wear their best country clothes and polished tan leather gaiters. If the farmer was accompanied by his wife they may have made the journey to market by horse and trap. Market day was an opportunity for the farmer's wife to rent a stall to sell her farm produce, for example clotted cream, butter and poultry. Villagers travelled to market by local bus which served many of the scattered communities. The nearest railway station in the Slapton area of South Hams was at Dartmouth. Here it was necessary to take the ferry across the River Dart to catch the train at Kingswear that could take travellers directly to London. Alternatively trains might be taken from the GWR branch line at Kingsbridge.

Dartmouth owed its maritime history to its deep-water anchorage. During the 1930s, although the picturesque town attracted visitors, the ancient borough was in decline with the population falling to 6000 residents. The centre of Dartmouth retained its medieval look, but many of the wooden-beamed and gabled properties had been neglected and were in need of repair.

Unemployment was a problem. Some local men worked as uniformed stewards, a poorly paid job, at the Royal Naval College overlooking the riverside town. There was little other work for them to do. Better wages were paid at Phillip & Son, the local boatyard where skills befitting qualified tradesmen were required for the construction of metal or wooden vessels. However the boatyards were experiencing a decline in orders in this period.

As in many other areas of Devon, local women, some girls of fourteen years of age, were employed as day servants by middle class families, while the wealthier Dart valley families required their servants to live in. Dartmouth had its share of impoverished families who were partly fed by the town's soup kitchen set up in the market place. In contrast money was no problem for Vernon McAndrew, a retired millionaire who lived in a grand house at Warfleet, overlooking the river.

Dartmouth Town Council considered ways to stop the decline of the town's population and to improve Dartmouth's economic situation. One proposal was to bridge the River Dart,

Foss Street, Dartmouth, one of the narrow streets found in this small riverside market town. In the distance is the ancient church of St Saviour's.

A 1930s panoramic view of the village of Torcross, Slapton beach and the freshwater Ley.

The Slapton Ley, seen here in the mid 1930s, was once a fisherman's paradise. In parts of the Ley tall rushes grew and these were scythed, harvested, stacked and dried, then used to thatch the roofs of local houses.

a subject that had been debated on many previous occasions. Opponents of a bridge being built argued that whatever asset this might have for the town, the peaceful environment of the South Hams would be ruined; these opponents eventually won the day.

The main attraction for visitors to Dartmouth was a trip up the River Dart on a paddle steamer. Travelling up the river in the 1930s would mean passing the ocean-going mercantile ships that were laid up because of the international surplus of shipping.

To the West, above and beyond Dartmouth the fertile land of the South Hams is revealed, with graceful undulating hills. The main road out of Dartmouth to Torcross winds up and down, passing Stoke Fleming and the village of Strete and offering glimpses of coves and bays. The peaceful panoramic view is superb as Blackpool Sands comes into view.

As Dartmouth lacked its own beach many townspeople would choose to travel by bus to nearby Blackpool Sands as their local seaside, in preference to the crowded Torbay resorts. From Strete Gate the long road runs close to the sea and separates the fresh water Ley from Slapton beach. Up to outbreak of the Second World, the Royal Sands Hotel was the best known hotel in the South Hams. The hotel, which stood approximately where the American evacuation Memorial now stands, was destroyed during the Second World War. On a fine summer's day a small steamer would arrive and sail up to the floating jetty where the

A large family picnic on Slapton beach during the 1930s. Although the area had yet to developed as a popular tourist venue, there was a growing number of motorists who ventured in to the area seeking new places to visit.

The Floating Bridge higher ferry, Dartmouth c.1930s.

The opening of the North Devon Aerodrome, Heaton, in 1933. The air service offered schedule flights to Lundy, Cardiff, Plymouth and Jersey. When it closed early in the Second World War adjacent land was used to build RAF Chivenor.

passengers would disembark and enter the hotel for a Devon cream tea, after which the passengers reboarded the boat and would sail away across Start Bay. These were halcyon days of the thirties.

At Slapton beach the sea breaks with a pleasant sound as the surf ceaselessly washes back the pebbles. Yet the magnificent scenic setting of Start Bay hides the grim history of the Bay. In the First World War, Start Bay was a lair for German U Boats; it is the graveyard for many ships and their crews that were lost in the area by enemy action. No wonder the beachcombers of Slapton Sands were able to find so many personal items. One particular naval disaster settled the fate of the crew of cruiser HMS *Formidable*, torpedoed by a German U boat on New Year's Day 1915, 20 miles off Start Point, with the loss of 547 lives. Of two of HMS *Formidable* boats that had been launched, one was found upside down on the beach at Abbotsbury, the other with sixty men landed in thick fog at Lyme Regis, although nine men had died of exposure or wounds. This incident had certain features similar that were to take place 29 years later in the English Channel.

The sinking of the warship was disastrous enough, but was compounded by serious errors of communication as news of the incident did not reach the Plymouth naval base until one and a half hours after the first torpedo had struck the cruiser. Furthermore the position of the *Formidable* and the enemy submarine were inaccurately transmitted, further delaying rescue. The loss of the *Formidable* shocked the country and Vice Admiral Sir Lewis Bayly was relieved of his command.[9] However U boat attacks in the area of Start Bay continued. Devonport Naval Command suspected that the U boats were using the Channel waters around Start Point as a laying-up place. In an attempt to confirm their suspicion, the Royal Navy strung nets across part of Start Bay and maintained a watch. On the 1 March 1916, parts of the netting were seen to sink and move with violent pulling and vibrations. The Royal Navy carried out an explosive sweep over the suspected area resulting in large quantities of oil appearing on the surface of the water, leaving no doubt that an enemy submarine had been destroyed. The Royal Naval Air Service organised anti-submarine patrols to cover Start Bay and Lyme Bay using a flight of Sopwith aircraft based at RNAS Prawle, a small airfield close to the village of East Prawle.[10]

Dartmouth harbour with Kingswear in the background showing two paddle steamers on the River Dart and three Bibby troopships at anchor. One of these ships was used in the 1938 amphibious exercise held at Slapton Sands.

In April 1936 there was considerable interest and publicity given to the plight of the Finish barque *Herzogin Cecilie* that ran aground in thick fog after striking the Ham Stone off Sewer Mill Cove, near Salcombe. The four-masted sailing ship was a graceful sight even as she lay on the rocks. Thousands of people were attracted to the Bolt Head area to view the wreck. Attempts were made to save the ship, but she was eventually broken up for scrap.

The small village of Torcross lies at the westerly end of Slapton Sands and has a history of being battered by stormy seas. Beyond the village the road continues inland passing the village of Stokenham and continuing through Chillington to Kingsbridge. This small country town nestles on a steep hill above the Kingsbridge estuary. A GWR branch line served Kingsbridge in the 1930s running to Brent Station which connected to the main line service to Plymouth, Exeter and London.

Near to Kingsbridge is Salcombe a place out on its own. It is the most southerly town in Devonshire. In the 1930s it had a population of 2000 inhabitants and was already an estab-

In the 1930s Britain still possessed a powerful navy even though many of the First World War warships had been scrapped. This 1936 picture of the mighty HMS *Rodney* was taken at Devonport dockyard during Navy Week. The Battleship was in action during the Second World War.

This nostalgic picture, showing part of the city of Plymouth in the background was taken from what was RAF Mountbatten (RAF Cattewater). To the right of the fishing boat a ferry makes its way from Plymouth to the village of Turnchapel.

lished venue for yachting and beach holidays as the small sandy coves and creeks in the area were ideal for picnics and sunbathing. Quality hotels attracted a rich clientele, while on the hills surrounding Salcombe stood large houses owned by the wealthy. One visitor to Salcombe in the early 1930s was Lawrence of Arabia who at this time was stationed at RAF Mount Batten, Plymouth.[11] He had come to Salcombe at the invitation of Lady Waring, a friend of Mrs Winston Churchill, to meet up with his friend Clare Sydney Smith, the wife of Wing Commander Sydney Smith who was staying at the Mount, a grand 18th century house that stands high up on the cliffs near North Sands.

Among the famous visitors to stay at Salcombe prior to the Second World War was Charles Laughton, one of the stars of the film *Jamaica Inn*. The smuggling scenes for the film had been shot at nearby Blackpool Sands.

* * *

At Slapton Beach on 6 July 1938, a few weeks before the infamous Munich Agreement, there occurred what arguably was the most visionary amphibious military exercise held in Britain, although it would have passed into obscurity but for future wartime events. Few contemporary documents about the exercise survive.[12] The object of the exercise was 'to investigate the tactical and technical aspects of an approach from seaward and the landing of a force on an enemy coast'. The Slapton Beach assault exercise was the first of its kind since the amphibious Gallipoli landings during the First World War. One feature of the exercise was the use of motorised landing craft. These had been designed in 1922, four years after the First World War ended.[13] Of three that had been built, two were known to have been used in 1938 at the amphibious exercise on Slapton Sands. In the 1920s a Landing Craft Committee had been formed and during the 1930s an inter-services training arm and training centre reported directly to the Chief of Staff to further the development of combined operations. It was the Landing Craft Committee that was the first to request a landing ship that was

A 1930s view of a long stretch of Instow beach that was used by the Americans in 1944 for amphibious exercises.

capable of lowering landing craft loaded with soldiers from davits. Brigadier Bernard Montgomery had been pressing for a divisional exercise involving the three services to be held in the summer of 1938. Montgomery was chosen to organise the event and placed in charge of the exercise. The planning took place at Portsmouth and Montgomery's son, on leave from India, was given the task of making two models of the Slapton shoreline that was used to instruct members of the task force.

Brigadier Montgomery was asked by a General to explain his ideas on inter-service co-operation to which Montgomery replied, "co-operation my dear chap, no problem there, I tell them what to do and they do it". Part of the Slapton exercise was for the assault to take place on three of the five sections of the beach, section C was an area nearby the Royal Sands Hotel where now stands the American memorial dedicated to the villagers who were evacuated in 1943.

DEVON IN THE THIRTIES 23

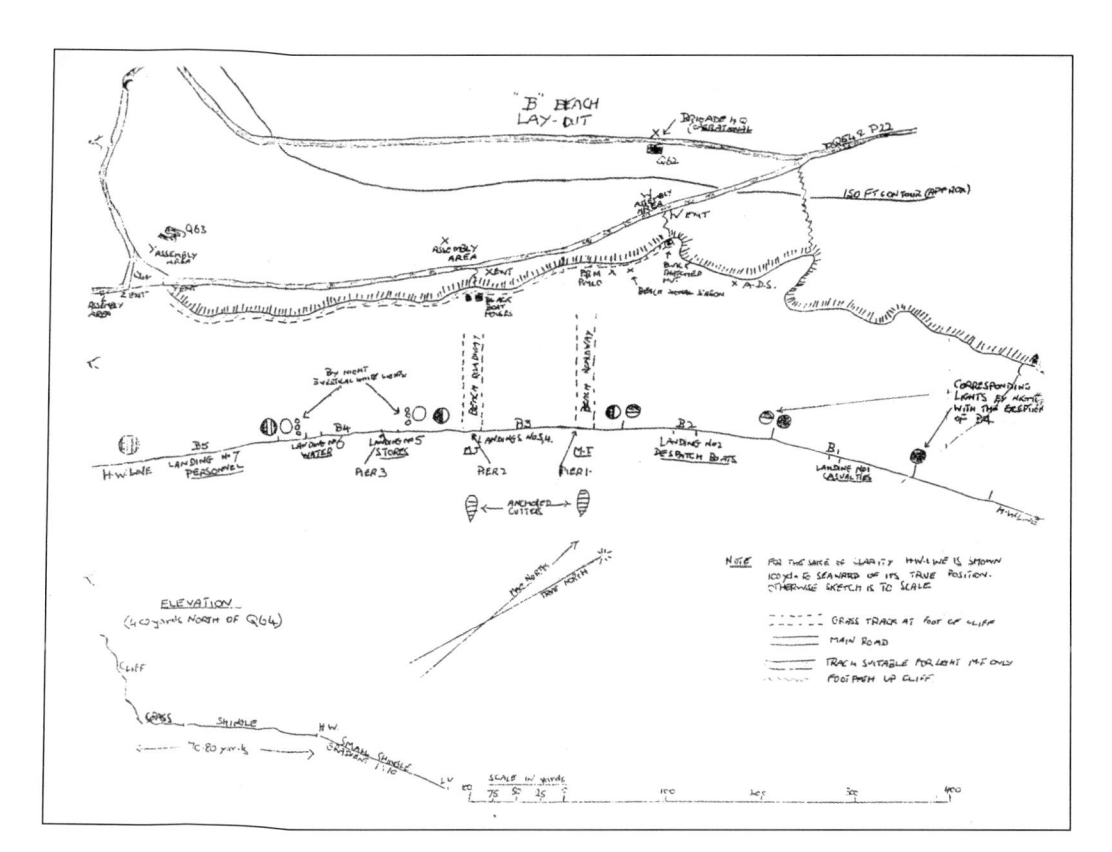

During 1938, Brigadier Bernard Montgomery held an amphibious exercise on Slapton Sands. This is a facsimile of the layout of B beach, The sketch shows the exercise was held on the beach area near Strete Gate.

A Vickers light tank on Slapton beach at the time of the 1938 amphibious exercise.

A rare photograph of a Fairey Swordfish biplane, participating in the 1938 amphibious exercise. The aircraft is about to land on Slapton beach, having flown off the Royal Navy aircraft carrier HMS *Courageous* anchored in Slapton Bay.

Two soldiers of the Kings' Own Scottish Borderers with a Vickers machine gun by the side of Slapton Ley during the 1938 Slapton Sands amphibious exercise.

This silver-bronze statuette of a British infantry soldier, dressed and equipped in contemporary style was presented to HMS *Britannia*, Royal Naval College, Dartmouth, by Brigadier Bernard Montgomery as a token of his gratitude for the hospitality received by his troops on the night of the 6 July 1938 when the Slapton amphibious exercise was cancelled due to bad weather.

The assault force referred to as the 'Eastland Army' comprised three battalions of the 9th Infantry Brigade totalling 1850 troops together with tanks, transport and stores. The naval force included the battleship HMS *Revenge*, two cruiser class warships and a flotilla of destroyers. Twelve Fairey Swordfish torpedo bombers that participated in the exercise were flown from the aircraft carrier HMS *Courageous*. The defending force the 'Wessex Army' was made up of the 8th and 9th Infantry Brigade with the 10th Infantry Brigade in reserve. The invading force set out from Studland, Dorset and sailed to Slapton Bay. Local people had been aware that something unusual was taking place in the area as throughout the previous night a continuous drone of aircraft engines had disturbed the sleep of many villagers. The following day the aircraft could be seen flying above the local countryside. The appearance of the Eastland Army completely surprised the Wessex defence force. The plan after the exercise, was to re-embark the troops later in the day, but in the evening the weather broke and a severe gale developed making it impossible for the soldiers to return to the ships without the risk that the ships would be blown towards the shore. Consequently the exercise was abandoned.

The men were tired, wet and hungry, and there was no alternative accommodation. The situation appeared desperate until a naval office suggested that the Royal Naval College, Dartmouth should be contacted to assist. At 11.15pm the college officers were told to expect 1100 troops and 80 officers, with other members of the force and the sailors being sent to Plymouth naval base. The College employees living in Dartmouth were urgently called from their homes and by midnight the Royal Naval College was ready to receive the first troops. There were remarkable scenes that had never before been experienced at the College. The quarterdeck, gunrooms, cinema and changing rooms were used to accommodate the troops that were packed 'like sardines in a tin'. The order was then given 'Tea for a thousand' resulting in beef and biscuits being produced and distributed.[14] The following morning the troops were up and dressed and away in the pouring rain, marching to the ferry to take them across the River Dart to Kingswear Station. By 8am the Naval College was clear except for the Lincolns who were reluctant to march out in the pouring rain. The exercise had ended disappointingly, but lessons learned were forgotten by Brigadier Montgomery, who returned three months later with three officers from the 9th Infantry Brigade to present the Commanding Officer of the College with a silver and bronze statuette of a British infantry soldier as a token of gratitude for the hospitality received on the night of 6 July 1938.[15]

The 1938 Slapton Sands amphibious exercise was held at the time of the developing European crisis that resulted in the infamous Munich Pact that was signed on 28 September 1938. Two days later the nation's attention had been focused on the return of the Prime Minister, Neville Chamberlain to Heston Airfield, Middlesex, to learn what agreement if any, he had made with Adolf Hitler. The 1938 Munich Agreement had bought relief to the country in the misleading belief that peace would be maintained and the anticipated large-scale air attack on England had been averted. The Government's immediate response to the Munich Agreement was to carry on as usual, but this was quickly followed by a decision for the country to restart rearming and for local authorities to continue preparing their civil defence.

Earlier, around the time of the Silver Jubilee in 1935, the Home Office had sent out its first Air Raid Precautions circular to each Devon local authority inviting them and the public to co-operate with the Government in creating ARP machinery for the purpose of protecting civilians and property from air attack. To establish a local ARP scheme required the approval of an official committee but many Devon local authorities had been slow to develop their schemes; furthermore there had been a limited response from the public to join ARP units. This situation change with the introduction of the ARP Act of 1937, that came into force on 1 January 1938. This Act stated that each local authority was required to establish its own Civil Defence Service.

In the South Hams, as with the rest of the Devon, communities were, from 1938, preparing their passive defence for air raids. Civil Defence schemes that were implemented were based on approved local authority ARP schemes. Dartmouth people were informed that in the event of a possible air raid on the town they would be warned by the blowing of the local gas works steam whistle. Later the town had an electric air raid warning siren installed. However seriously Devon people took preparations for air raids, there were many at the time, including the Government, who believed Devon was immune from air attack. As local authority ARP preparations continued, Devon resorts were packed with holidaymakers during the fine summer months of 1939, while a Royal Visit to Dartmouth took local thoughts further away from anxieties of impending war.

Below left: There is a legend that the ghost of the pirate Tom Crocker makes a circuit of Burgh Island on the date of his hanging in 1395. To commemorate his capture and hanging it was the custom for people to dress up in pirate clothes and visit the Pilchard Inn, where Crocker lived and hoarded his treasure. This picture records the festivities held at the Pilchard Inn in August 1939, two weeks before the outbreak of the Second World War.

The Royal family during their visit to Dartmouth Naval College on the 22 July 1939. It was an occasion when Princess Elizabeth met up with naval Cadet Prince Philip.

1. Berberich, C, *The Image of the English Gentleman in Twentieth Century Literature,Englishness and Nostalgia,* 2007. Ashgate publishing Ltd. p.102.
2. Geddes Axe (1922), *A Dictionary of Contemporary World History*, 3rd Edition. Oxford University Press.
3. Devon and Cornwall , *A Preliminary Survey,* 1947 Wheaton. p.174.
4. Devon and Cornwall, *A Preliminary Survey.* p.6.
5. Chapman T, Outbreak 1939, *The World Goes To War,* 2009 Virgin Books. p.xv1.
6. Bradbeer, G, *The Land that Changed its Face,* 1973 David & Charles. p17.
7. Devon and Cornwall, *A Preliminary Survey.* p.28.
8. Devon and Cornwall, *A Preliminary Survey.* p. 30.
9. Wasley, G. *Devon in the Great War 1914-1918*, 2000 Devon Books pp 57-58.
10. Wasley, G. *Devon in the Great War* pp.112-113.
11. Smith, Sydney Clare, *The Golden Reign, The Story of My Friendship with Lawrence of Arabia,* 1940. Cassell. p.208.
12. Pack, S.W.C. Captain, *Britannia at Dartmouth*, 1966 Alvin Redman. pp234- 235.
13. Yung, Christopher, *Gators of Neptune, Naval Amphibious Planning for the Normandy Invasion,* 2006. Naval Institute Press. USA. p.24.
14. Wasley G. *Devon in the Thirties; The Way We Were*, 1998. Halsgrove. p.123.
15. Davies, E. and Grove, E. *The Royal Naval College, Dartmouth*, 1980. Gieves and Hawkes p.62. 24

2 The Home Front: Devon

THE SECOND WORLD War experience was different for civilians on the Home Front than in previous conflicts in which Britain had been involved. In the past the country had fought its battles from a distance, causing little concern among the people at home who often did not know what had happened or what was happening. This made them feel completely remote from their loved ones fighting abroad. In the present century the instantaneous and unceasing reporting of a distant conflict has to a large degree significantly altered the situation. The 'close war' experienced by Britain during the Second World War placed non-combatants in the front line, blurring the distinction between civilians and the fighting forces, a situation that had never happened on any scale before. Civilians in Devon were directly exposed to the enemy by bombing, inflicting serious injury or violent death. This is evident from the 7000 civilians who were killed or injured in air raids on Devon communities. Furthermore thousands of people had their homes demolished.

On the morning of the 3 September 1939 the Prime Minister, Neville Chamberlain, announced on the radio that Britain was at war with Germany. Unlike the declaration of the First World War there were no expression of public emotion in Devon. In 1914 people had congregated and cheered at the news that the country was at war. Yet listening to the Prime Minister speak on the radio on this September Sunday morning there would have been many people privately frightened and concerned how the war would affect their lives.

The glorious summer weather of 1939 had attracted thousands of holidaymakers to Devon, who seemed to have marginalised the real threat of war with Germany. But with the declaration of hostilities these people were now desperate to return home. In contrast to this mass exodus of holidaymakers, thousands of Government and private evacuees, mainly from London began to arrive in Devon. By the end of September 1939 over 82 000 Government evacuees had arrived in the county. In addition, those privately evacuated to Devon outnumbered the Government evacuees by 700 per cent.[1] There are many stories told of how evacuees were received and settled down in their Devon billets. The challenge for many Devon local authorities in coping with so many evacuees was often formidable and the local councils had to quickly adapt to deal with an entirely new set of circumstances. Many evacuees were happy and contented, others quickly returned to their parental home.

Preparing for air raids c.1939. Filling sandbags at Victoria Road, Dartmouth to protect Dartmouth Guildhall. Until the provision of shelters, sandbags were the only means of passive defence against bombs.

The problems associated with some evacuees arose from the social differences that were manifest from mixing people of different class levels.

Evacuating vulnerable people from London and other provincial cities was not only to offer them physical protection from bombing but to maintain the morale of the civilian population. Civilian evacuation was part of the Government's policy of population dispersal, a lesson it had learned from the experiences of air raids on Britain during the First World War. These raids had caused casualties, destruction to property and panic among sections of the population. The belief was that in the future, if the country was involved in another European war, aircraft would in all probability be used to attack Britain. The Air Staff

Evacuees from Bristol who had just arrived at Brent Station, south-west Devon. From here they were taken to their billets at Kingsbridge.

A group of young evacuee children with their nurse in the grounds of the children's home at Tapley Park, North Devon. Later in the war Tapley Park would be occupied by the American Forces.

predicted that if another war was declared, London would immediately be devastated by a 'knockout blow' by the German Air Force using a massive air attack on the city in an attempt to break the morale of the British people.[2] Why was morale important? Captain Basil Liddell Hart was acknowledged by Field Marshall Bernard Montgomery as the leading British military strategist of his time.[3] Liddell Hart stated: "A nation at war depends on the morale of its citizens, if this is broken the resistance of its army will also crumble as an inevitable sequel".[4] The same threat hung over Paris where the French Government also believed their capital at the outbreak of another war would be destroyed by bombing.[5] The expectations of a 'knockout blow' soon after the declaration of the Second World War resulted in the Government introducing a ban on the gathering of crowds throughout the country, to reduce the casualty rate when the bombs began to fall. Attendances at football matches, cinemas and theatres were forbidden, but churches and public houses were allowed to remain open. In North Devon the annual Barnstaple fair was cancelled, as was the Bideford regatta. But the German Air Force waited six weeks before dropping the first bomb on British soil during the Second World War and eight months before attacking the civilian population.[6] The anticipation of a devastating enemy air attack on London at the beginning of the war that raised so much apprehension was, according to the official history *The Defence of the United Kingdom*, speculation based on Air Ministry predictions.[7]

With the declaration of war, a wide range of emergency services came into operation. These were the result of planning by the Government and local authority departments. For example, the introduction of Air Raid Precautions for the civilian population began in 1922, just four years after the end of the First World War. The planners were concerned of the possible effects that air raids may have of the morale of the British people, and the Government's problem was to maintain the resilience of the nation.[8] Would the effect of bombing the civilian population break the morale of the British people?

Many of the wartime measures on the Home Front were the responsibility of the local council authorities who were called upon to implement Government policy that often deeply intruded into people's lives. An immediate impact on the people living in Devon was the compulsory blackout that was introduced two days before the declaration of war. Anyone failing to conform to the regulations was liable to be fined or imprisoned. In Germany persistent blackout offenders were sent to concentration camps. The Lord Mayor, Alderman and citizens of Plymouth were collectively fined two pounds for not properly blacking out their city's Guildhall.[9] To assist the motorist and pedestrian, towns and villages throughout the county had been transformed with white paint daubed on kerbstones, telegraph poles and the corners of buildings. The blackout was difficult to bear, it affected the lives of the people and the accident rate soared; although some urban dwellers likened the blackout to living in the countryside. Blackouts affected the local economy as shops and markets closed early, with shoppers wanting to get home early before dark. Deliveries of the post and essential supplies were often held up. The time of evening worship in many churches and chapels was brought forward.

On the eve of the outbreak of war Devon agriculture was a depressed industry and relatively unimportant. By noon on the day following day the declaration farming had, because of the importance of food production, become an element of National Defence. Devon farmers were immediately urged by the Ministry of Agriculture to increase their yields as part of the war effort.

Men who had been conscripted now left behind a wife to fend for herself, which for her was a new experience, more so having to live on a paltry Government allowance. For example, in 1939, a private soldier with two children received a total allowance of 32 shillings (£1.56p). However there were employers who continued to make up the wages of their staff.

The transition from peace to war continued. The Chancellor of the Exchequer in his first wartime budget increased Income Tax. Food rationing for civilians was introduced. Butter, bacon, sugar and cooking fat were the first foods to be rationed. Three months later meat was rationed. Sausage and processed meats were not officially rationed, but only became available to people according to supplies the butcher received. Meat rationing was not a question of ordering over the counter, but relied upon what your butcher was prepared to sell you, the quality depending on the source. Distribution varied widely from one region to another. The traditional family Sunday roast joint disappeared from the table. What continued to be available throughout the war was fish and chips.

Whatever the Government's policy of fair shares for all, some people fared better than others. People who lived through the Second World War tell their own stories of how they ate during the war. The late Miss Piper of Holsworthy, told the author of this book that

Working on the land during the Second World War meant intensive toil for farm workers. This picture taken at Mount Barton Farm, near Totnes, shows farm workers building a haystack.

Below left: A familiar sight on the Home Front was queuing for food. News would soon spread that a shop had received a consignment of unrationed 'goods' that were in short supply resulting in the formation of a queue of people. Plymouth c.1941.

Below right: Mrs Daisy Cook with her daughter handing over her ration book after collecting groceries from the village store at Bishop Nympton.

A knitting circle at Torquay, 13 August 1940. An early popular local war effort on the Home Front was for women at home or in social groups to knit garments for members of the services, for example, woollen socks for naval crew. It was an opportunity for women to show their patriotism by doing something worthwhile, Other women would volunteer to repair the uniforms of servicemen.

throughout the war, she and her family never had an opportunity of buying any extra food although she lived next to the cattle market and knew many local farmers. In contrast Norman Howard, an evacuee from Acton to Dartmouth, recalls that when he went shopping in Paignton with the family with whom he was billeted, he was taken to Dellers' Café for an enjoyable hot meal, while listening to a three-piece ensemble playing popular melodies. Not everyone could afford to eat out in a cafe or restaurant, but if you could there was plenty of food to be had. For those who had money there were many choices in wartime Devon: at the Grand Hotel, Plymouth the wartime breakfast menu included a choice of 14 different dishes. Grapefruit or cereal was followed by haddock or grilled sole, or as an alternative there was cold ham or tongue; the mixed grill however could only be served with one egg. The Government decided to ban the manufacture of clotted cream, and housewives, not to be denied of one of their simple pleasures of life, scolded their milk in order to take off the cream. There is no evidence, in spite of rationing and shortages, that anyone in wartime Devon was starved of food.

The war infiltrated into the daily lives of people and could not be separated from their everyday existence. For people who owned a car their journeys were severely restricted as petrol was rationed.

The reality of war soon came to many Westcountry families when the aircraft carrier HMS *Courageous,* that had recently joined a naval force to hunt enemy U boats, was sunk by two torpedoes fired by U29 on 17 September 1939, off the west coast of Ireland. The casualty rate was high, 519 crew members lost their lives. The ship had only a few days earlier sailed from Devonport. Disaster struck again on the 14 October 1939, when the Devonport built Battleship HMS *Royal Oak* was sunk by U47 that had managed to penetrate the defences of the Home Fleet anchorage at Scapa Flow in Orkney, Scotland. The loss of life was high, 813 sailors lost their lives, including 120 boy sailors. These deaths occurred during the period referred to as 'the phoney war', because of the lack of military action in France.[10]

The face of Home Front Devon began to change early in the war as more women went out to work due to the shortage of men. Women for example, worked in the shops and factories, delivered the post, milk and bread, taking on jobs that were once the domain of men.

As the war proceeded the scale of volunteerism entwined with patriotism increased. The women of the Land Army toiled on farms and local women volunteer organisations came forward to make their contribution on the Home Front, including setting up and serving in canteens and at a railway stations to offer refreshments to the servicemen. Among the larger voluntary organisations that made important contributions to the war effort was the Woman's Voluntary Service and the Woman's Institutes. In towns and villages there was great activity in raising funds for service charities. Women's patriotism on the Home Front extended away from their gender role of domestic duties into their leisure hours. The contributions to the war effort made by women who were members of a local church or voluntary organisation, who worked at home or in a local group activity, could be described as 'local patriotism'. For example they knitted thick woollen socks for men serving on naval minesweepers or repaired clothes and sewed buttons on to soldiers uniforms.

Rumours had spread throughout Devon that the war would be over by Christmas. Morale was low because nothing was happening. The Civil Defence, in particular Air Raid Wardens, were criticised by the public for having nothing to do and were considered a waste of public money. People were bored. Property throughout the county began to look shoddy, as there was a shortage of paint. The appearance of many high streets became nondescript due to sandbagged buildings. Yet the first wartime Christmas in Devon was one of plenty. Christmas poultry was plentiful as was beer, wine and spirits. The shops were stocked with presents and children's toys. Winter had set in; the weather was as bitterly cold and bleak as anyone could remember. At Slapton the Ley had frozen, enticing people to come out and skate on the ice. On 16 January 1940, the closeness of war was seen when hundreds of people watched from the North Devon clifftops the scene of the blazing oil tanker *Inverdargle* with a cargo of aviation fuel that had hit a mine off Foreland Point, near Lynmouth. The oil tanker eventually sank with the loss of 42 members of her crew.[11]

The radio was an important source of war news and entertainment. It was a common ritual for families, particularly on a Sunday evening to sit by their wireless and listen to a comedy program. During the early part of the war the BBC broadcast a considerable amount of orchestral and organ music. American-style popular music had yet to reach Britain. Wartime culture, although not at the level of peacetime, provided a welcome break for many people. Some communities continued to produce art exhibitions. Many people because of the blackout and loneliness took to reading and there was a significant increase in book loans from public libraries. Professional and amateur dramatics continued to be popular, as were light operettas.

The British cinema at this period was dominated by American films and the blackout did not stop young people in the towns and villages visiting cinemas or dance halls. It was a common feature for a wartime cinema audience to clap when Winston Churchill or the Royal Family appeared on the screen. Later in the war this applause extended to Stalin.

A Devon wartime Sunday was a solemn occasion, although chapel and church attendances continued to fall. With few exceptions cinemas and shops were closed on Sundays. Devon people at this period wore their best clothes on the sabbath. Some local communities continued their Sunday evening tradition of strolling around the local streets.

Above left: During the war women were employed in jobs that in peacetime were the domain of men. This picture shows two women employed as projectionists at an Exeter cinema.

Above right: Plymouth women registering for war service at the local Labour Exchange. Although voluntary at first, as the war progressed registration became compulsory. The choice was to serve in one of the women's uniformed services or work in one of the essential war factories.

In February 1940 the country's morale was lifted with the arrival of the cruiser HMS *Exeter* at Devonport. This warship, along with HMS *Ajax* and the New Zealand Cruiser HMS *Achilles,* was involved in the first sea battle of the war, the Battle of the River Plate, fought in the South Atlantic. Although severely damaged HMS *Exeter* eventually made its way back to Devonport to be greeted by the First Sea Lord, Winston Churchill. The crew of HMS *Exeter* then went on to the city of Exeter to a hero's reception.[12]

In the early months of 1940 there were people in Britain who continued to feel that the nation was not at war because of the continued lack of military activity in France. This created a mood of complacency and scepticism among the population. But in April 1940 the conduct of the war quickly changed when the German army using their blitzkrieg tactics rapidly advanced through Holland and Belgium. Overnight Belgian fishing boats began to arrive in Dartmouth and other Westcountry ports. The Belgian fishermen bought their families and furniture with them before settling in coastal towns such as Brixham and Falmouth for the duration of the war. Devon became multinational with, for example, Australian, Dutch, French, Indian, Polish and Norwegian servicemen based in the county.

1940 was a very important period of the war on the Home Front as there was a real threat that England would be invaded by the enemy. Various defences were established along the north and south Devon coast. The call went out for Local Defence Volunteers to resist the invader. The picture shows a small band of men ready to defend the Great Hill reservoir, Torquay in May 1940.

The German army continued its advance into France culminating in the British retreat from Dunkirk. Small ships from Devon joined those from other ports, making their way across the English Channel in order to rescue the stricken troops. Events moved quickly as Holland, Belgium and France capitulated to Germany.

A grave threat now existed for Britain as the Germans occupied northern France and were in flying distance of south-west England. The Battle of Britain was extensively reported on the radio and in the newspapers. The epic air battle extended to the Westcountry as the enemy attempted to block the port of Plymouth by laying magnetic mines in Plymouth Sound. On 13 August 1940, 213 Squadron from RAF Exeter and 238 Squadron RAF Middle Wallop, part of Churchill's 'Few', intercepted a large formation of German fighters off Portland that had followed two waves of enemy bombers.[13]

The air raids started again (intermittently) in November until August 1943. The raids varied in time and intensity resulting in casualties, destruction of property and creating huge social problems. These air attacks were traumatic for the Devon communities who suffered under them and the ARP services were called upon throughout the day and night to warn of the presence of enemy aircraft. Many Devon authorities since the beginning of the war had built public air raid shelters, but few civilians had been provided with a domestic shelter.

A familiar sight in many Devon communities was the brick-built public air raid shelters such as these shelters built in King's Garden, Plymouth. Up to the time of the Plymouth Blitz many of the public shelters were vandalised. Later, however they were restored and local people would stay and sleep in them overnight.

The German land victories changed the mood of the British people and now the British Government were fearful of the Germans determination to invade England. Anticipating the Germans would attempt a landing in Devon using seaborne and airborne troops, anti-invasion defences were constructed (see the author's book *Devon at War*). Possible landing beaches were sealed off and land mines were laid. Scaffold structures were erected on many seaside beaches along with miles of barbed wire.

However, the prospect of German parachutists being dropped from aircraft, or the enemy landing on a local beach, did not deter people from important events such as getting married or even going on holiday. Whatever people's concern regarding the threat of invasion community life in the towns and villages of Devon carried on.

The defence of Devon was limited by a shortage of troops and equipment, because of what had been abandoned at Dunkirk. The Order of Battle placed Devon under Southern Command. Along with the mining of beaches, obstacles were erected in fields inland to prevent enemy aircraft and gliders from landing. Place names had been ordered to be removed from road signs so not to assist the enemy. As part of the military defence certain towns and villages had concrete pillboxes, barbed wire entanglements and tank traps constructed. Units of the newly formed Local Defence Volunteers, later known as the Home Guard were ordered to be the first line of defence and would be expected to hold the line

At the time of the expected invasion of England, unarmed mounted patrols made up of men and women of the Dartmoor Hunt went out in daytime to the remote moorland areas looking for enemy parachutists.

until the arrival of regular army troops. The men of the Home Guard were local men; it took courage in their commitment to face and fight a powerful well-armed enemy. While waiting for the enemy to arrive, a watch was kept on the air, land and at sea. A vigilance was maintained on Dartmoor where young unarmed women of the Dartmoor Hunt went out on their horses to spot enemy parachutists; elsewhere-ancient church towers were used as observation posts.

There were no wartime local Devon council elections as the main political parties had, since the beginning of the war, agreed to keep the status quo of elected councils, the Mayor retaining his dignity as the leading citizen. Local authorities in the Second World War had a formidable task, particularly in the extra work involved in those communities which had suffered casualties and destruction to property.

The war thus brought about many changes in local authority affairs. The scale and frequency of raids and the post-raid care were to be dominant issues among those Devon authorities who had suffered air attacks. There is no simplistic model to describe how individual authorities operated in wartime amid the complex problems they often faced. Throughout the war the traditional work of the local councils, for example, the collection of rates, refuse and road sweeping, continued alongside the council's new wartime responsibilities. As the war progressed and male council staff were conscripted so this significantly changed the ratio of staff, with many more women employed. The co-operation of regional councils with central Government and voluntary agencies increased the burden of their work. Local councils were also involved in collaborating with the WVS and other charitable organisation in raising funds for the armed services. These events, were based on a military theme and usually lasted a week, For example in 1940, Dartmouth achieved its set financial target for 'Warship Week'. The opportunity was taken at these fund-raising events to make it a social occasion, the purpose to maintain the morale of the population.

Devon authorities had been preparing for air raids since the Munich Crisis of 1938. Some Councils were more advanced in their ARP schemes than others. A challenge to some of the Devon Civil Defence services was the protection of the rural communities and their properties. Many Devon villages and hamlets did not have mains water supplies or hydrants to connect hosepipes. As previous mentioned, during the early period of the war, because of the lack of military activity, the Air Raid Precaution service was criticised by the

Below left: A wartime picture of two Brixham Girl Guides sitting on the base of the William of Orange statue at Brixham Harbour.

Below right: A wartime picture of an almost deserted street in Brixham. It shows three naval officers with a jeep, a vehicle more associated with the American forces.

public as it had nothing to do and many people thought it was a waste of public money. However as a result of the change in the conduct of the war with air raids on the county increasing, people were able to witness the devotion and bravery of the Civil Defence personnel, and this changed public opinion. It should be appreciated that ARP was a new and untried concept in the history of the defence of the United Kingdom.

Although more Devon farmers used tractors during the war, the horse-drawn plough was still in use and hand-sowing of seed continued. Farmers were unhappy about the Government regulations that were being imposed on them. 'Ploughing for Victory' was a theme used in the many propaganda posters that seem to be pasted up everywhere or

Above left: 'A Daylight Raid on Plymouth' by the Polish artist Felix Topolski.

Above right: A painting of fire fighters attending a crashed aircraft somewhere in Devon. The scene reveals the challenges faced by rural Air Raid Precaution services, one being the scarcity of fire hydrants to connect hoses. This could result in extremely long lengths of hosing require to fight a fire.

The Duke of Kent inspects boy messengers of Plymouth's Civil Defence on Plymouth Hoe. The picture was taken a few days before the intensive air raids of March 1941.

Pilot Officer Hayes, a fighter pilot of no 247 Squadron stationed at RAF Roborough who contributed in the air defence of Plymouth during 1941.

published in the newspapers. The Ministry Agriculture Scheme urged Devon farmers to plough up the land; to plough for milk, plough for corn and potatoes. Many young people, local and evacuees earned pocket money potato picking, a physically tiring job.

According to the National Archives, there were in Devon 12 000 smallholdings of fewer than 100 acres. Land Girls many from urban families were beginning to work on farms and smallholdings although at first there had been a reluctance for Devon farmers to employ women, as they were convinced women were not up to the rough and tough physical task of farming, but slowly this attitude change and the gender discrimination waned as Land Girls became an important part of the Devon farming community and played a vital role in the war effort by their contribution in food production.

In the countryside wild rabbits were a common pest and a major problem for farmers. However wild rabbit meat, that had been part of the diet for many Devon households in peacetime, was during the war a much-sought source of food by the housewife. Rabbit was not unlike the taste and texture of a chicken; it could be stewed or baked as a pie.

Early in 1940 the ice of the bleak cold winter had began to thaw. The monotonies of everyday life at this time must be seen in the context of the drab lifestyle that the war had produced. The labour shortage on the Home Front resulted in the introduction of The National Service (No2) Act that compelled women under the age of 40 to register for war work. Provision was made for mothers with children under fourteen to be exempted. The small number of industrial factories in Devon meant that many conscripted women were sent outside the county for war work. A continuing frustration on the Home Front for the housewife was the shortage of domestic and small goods, for example, combs, razor blades, and soap and torch batteries that meant searching around the shops.

During 1940 there was a brief but golden literary period in the lower valley of the River Dart where three talented authors lived close to each other. One was the poet Robert Graves who in 1940 came to live in the village of Galmpton, near Brixham. One of his neighbours who visited him was the crime writer Agatha Christie who lived at Greenway on the banks of the River Dart, opposite the village of Dittisham. Flora Thompson, author of *Lark Rise to Candleford* lived three miles away in Above Town, Dartmouth.

On the 6 July 1940 enemy aircraft appeared over Devon and dropped bombs on Galmpton, Barnstaple and Plymouth; the first time Devon communities had suffered air attacks. These raids marked the beginning of the first phase of air raids on Devon communities that continued up to July 1941. The raids restarted in November 1941 and continued until the summer of 1944. When the air raid warning sounded people would anxiously listen for the sound of approaching aircraft and experience relief at the receding drone. People learnt to distinguish the sound of an enemy bomber aircraft from a friendly one as the Germans had desynchronized the twin engines of their bombers to make it more difficult for the British sound locators to detect them.

During the Plymouth Blitz, the people suffered as street after street of their homes were demolished. The picture records the devastation of a street that is now Garden Street, Devonport in 1941. It shows why the need for post-raid Civil Defence services were vital to offer the victims, care, shelter and food.

Plymouth children collecting free firewood from the huge wood pile created from the houses and buildings demolished in the Plymouth air raids. This was a useful supply of fuel for householders as coal was scarce and rationed.

During the Plymouth Blitz of 1944, thousands of people trekked out from the city each evening to seek safe shelter. Some walked, others travelled by bus or lorry as shown in this picture.

PRELUDE TO D-DAY

Winston Churchill and his wife Clementine photographed outside Lady Astor's house on Plymouth Hoe during their visit to the bombed city of Plymouth in May 1941.

This letter, referring to a request to use certain railway tunnels as air raid shelters, is of particular interest as it mentions the expected increase in rail traffic in the area, an early indication of the build up to Operation *Bolero*, in which US armed forces and equipment arrived in Britain prior to the eventual invasion of Normandy.

The second wartime Christmas in Devon was celebrated free from enemy air raids. People were still able to enjoy a traditional Christmas dinner, but the seasonal fare was limited because of rationing and the absence of festive luxury items. The church bells had been silenced in 1940 as the Government ordered they should only be rung as a warning if enemy parachutists had been seen to land. During March and April 1941, Plymouth, having previously experienced a number of heavy air raids, suffered a series of intensive fire raids that destroyed the city centre. There were shared dangers as civilians came out on to the streets along with the Civil Defence to douse the dangerous incendiary bombs that had been dropped in their thousands on the city by the enemy aircraft. One of the understated aspects of Home Front Devon during the Second World War was the contribution of local residents during air raids in defence of their homes and local property.

Alongside the casualties suffered by the bombing, thousands of people were made homeless and required emergency feeding. As there was no secure base in Plymouth for people to rest and sleep, there were on occasions up to 60 000 people that trekked out of the city. These 'trekkers' are known to have slept in the open on Dartmoor.[14] Other trekkers made for the Dartmoor towns and villages that were sometimes overwhelmed by sheer numbers, but to their credit many willingly provided shelter and food.

On 7 December 1941, the war dramatically changed again for the British people when the Japanese air force attacked the American Pacific Fleet at Pearl Harbor. Japanese forces also attack the British possessions of Hongkong, Malaya and Burma. America and Britain declared war on Japan. Germany and Italy declared war on America that was now to fight the Axis powers on two main fronts: the European and Pacific. On the 10 December 1941 disaster struck for Britain when Japanese aircraft sunk two of the largest ships of the Royal Navy, HMS *Prince of Wales* and HMS *Repulse* with the loss of 600 men. The ships were without air support that had been declined by Admiral Tom Phillips.

Prime Minister, Winston Churchill travelled across the Atlantic on 12 December 1941 to meet President Roosevelt to discuss strategy for the combined war effort. America, Britain and Russia whatever their fundamental political differences, decided the Allies would have to land in occupied Europe to confront the German land forces. America agreed that the European theatre of war should have priority over the Pacific war zone. A decision was made to send an American Expeditionary force to Britain. This was the first step in the huge build up of American Forces and supplies, code named Operation *Bolero*. Part of the America Force would be based in Devon and Cornwall. As the Americans started to arrive in the south west of England, there were to be many high levels meetings between the Allies, before an agreement was made on plans to liberate Europe from the Germans.

Devon had not, since the summer of 1941, been troubled by the German Air force until 27 March 1942 when four Messerschmitt Bf109 fighter-bombers appeared over Torquay and bombed the town (a day later the epic St Nazaire raid took place). The attack on Torquay puzzled the British authorities as the town had little value as a military target. Four days later Brixham was attacked. This was followed by raids on Exmouth and Budleigh Salterton. The raids took place on undefended towns and these fringe attacks appeared pointless, as they did not impinge upon the war effort. Nine months later after the Torquay attack, the area was reinforces with a huge armament of anti-aircraft guns referred to as the 'Paignton fortress' for the defence of Torbay.[15] This newly created AA defence system extended to Brixham, Kingswear, Dartmouth and down to Salcombe, and to the east of the county at Exmouth and Teignmouth.

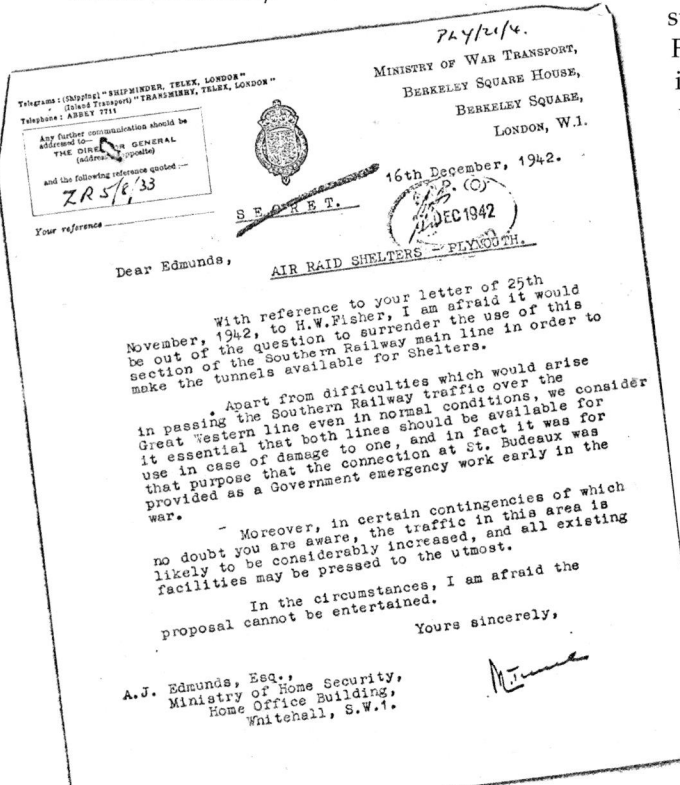

THE HOME FRONT: DEVON

Above left: The result of the Baedeker raid on Exeter on 3rd May 1942. Many of the enemy bombs fell in the city centre where buildings were densely packed as shown in this picture of the aftermath of the raid in High Street, Exeter.

Above right: After the bombing. Exeter Cathedral is seen over the rooftops of ruined property caused by enemy air raids.

The WVS were quick to respond to the major attack on Exeter during May 1942. As the city's bakeries had been destroyed, the WVS set to and provided sandwiches for the homeless using emergency stocks of bread.

Above left: This classic painting depicts an Exeter fire guard team equipped with a stirrup pump and a bucket of water. The picture is set against the levelled ruins of part of Exeter with the Cathedral in the background. Firemen artists such as William Clause, together with the men and women of the city, shared dangers in defending the city and its residents when it suffered air raids.

Above right: Many small communities in South Devon were bombed in the Second World War. This picture shows the ruins of St Andrews Church, Aveton Gifford that was demolished by a bomb when five Focke-Wulf 190 fighter-bombers attacked the village on 26 January 1943.

On 24 April 1942 Exeter experienced the first ever Baedeker raid. The raids had been ordered by Hitler as retaliation for the RAF raids on Lubeck and Rostock. Exeter was a soft target. The city had no substantial ant-aircraft defence. A record shows that on 25 May 1941 there were four anti-aircraft guns in place for the defence of the city, but there is no evidence to confirm if they remained in Exeter during April 1942.[16] The first air raid on Exeter was made by a force of enemy bomber aircraft and most of the bombs fell on civilian property. Two days later a single enemy aircraft flew over the city and released several hundred incendiary bombs. The enemy then resumed its attack in force. As there was no balloon barrage defence, the German bombers were able to fly low over the city and the terror of the raids was magnified as the aircraft machined-gunned the civilians.

From 1942 American servicemen were seen in various places in Devon before the massive build-up described in the following chapters. The first of these forces were naval personnel whose task was to establish advanced US naval bases. Although there had been an improvement in the war situation for the Allies, enemy air attacks on Devon communities were persistent, with bombing raids continuing every month throughout 1943. There was

The war appears to be a long way away from Bampton, in mid Devon as recorded in this peaceful scene of a farmer driving his sheep through the village to Bampton market c.1943.

A Women's Voluntary Service Civil Defence ABC guide issued to Devon village representatives c.1944. The booklet contained 14 pages of information that included what to do if an aircraft crashes, the location of the ARP control and report centre, and message writing.

Opposite, bottom: On the Sunday afternoon of 30 May 1943 Torquay suffered a disaster when forty-three people were killed in an air raid on the town. The dead included twenty-one children and three Sunday School teachers when a bomb fell and exploded on the church of St Mary's. Three hundred houses were completely demolished or damaged.

no respite for people living in the coastal communities of Devon. On the 26 January 1943 during a raid on the South Hams village of Aveton Gifford by five Focke-Wulf 190 fighter-bombers, St Andrew Church was badly damaged by a bomb. On 30 May 1943 Torquay was bombed killing 43 people. This included 21 children and three Sunday School teachers attending a service at St Mary's church.

Against this background of tragedy and upheaval, Christmas 1943 was celebrated in Devon with carol singing, and church services. Traditional parties were held for the children and a Christmas dinner given to many of the old folk. But wartime life on the Home Front in Devon had become more austere. A paper shortage meant there were no decorations to be bought. There were few toys in the shops and many of the toys given as presents were home made. There were plenty of chocolates and sweets in the shops but they were on ration. And while there was no severe shortage of food, other than the items that were already rationed, poultry such as turkey or duck for Christmas dinner was difficult to obtain, as was wine and spirits. Rationing restrictions meant bread was no longer white but an insipid pale brown colour, said to be more nutritional. To save fuel a Government campaign had been introduced that any person taking a bath was requested to use no more than five inches of water.

From early 1944 Devon had become 'occupied' with American servicemen whose numbers increased up to their departure for D-Day. In spite of this huge influx, life on the Home Front went on without great interference from their presence.

1. Titmuss, R. M. *Problems of Social Policy*, 1950. HMSO p.102.
2. O'Brien, T. *Civil Defence*, 1955. HMSO p.282.
3. Montgomery of Alamein. *A History of Warfare*, 1968. London: Collins p.20.
4. Hart Liddell, L.H. *Thoughts on War*, 1944. London : Faber & Faber p. 20.
5. Charman, T. *Outbreak: 1939. The World Goes to War*, 2009. Virgin Books p.224.
6. O'Brien.*Civil Defence*. HMSO p.294.
7. Collier, B. *The Defence of the United Kingdom*, 1957. HMSO p.48.
8. Mackay, Robert. *Half the Battle: Britain during the Second World War*, 2002. Manchester University Press. p31.
9. Charman, T. *Outbreak 1939, The World goes to War* 2009 HMSO p. 333.
10. Turner, E.S. *The Phoney War on the Home Front*, 1961. Michael Joseph. p.180.
11. Young, J. *Britain's Sea War, a diary of ship losses 1939-1945*, 1969. Patrick Stephens p.24.
12. Walling, R. *The Story of Plymouth*, 1950. Westaway Books p.272.
13. Collier, B. *The Defence of the United Kingdom*, 1957. HMSO P.185.
14. Piper, Lilian. *Report of Plymouth Evacuation*, 1944. Friends War Victims Relief Committee. p.10.
15. Dobinson Colin. *AA Command: British Anti-Aircraft Defences of the Second World* War, 2001. Methuen p.369.
16. Dobinson Colin. *AA Command* p.517.

3 Establishing US Naval Bases

THE HISTORY BEHIND why part of the American forces participated in the major amphibious exercises at the Slapton Battle Training Area was the result of the August 1943 Quebec meeting between President Roosevelt and Prime Minister Winston Churchill. Here they had agreed to mount a cross-Channel invasion of France to liberate Europe from Nazi Germany, with the code-name *Overlord* assigned to this major military operation. The agreement was reluctantly made by the Prime Minister who was well aware of his controversial First World War amphibious operations at Gallipoli where the British had sustained high losses, creating doubt in Churchill's mind about an amphibious attack on the shores of France. Churchill had preferred what he called the underbelly strategy suggesting the Allies attack Germany through Italy and the Balkan countries. Churchill in pursuing this policy was reported to go around referring to corpses floating in the Channel, a correct prediction as fate would have it.

With the Quebec Agreement in place, *Operation Bolero* that had been proposed by the American planners as early as 1942, was set in motion. This was for a large-scale build up of American Forces in Britain for the eventual liberation of Europe.[1] Plans and preparations for the eventual amphibious assault had been made during March 1943 culminating in setting 1 May 1944 (this was latter changed to the 6 June 1944) as the date for the major sea invasion of France code named *Neptune-Overlord*. The final Allied agreement was set out in the Combined Chief of Staff directive of 12 February 1944 to General Eisenhower, that stated, "You will enter the Continent of Europe, and in conjunction with other United Nations undertake operations aimed at the heart of Germany and the destruction of her armed forces".[2] This required the build up and concentration of forces for a powerful drive at the earliest possible date. Admiral Leatham, Commander in Chief Plymouth, had learnt as early as June 1943 that all the assault forces that were to operate in his area of Command were to be American, with six new amphibious bases established within the Plymouth Command.[3] In the early summer of 1943 Admiral Stark of the American Navy requested the use of the facilities of the Royal Naval College, Dartmouth for the training of US naval personnel.[4] American Forces started to arrive in Devon during 1943 as part of the huge Allied force that would depart from Britain in June 1944 to land in Normandy.

Opposite: The presence of the United States Navy in Britain during the Second World War, particularly in south-west England has always been understated as the history of these dramatic times was focused on the overwhelming numbers of US soldiers who were stationed in the country before D-Day. The map shows the US naval bases and facilities that were established in south-west England before D-Day.

Right: Table showing the number of on-shore naval personnel who were accommodated in south-west England in all forms of accommodation: houses, hotels, Quonset huts and tents.

Location	New camps				Alterations				Total	
	Huts		Tents		British barracks		Houses and hotels		Total	
	Officers	Enlisted Personnel	Officers	Enlisted Personnel	Officers	Enlisted Personnel	Officers	Enlisted Personnel	Officers	Enlisted Personnel
Falmouth	48	2059	---	1146	---	---	120	528	168	3733
Fowey	104	1500	---	---	---	---	101	930	205	2430
Plymouth	482	4172	---	186	106	296	45	371	633	5025
Salcombe	32	900	---	---	---	---	105	893	137	1793
Dartmouth	138	750	---	462	150	1750	90	344	378	3306
Teignmouth	8	---	---	---	---	---	48	817	56	817
Milford Haven	71	800	---	---	---	102	---	---	71	902
Penarth	28	425	---	---	---	---	47	514	75	939
St. Mawes	8	264	---	---	---	---	62	530	70	794
Saltash	0	150	---	---	---	---	30	150	30	300
Calstock	---	---	---	---	---	---	20	125	20	125
Weymouth	---	---	80	500	120	1113	26	679	226	2292
Poole	---	---	---	402	150	1160	19	100	169	1662
Southampton	24	34	---	250	---	---	53	366	77	650

ESTABLISHING US NAVAL BASES

U.S. NAVAL BASES AND FACILITIES
(With Headquarters of principal U.S. Army units)
BRITISH ISLES
June 1944

- Advanced Naval Base
- Advanced Amphibious Base
- Amphibious Training Base
- Naval Hospital
- Naval Ammunition Depot
- Naval Facility
- Supply Depot

HMS Britannia, Royal Naval College, Dartmouth, used by the US Navy as its Headquarters.

Arrangements to prepare shore bases in Britain for the USA Naval Forces can be traced back to 1942, a long time before a firm date had been agreed for the invasion of France.[5] In that year agreement was made between the British and American Governments that two recently constructed British Naval bases at Londonderry, Northern Ireland and on the Clyde at Rosneath, Scotland could be used by the US Navy escort forces engaged in defence of the trans-Atlantic and Russian convoys. With reference to training US naval personnel in the UK, the American Admirals Hall, King, Kirk, Stark and Wilkes had agreed that they would not concentrate on providing basic training in amphibious warfare for them as this was given in America.

There were two assault-training centre's used by the British navy participating in *Operation Neptune*, the amphibious component of *Operation Overlord*. One centre was at Hayling Island, Hampshire, used to introduce the assault forces to the basics of amphibious assault. The other at Inverary, Scotland that became the centre for advanced combined-operation training for the three services.

The build up of the American naval presence during 1943 in Devon and Cornwall resulted in the arrival of high-ranking American officers and their staff who were involved in planning and training men before they faced the challenge of combat with the enemy. No great military enterprise can be free from frictions caused by individual personalities and *Neptune* was no exception. What did these high ranking naval offices think of each other? The outspoken American Rear Admiral John Hall, a student of amphibious war, was nicknamed 'Viking' by General Eisenhower. In November 1943 he had been appointed Commander of the 11th Amphibious force, and his orders were to plan, oversee and execute the training and readiness of the armed forces that were to assault the shores of the French coast. Rear Admiral Hall established his command at Devonport, Plymouth. This Command also gave him operational and administrative control over nine US naval bases in the UK and 235 landing craft that as D-Day got closer significantly increased in number.[6] Rear Admiral Kirk, whose personality and methods caused friction with his peers and colleagues, had been assigned as Commander of Task Force 122 'O' (Omaha). Admiral Ernest King, Commander-in-Chief of the Atlantic Fleet, described as the most disliked Allied leader of the Second World War: 'he was always in a rage'. King eventually reached the rank of US Fleet Admiral.

Admiral Harold Stark, nicked name 'Betty' was appointed Commander of the US naval forces in Europe and was ordered by President Roosevelt to be based in London to make use of his naval experience, but also to get him out of the way. Admiral King was a critic of Stark who for some reason believed that he was distracting and eroding the war effort.

Over 2000 American naval personnel were based in and around the small riverside town of Fowey, Cornwall. This contemporary painting by Dwight Shepler, c.1944, at first conveys a peaceful scene, but on further examination one can depict an American jeep, US servicemen and a harbour full of American amphibious craft of different sizes.

Falmouth was very much involved in the activities of the American navy leading up to D-Day. This watercolour by Dwight Shepler which he titled 'Platypus of Falmouth' is of a landing craft on a Falmouth slipway.

However Stark made a significant contribution to developing the Advanced Amphibious training bases. It was Admiral Stark who decided on establishing Appledore as a major training base. Rear Admiral John Wilkes was a highly skilled and competent US Navy Commander. Up to the outbreak of war Wilkes had served most of his career in submarines. In July 1943 he was appointed Commander of Landing Craft and bases in Europe. From the summer of 1943 he had organised the US naval bases in the west of England. Wilkes had established his headquarters at Falmouth before transferring his base to Plymouth.

Rear Admiral Don Moon was Commander of Force 'U' that planned to land on Utah beach on D-Day. At the end of 1943, as Captain Donald Moon, he was serving in the War Plans Division of the staff of the Chief of Naval Operations when Admiral King promoted him to the rank of Rear Admiral.[7] According to Yung, an American senior research analyst, Rear Admiral Moon was the least qualified to participant in amphibious warfare and had the least amount of time to train and prepare his amphibious Assault Force. In the opinion of Admiral Hall, Rear Admiral Moon was unsure of himself, a workaholic, he would not delegate his work and rarely took time off to relax and socialise.[8] He was in charge of Exercise Tiger, referred to in chapter eight, and an important figure associated with the ill-fated operation. Before the arrival of Rear Admiral John Hall a huge amount of preparatory work was carried out in the constructing of the naval bases for the arrival of the landing craft. By the end of July 1943, the Americans had conducted a survey of possible naval bases in south-west England and had decided on nearly all the locations that the US Navy would want to use to assemble, train and prepare for the invasion of France.

Co-operating with the American naval force was the British Admiral Sir Bertram Ramsay. During the First World War he commanded the destroyer HMS *Broke*, synonymous with 'Evans of the Broke'. Ramsay retired from the Royal Navy in 1938 but returned with the encouragement of Winston Churchill to help deal with the threat of war. During the Quebec Conference of August 1943, the First Sea Lord, Sir Dudley Pound, recommended to the Prime Minister Winston Churchill that Sir Charles Little, the Commander in Chief Portsmouth, be appointed as the Allied Naval Commander, Expeditionary Force, but Churchill objected and proposed Ramsay for the post, as Vice Admiral Ramsay had been responsible for Operation Dynamo, the Dunkirk evacuation of 1940. Later in 1944, he was promoted to the rank of Admiral and appointed Naval Commander-in Chief of the Allied Naval Expedition for the Allied invasion of France.[9] The US Admiral Hall and other

Admiral Sir Bertram Ramsay (centre) on a tour of the US *Ancon*.

A propaganda poster depicting the friendly relations that had been formed between American and British naval ratings in the fight against the enemy.

US naval commanders were critical of Ramsay perhaps because all sea movements were placed under his control. Both Admiral Hall and Admiral Stark felt Ramsay and his Staff planned in too great a detail. Ramsay found Stark 'a shrewd old man'. Ramsay had confided in a letter to his wife that there were many pitfalls and in an Allied operation there were bound to be jealousies. Before the end of the war Admiral Ramsay was killed in a plane crash.

The decision to mount the United States invasion forces in south-west England meant many naval facilities were required. The establishment of US naval basis required the provision of adequate living and office accommodation, for example 15 000 USN officers and men were based within the Plymouth Command. This included the crews of the numerous small landing craft. The responsibility of making these craft available to the US Navy was given to Plymouth's Commander-in-Chief, Admiral Leatham, who controlled all sailings and movement of shipping under his Command. The C-in-C Plymouth also provided many bases for the US Navy, facilities of varying sizes.

Setting up these bases was one of the earliest undertakings leading up to the training and eventual departure of the American forces for Normandy.[10] This was a huge challenge, as the south-west ports did not, at first, have the facilities for loading and accommodating their craft. To overcome this problem concrete embarkation hards, known as 'chocolate blocks', were constructed. These were constructed with a slope that led down to the water, below the low-water mark. The design was made so that a landing craft could run its bows onto the hard whatever the state of the tide, open its ramp and load or unload vehicles by simply driving them on or off the craft. The hards were equipped with a pipeline for supplying vessels with fuel and water.

Most of the naval bases in south-west England had been commissioned by December 1943. As the naval bases had not been ready until December 1943, only a few US amphibious craft had arrived in the Westcountry, thereafter they arrived in large numbers. The appearance of the different types and sizes of landing craft was somewhat strange at first to the local seafaring communities. Westcountry people had never seen the like of these strange-looking craft that arrived in their port. Those who lived by the sea had been used to seeing boats with a pointed bow and keel, whereas what had arrived were flat-bottomed craft that opened at the front. Furthermore landing craft were not named but identified by a letter(s) and a number on the bow.

The craft were designed to enable troops and cargo to load or unload from their bows and were seen as a means of landing a mass troops on shore. These boats became a familiar sight in the harbours and ports throughout the South West as they performed a vital role in the amphibious exercises and for the D-Day landings.

There were many different types of craft, each with its own variants. The large ocean-going flat-bottomed Landing Ship Tank (LST) was a familiar sight in certain Devon

The American servicemen were known for their generosity towards children. This picture shows a naval officer surrounded by Devon children prior to them attending a party organised for them by a naval unit.

harbours. The LST was the largest beaching vessel capable of discharging military cargo directly on to the shore without having to dock or use a crane to unload. An LST had the capacity to carry 70 trucks or 20 M4 Sherman tanks. The second deck of a LST was used to accommodate troops, including bunk beds and messing. There were bathrooms, showers, toilets and a galley that could cater for up to 250 troops. The LSTs were armed with anti-aircraft defences. Naval officers had their separate accommodation and mess. LSTs were organised into flotillas of 18 ships, each flotilla was subdivided into three groups of six LSTs, and each group had a commanding officer. The size of a LST crew could vary but was in the order of 10 Officers and 15 men.

The Landing Craft Tank (LCT) was a smaller vessel than the LST; it could carry 5 medium tanks. It had a tendency to roll when out at sea.

Landing Craft Infantry (LCI) was a follow-up vessel, designed to come up to a beach and to allow troops to disembark rapidly using a gangway. Arguably the most familiar image of a landing craft was the Landing Craft Personnel (LCVP) or the Higgins Boat, named after the designer and manufacturer. This form of craft was not entirely new in the Westcountry for Brigadier Montgomery had used flat-bottomed craft in the 1938 amphibious exercise at Slapton Sands. Furthermore in 1940 the Commandos used them at Plymouth and for training on the River Dart and, with the arrival of the US troops, they became a common sight in the Westcountry ports. These small mass-produced craft carried 35 troops, or a jeep and 12 men. Its disadvantage was that the boat did not handle like a conventional vessel. Its flat bottom and shallow draft made it susceptible to drift to leeward or get pushed sideways by the wind. But its shallow draft allowed them to move right on to the shoreline. and the steel ramp could quickly be lowered to allow the rapid disembarkment of troops. The US LCVPs were organised as flotillas each of twelve craft and were used for both small and large landing exercises. The British equivalent to the LCVP was the Landing Craft Assault (LCA).

DUKWs were a cross between a truck and a boat. This form of amphibious transport was used at the assault-training centre, North Devon and at Slapton Sands. Its advantage over other craft was to carry supplies or troops between ships and shore without having to unload its cargo on the beach. One disadvantage was moving from sand to a hard surface meant having to raise the tyre pressures for efficient operation.

Assault ships, many were adapted peacetime passenger liners, were used to transport troops en masse. The troops were transferred from ship to small landing craft sometimes by climbing down the rope netting that had been slung down the side of the ship.

From the beginning the Americans suffered casualties. Security initially was lax, for example, the *Western Morning News* was allowed to report the deaths of fourteen American soldiers who, on an exercise, had drowned in a river estuary.

US NAVAL AMPHIBIOUS BASE SALCOMBE

Salcombe is the most southerly town in Devon, it is situated on the Kingsbridge estuary and close to the Slapton Battle Training Area. The Salcombe Naval base, established on the 23 September 1943 although not the largest, was one of the earliest bases built by the US Construction Battalion for the repair and maintenance of landing craft.

All available hotels, houses, garages, and workshops in the town were requisitioned, as were the boat stores and waterside workshops. Preparations had been made to receive an intake of 2000 naval personnel. Hutted camps were erected on the rugby field and at Kingsale Road. The presence of the US personnel eventually equalled the civilian population.

Commissioned on 23 November 1943, Commander H. Henszen was the officer in command; his headquarters was The Salcombe Hotel. The Americans built a large slipway and took over nearly all the boat stores. The St Elmo Hotel was used as a hospital.

During 1943, the barge organisation HMS *Salcombe* was transferred to Exmouth as HMS *Tennyson*.[11] Other than the work associated with marine craft, Salcombe Naval Base was involved in amphibious training. It functioned as an advanced training base for landing craft crews. The US 6th and 7th Beach Battalion that had arrived from Falmouth were accommodated in a hutted camp on Salcombe Hill. Their task on D-Day would be to clear beach obstructions and act as Beach Masters to enable assault landing craft to unload their men on the beaches.[12] The beach battalions practiced landings on the small beaches near to Salcombe that included Fisherman's Cove at East Portlemouth.[13] The Salcombe Beach Battalions also participated in the major Slapton Sands Amphibious exercises.

Below HMS *Britannia*, Dartmouth is Coronation Park which the US Navy took over and used as a maintenance and repair depot.

US NAVAL AMPHIBIOUS BASE DARTMOUTH

On the 22 November 1943 the US Dartmouth Naval base was established. The lack of available accommodation at Dartmouth had resulted in the Amphibious Base being first set up at Sandridge Park, located on the other side of the River Dart, between the villages of Galmpton and Stoke Gabriel. As the base expanded various local properties were taken over by the American Navy. They included Maypole House, Hunters Lodge and Greenway, the latter once the home of the author Agatha Christie. These were used as staff headquarters for many of the marine craft flotillas. These scattered units made it very inconvenient for the American Naval base to carry out its tasks. After the Dartmouth naval cadets had been evacuated to Cheshire, the Americans amphibious units moved to the Royal Naval College, Dartmouth where a school for amphibious training and gunfire support was established. The Naval College then became the headquarters for the Americans. Below the Naval College by the River Dart, the US Navy opened a repair division at Coronation Park and this became increasingly busy with the large number of marine craft requiring repairs or servicing. The riverside embankment and Coronation Park was a restricted area for civilians who required a pass to enter.

One of the most remarkable means of transport that was used in the invasion of Normandy was the Rhino. These were ferries sufficient to take up to 40 vehicles and were propelled by two heavy outboard propulsion units. The assembly of these Rhinos by the US Navy Construction Battalion took place at Falmouth, Cornwall; later they were built at

A view of a loaded Rhino barge out in the English Channel These self-propelled ungainly barges were made of steel and girders.

Plymouth and Dartmouth.[14] The construction site at Dartmouth was upriver at Waddeton where slips had been built to repair landing craft. The US Naval Authorities decided that twenty Rhinos would be needed at Omaha and eleven at Utah beach. The display of landing craft tied up in any of the Westcountry ports could at times be a bewildering sight, as the ports were used for both major and minor amphibious exercises. Landing craft would come and go and sometimes up to 500 small craft in rows of four were tied up alongside the Dartmouth Embankment. On dry days it was a common site to see long lines of American servicemen sitting on the Embankment waiting to embark. Practice runs and small-scale exercises started each morning with trainee sailors being directed to a particular vessel.[15] The boats would take on troops, then sail out of the River Dart and make their way to Slapton Beach. Many of the coxswains of these small landing craft were British naval personnel. The larger craft at Dartmouth were moored in mid river and stretched as far as one could see and beyond.

US NAVAL AMPHIBIOUS BASE PLYMOUTH.

By the end of 1943, the arrival of so many US Army and Naval personnel in the Plymouth area gave the impression there were more of them than local residents. By early 1944 every port, river estuary and creek became full of landing craft of every shape and size reflecting the build-up for action at sometime in the near future.[16] On the 8 November, 1943 a US Naval amphibious base was commissioned in Plymouth with Queen Anne's Battery as the headquarters. One of its many functions was to train naval personnel for the D-Day landings. The American Manadon Field Hospital, Plymouth, had already been built to cope with the expected casualties that were anticipated to arrive from the fighting in France and to provide medical care for the increasing number of American servicemen that continued to arrive in this part of Devon. The base was also concerned with the service and repair of all types of marine craft. A large assembly of different workshops, for example a blacksmith, carpenter, and a machine shop were set up at Queen Anne's Battery, Coxside.

This US Naval presence at Plymouth, not only grew, but spread across the city to Devonport and its fringes. Many American personnel were employed at the Royal Naval Dockyard in Devonport. The Commanding Officer, Captain Quimby was resident at Hamoaze House, Mount Wise. Alongside the River Tamar at Saltash and Calstock sub-bases to service and repair small craft were established. The US Edinburgh Road Camp, Devonport, consisted of large galvanised Quonset huts that had been hastily built to accommodate the personnel of Rear Admiral Moon who had been appointed Commander of Force 'U'.

Opposite, bottom left: Waddeton shipway located up the River Dart near Noss Mayo was used by the US Navy as a repair base for amphibious craft. This painting by the American war artist Dwight Shepler shows a damaged LCI (Landing Craft Infantry) under repair after attempting to rescue a sister ship from the rocks near Paignton. March 1944.

Opposite, bottom right: Rhino barges were self-propelled and had a shallow draft. They were capable of carrying huge loads of equipment including tanks, trucks, jeeps and other military items which could be unloaded directly on to flat beaches, Originally built in Cornwall they were eventually constructed at Coronation Park, Dartmouth. This Dwight Shepler painting is of a Rhino by the side of the River Dart with its propellors swung clear of the water March 1944.

Queen Anne's Battery, was the centre of operations for the US Navy amphibious craft based around Plymouth. This picture shows the location of the base with an amphibious craft laid up. In the background is Plymouth Citadel and Drake's Island.

A US navy shore patrol outside their headquarters at St Georges Hall, East Street, Stonehouse. The patrol men were renowned for their smartness. In this picture they are standing by their jeeps, used to patrol across the city.

A superb close up picture of LST 490 stranded on the rocks alongside the Plymouth Breakwater after D-Day. It was eventually refloated.

It was at the Edinburgh Road Camp that Admiral Moon spent long hours planning Force 'U's part in the landings on Utah Beach, Normandy. Admiral Moon's flagship was the USS *Bayfield*, APA-33, that had been launched on 15 February 1943 and was moored on the River Tamar, opposite the Royal Dockyard. An important if unobtrusive construction was the Turnchapel Hard laid down at Sycamore Beach on the River Plym.

EXETER US NAVAL SUPPLY BASE

By November 1943 all the Seabee units (United States Navy Construction Battalion) in Britain, with the exception of one were involved in constructing new bases in Devon, Cornwall and Wales. The largest single base construction undertaken by the Seabees in southwest England was the Exeter supply base, commissioned on 4 February 1944. The base was built on a golf course, located south of the city and eventually grew to cover ninety-five acres of land. In addition seventy-five acres of storage space was utilised in other parts of the city. Over 80 warehouses were erected, together with administration and personnel accommodation that was provided for 2700 officers and men. Most of the storage buildings were Quonset huts. A purpose-built railway siding was constructed to bring the enormous quantities of essential supplies to the store. Seven miles of roadway was laid to serve the base. A retired US Navy Chief Petty Officer recalls that in an adjacent hut were he was based in Exeter, there were two men who had been awarded German Iron Crosses in the First World War, who he and his friends never trusted.

EXMOUTH

HMS *Tennyson* was a shore establishment based at the Imperial Hotel Exmouth that was responsible for the Landing Barge Vehicles (LBV) that were moored between the Exmouth Bight and Powderham. At first as the barges lacked power they were moved by tugs. The warehouses that backed on to Victoria Road were used as naval workshops that fitted each of the barges with engines. The barges played an important role by providing food, water and fuel and for the repair and maintenance of allied landing craft.

APPLEDORE AND INSTOW, north DEVON

The area around Appledore with its flat beaches was selected in July 1943 by the American Admiral Stark to establish a major amphibious training base for naval landing crews and in assisting the army in accustoming its troops to boat work. An old Chesapeake Bay steamer S.S. *Warfield* that had made its way across the Atlantic to provide living quarters for many of the officers and men. Nearby Appledore was the Combined Operations Experimental Establishment (COXE) where British Royal Marines and naval personnel were trained in placing charges to destroy obstacles.

A panoramic view of Instow Beach c.1944, used by the American forces for amphibious trials and exercises.

Top left: The US Instow amphibious base was occupied keeping tank and infantry landing craft operational. The tidal flow could leave a landing craft high and dry as shown by this painting that depicts a Le Tourneau mobile crane hoisting the stern of a craft to replace a propellor. Dwight Shepler, February 1944.

Top right: Near to the town of Appledore, north Devon, the rivers Taw and Torridge converge to flow into the Bristol Channel. It was an area used by the US Army and the Combined Operation Experimental Establishment (COXE) to test and evaluate various weapons of war for the forthcoming invasion of France. One was the Great Panjandrum. Dwight Shepler's watercolour shows the American army practicing loading Sherman Tanks. May 1944.

Above right: Two beached landing craft with Appledore in the background.

TIVERTON NAVAL STORE AND SPARE PART DEPOT
ESTABLISHED SEPTEMBER 1943

By January 1944, many US Naval bases had been commissioned and there had been a gradual increase in American Forces in south-west England, with the US 29th Infantry Division actively involved in training exercises. The greatest speed in the build-up of American forces occurred in the six months prior to D-Day (6 June 1944).

---

1. Morison Samuel. *The Invasion of France and Germany. History of United States Naval Operations in World War Two*. Volume Eleven, 1953. Navy Institute Press p.9.
2. Morison Samuel. *The Invasion of France and Germany*, Volume Eleven p.3.
3. Yung, Christopher, *Gators of Neptune*, 2006. Naval Institute Press USA. P.14.
4. Yung Christopher, *Gators of Neptune* p.14.
5. Morison Samuel. *The Invasion of France and Germany*, Volume Eleven p.51-52.
6. Yung, Christopher. *Gators of Neptune*, 2006.
7. Yung Christopher. *Gators of Neptune*, 2006. p.18.
8. Yung Christopher, *Gators of Neptune*, 2006. p.18.
9. Lowe, Robert and John, Major (eds). *The Year of D-Day. The 1944 Diary of Admiral Sir Bertram Ramsay*, 1994 The University of Hull press p.xxxv.
10. Yung Christopher, *Gators of Neptune*, 2006. p. 14.
11. Murch David and Muriel. *American and British Naval Forces at Slapton*, 1943-1945. 1994 Phantom Press p.5.
12. Murch David and Muriel. *American and British Naval Forces at Slapton*. p.10.
13. Murch David and Muriel. *American and British Naval Forces at Slapton*. p.10.
14. *Assembling the Rhinos and Causeways. US Navy Construction Battalions during World War Two* p.105. Naval Historic Centre, Washington Naval Yard. USA,
15. Leading Seaman George Cox. *We Remember D-Day*, 1994 , p.11. Dartmouth History Research Group, Dartmouth Museum.
16. Letter ex P.O.Wren, Hilda Crowe to G. D. Wasley, 6 January 2001.

4 American Troops in Devon

THE ARRIVAL OF American troops in Devon could be described as low key. There was no marching through the streets with cheering crowds to welcome them. At first a certain amount of reserve was shown towards the GIs by the local communities.

Accommodation for the troops was scarce some units were based in old army barracks while others were billeted in people's homes. The Americans lost no time setting up their camps ('Little Americas') comprising large bell tents and/or Quonset huts. American officers were usually accommodated in requisitioned buildings, hotels or with families. The American servicemen who arrived in Britain from the United States had left their country where a booming economy had developed and where life for many was now so different from how they lived in the 1930s at the time of the Great Depression when people suffered from unemployment and a lack of money. When America entered the Second World War there were over three million unemployed in the United States yet the standard of living had risen and, despite the introduction of rationing, there were few shortages. More American people were better off than ever before.

The American troops had been primed about the British people by the issue of a booklet *Instructions for American Servicemen in Britain 1942*. The book stated that 'almost before you actually meet the people, you will hear them speaking English! At first you may not understand what they are talking about and they may not understand what you say'. For the British, they came to learn there was no such thing as the all-American male as America was comprised of many different races and cultures.

Racial tension existed in the American army with segregation and an alien attitude towards the black US troops. Black men were excluded from the US Marine Corps and the US Air Force. Because of the tensions that were created between blacks and whites it soon became evident to the Devonians that black American servicemen were treated as members of an underclass. Many Devon people befriended the black soldiers who found the locals friendly and polite. At home they were segregated from the white men and their discrimination was shown by the minor tasks they were given to perform. Not until the Battle of the Bulge in December 1944 were black American soldiers placed in the firing line of battle. The segregation of black troops from white troops often resulted in violence when both met

Every member of the US forces arriving in Britain was given a guide explaining many of the customs of the country and the social behaviour of the people.

American soldiers led by a flag bearer carrying the Stars and Stripes march pass Sherwell, Plymouth, towards the devastated city centre. This must have been a special occasion as evident by the crowds of people lining the streets and, usually, the American forces shied away from public parades

Bell tents viewed from a private house in a US marshalling area. The pictured resident, like many others who lived inside a marshalling area was, because of the strict security, forbidden to speak to the military personnel that were camped close by.

Popular, or 'Swing' music was introduced by the American servicemen during the war.

up when out in the evenings. An order was given that the black and white American soldiers went out at on different nights to prevent brawling.

Whatever information American servicemen had been given to establish good relations with the British people their arrival had little immediate impact on Devon society. However what people noticed about the GIs was the distinctive army forage cap and the quality and cut of their ranker's uniform compared with the rough texture of the British soldiers battle-dress. When wearing a uniform on leave the American soldiers always wore a tie. The design and appearance of an American officer's uniform was an added attraction to many British women as it gave them the impression they had just stepped out from a Hollywood film set. Many of the American GIs, described as 'overpaid and oversexed', were better fed and clothed than they had ever dreamed of during the recent American economic depression of the 1930s.

At first the local residents and American servicemen tended to keep their distance from each other. But the Devonians soon realised the Americans were friendly, with a tendency for some of them to be noisy, to brag and to speak with a drawl. Other American servicemen were more conservative in their behaviour and went quietly on their way. The *Exeter Express & Echo* published the text of a BBC broadcast given by a Major of the US Army. His first problem was 'getting use to the blackout', and he was surprised on visiting an English pub for the first time, how quiet and friendly it was compared to the noisy bars back in the USA.[1] What social barriers existed were eventually broken down and many Americans were invited by local people into their homes.

1939. "MAY I HAVE THE PLEASURE OF THIS DAWNCE?"

1944. "LET'S 'CUT A RUG', SISTER!"

Young women were charmed by these smooth-talking young men. One Plymouth woman remembers the dances at a church hall in Devonport with the sentimental wartime music associated with Glenn Miller who, after D-Day, arrived with his band at Plymouth and played at the Odeon Cinema. She recalls that soon after the Americans arrived the local dance band that had been booked failed to turn up resulting in some of the American boys contacting their barracks to organise and send a 'scratch band' to play at the dance. The standard of music was unbelievable and from then on they played every week without charge. They were not always the same musicians but were nevertheless excellent music makers and soon the church hall became jammed to the doors.[2] The Americans lost no time in romancing the local ladies. If it had been Victorian times it is likely many of the women because of their behaviour would have been submitted to censure.

Other American troops chose to spend their free time at their base perhaps reading, listening to music, watching a film in their camp cinema, or eating in the canteen. The Americans who visited the local pubs discovered they were friendly, sociable places. However they did not like the warm English beer; more to their taste was the Devonshire cider. They played their baseball or American football, but few understood the game of cricket.

A snapshot of a canteen inside an American army camp.

Troops lining up to enter the cook-house for a meal. Note that the black and white soldiers are in separate queues.

Opposite, top left: Units of the American Army arrived in Devon and Cornwall at a time when south-west England was experiencing air raids. To counter air attacks on Plymouth the Americans reinforced the city's defence by providing additional anti-aircraft guns. Here a pom-pom gun (quick firing) gun was sited on Plymouth Hoe close to the lighthouse.

Opposite, top right: A larger variant of a Quonset hut which, along with tents, were used to accommodate most of the American troops based in Devon during the Second World War.

At this period there were strong racial prejudices in American Society that was manifest in the American armed services in Devon. For example black troops were restricted with regarding to admission to certain venues and there were many serious brawls in Devon pubs when black and white servicemen met up. There were also fights between American and British servicemen, mainly over women. By 21 December 1943, the time of the completion of the civilian evacuation of part of South Hams there were 36 369 American troops stationed in Devon, and by the end of April 1944 this had more than double to 85 191 US servicemen in the county.[3]

THE US 29th INFANTRY DIVISION

In 1942, the year when Exeter was severely Blitzed, the Americans had started to build up their forces to prepare for the Allied invasion of Europe. The US 29th Infantry Division (the Blue and Gray), was a National Guard Division composed of men from the Southern states of Maryland and Virginia. After sailing across the Atlantic in the liner RMS *Queen Mary* was caught up in a disaster. On the 2 October 1942 HMS *Curacoa* had been detailed to escort the *Queen Mary* back to Glasgow. As the two ships zig-zagged into position, a common wartime manoeuvre to confuse any U-boats, there was an error of judgment as the *Queen Mary* struck the cruiser and sliced the *Curacoa* in half. The liner sailed on and did not stop to pick up any survivors: 338 British sailors lost their life.[4]

On 22 July, Major General Gerhardt was appointed the new commander of the 29th Division. From the 11 October 1942 until 27 May 1943 the 29th Division was stationed at Tidworth, Wiltshire. The 29th then moved on at the end of May to West Devon and Cornwall. The Division established its Headquarters at Abbotsfield Hall, off the Callington Road, Tavistock. Among the divisional units based in Devon were the 121 Engineer Combat Battalion stationed at Paignton, the 227 Field Artillery Battalion at Okehampton and the 116 Infantry Regiment camped in and around Plymouth, for example at Ivybridge.

On 11 February 1944, General Eisenhower arrived in Plymouth and travelled to Tavistock to inspect the US 29th Infantry Division.[5] The officers of the US 29th Infantry Division in Devon were accommodated in local hotels while the GIs lived in barracks or field camps of canvas tents or Quonset huts, a lightweight elongated prefabricated structure with a semi circular roof of corrugated steel.

An American army infantry division was composed of 14 000 troops. Each division had three infantry regiments and each regiment had three infantry battalions. In addition Infantry divisions could be reinforced with additional attachments, for example, field artillery and a chemical battalion, and these could increase the size of the division up to 22 000 men. Infantry Divisions were not specifically organised to conduct amphibious

General Eisenhower, Commander of Allied forces inspecting troops of the US 29th Infantry Division outside Tavistock Parish Church, opposite the market. To the left of the picture is Lord Tedder (with his fur lined collar turned up) the deputy Commander of the Allied forces, c. April 1944.

assaults and were required to undergo specialized training. The 29th Infantry Division based in south-west England consisted of three regiments (plus additional units):

115th Regimental Combat Team (RCT) based in Cornwall at Bodmin and Launceston.
175th (RCT) based in Cornwall at St Ives, Helston, Camborne, Penzance.
116th (RCT) based in West Devon.

The First Battalion of the 116th Regiment camped at Ivybridge. The Second Battalion camped at Bridestowe, near Okehampton. The Third Battalion of the 116th were accommodated in the district of Plymouth. The troops of the 116th exercised on Dartmoor often under the most appalling weather conditions. Dartmoor with its broad stretches of undulating land was recognised by some American soldiers from the Hollywood film *The Hound of The Baskervilles*. To the GIs it always seemed to be raining on the moors – a cold stinging horizontal rain.

A large concentration of troops of the 29th Infantry Division on exercise on Dartmoor near the Okehampton training camp.

C Battery of the 11th Field Artillery Battalion of the 29th US Division with a 105mm guns on exercise at the Okehampton range, Dartmoor. It must have been cold when this picture was taken as the gunners were wearing overcoats.

Out in the Devon countryside it was a common occurrence for people to come across columns of US infantrymen out on a training march.

Troops of the 3rd Battalion, 116 Infantry Regiment, 29th Infantry Division, laying chestnut paling at Ringmoor Downs, near Yelverton. 5th October 1943.

A fabular sight on many of Devon's roads and lanes leading up to the departure of the American troops for Normandy were the long processions of army vehicles. This picture shows such stationary transport camouflaged with netting alongside a road.

Training on Dartmoor was remembered by many troops of the 29th Division with loathing, because of the spongy soil, with the men having to battle against a strong wind that always blew. The alternative to cold driving rain was the drenching moorland mists.[6] The most expertly pitched tents were incapable of keeping their occupants dry and water would ooze up from the ground and the rain would loosen and wash out the tent pegs. In the winter month's temperatures would drop and the raw cold would penetrate the stoutest coat and the thickest blanket.

The notorious Dartmoor Prison, that during the war accommodated conscientious objectors, could be seen by many of the American troops camped out on the moor. They viewed the prison with envious eyes as they longed for the comforts enjoyed by the inmates behind the grey stonewalls. The Dartmoor tors provided the only visual relief for the Americans from the dull, drab surroundings. For some soldiers, Haytor bore a remarkable resemblance to an assault boat.

Troops of the 29th Infantry Division lining up in the middle of Falmouth to collect their meal. 31 December 1943.

A convoy of American army trucks carrying troops of the US 29th Infantry Division passing a camp of bell tents in Cornwall. c.1944.

"They won't let on who the camp is for."

Captain Maurice Clift of the 115th Regiment wrote a parody of John Masefield's poem *Sea Fever* about how he felt about Dartmoor (7). The first and last verses read:

I want to go out to the moors again,
To the fog and the rocks and the rain,
To the gorse and the marsh and the muddy pools
Wherein the boys had lain .....

Oh, I'll go out to the moors again.
But mind you and mark me well,
I'll carry enough explosives
To blow the place to hell.

Thousands of US troops were also billeted in tented camps along the stretches of the moorland roads. The whole of north Dartmoor had been requisitioned for military training, although artillery firing predominated. Both the US 4th and 29th Divisions trained intensively on Dartmoor where the sound of battle was constantly heard. Away from camping or training on Dartmoor, troops focused on weapon skill and small-unit training carried out in their camps.

The Ivybridge camp was where Company A of the 116th Battalion was accommodated. The Company had been selected to be part of the first assault wave to land on Omaha Beach on D-Day. Early in July 1943 the 29th Division received orders to commence preliminary amphibious assault training. The program was initially to suffer from a lack of equipment, the only craft available being a few landing boats that had been used by the British Commandos and US Ranger battalions on their raids on the Norwegian and French Coasts. Eventually landing craft were borrowed from the British. At this period barges were used as landing craft and mock-ups of ships' sides were erected. Six months before the first major amphibious exercise on Slapton Sands took place, in January 1944, units of the 29th Division loaded into these craft on the River Dart, Dartmouth and made their way out to sea to practice an assault landing on the Slapton beach.

Life was strict for the 116th Regimental Combat Team. For example, during March 1944, a private lost a water canteen in Slapton Ley. His officer a tough taskmaster and when heard

A wartime time aerial photograph of the village of Ivybridge showing the camp (outlined in black) where Company A (that included the ill-fated Bedford Boys) were based.

Below left: An historic picture of troops of Company A of the 116th Infantry, 29th Division marching through Ivybridge on the first stage of their journey to Weymouth where that would eventually depart, to land on Omaha beach early on D-Day. Few of the soldiers pictured would survive by the end of D-Day.

Above right: A formal photograph that includes images indicated with a cross of 16 of the 19 Bedford boys, all from the same small town of Bedford in Virginia, who were killed when landing in the first wave on Omaha beach on D-Day. The caption tells an even more tragic story.

what had happened he made sure he would learn to take better care of his equipment by punishing him. For seven days the private, who was a poor swimmer, had to jog up a two mile slope accompanied by his Sergeant to a private swimming pool and wade through the cold water that had a thin layer of ice on the surface, wearing all his clothes carrying his equipment and a water canteen.[8] Another place American troops exercised was in the Bableigh Valley, North Devon. The troops would advance a few feet among exploding thunder flashes, beneath a blanket cover of live heavy machine gun fire. Walter Isaac, author of *The Way 'Twas* describes when his father sold the Americans a rack of straw for their palliasses (mattresses), it resulted in a full military operation. A convoy that included every type of vehicle (other than tanks), dispatch riders and military police converged on the field to collect the straw.[9]

Compared to what the Division experienced in the next few months the training, although useful, was of a primitive nature. Men were taught to swim and trained to wade ashore in full equipment from neck-high deep water. The only boats available had been borrowed from the Royal Navy. These small craft and naval barges loaded with men sailed out from Dartmouth Harbour and made for Slapton Sands to assault the beach.

A convoy of heavy American transport, one armed with an anti-aircraft heavy machine gun, waiting at a check-point before proceeding to its destination.

One American soldier records: "again and again we loaded on to landing craft that pitched and rolled out into the Channel and then roared landward to drop ramps over ramps. We lumbered and floundered through surf to the beach and go through the assault drills. So often repeated, these drills became a ritual dance performed by flame-throwers and demolition teams displaying them advancing in stylised movement, to blast paths through barbed wire or through the apertures of bunkers with explosives. Battalion and regimental staffs entered on cue to direct further movements".[10] The 116th Regimental Combat Team were given endurance and strength tests. The criteria for being awarded the 'Expert Infantry Badge' was for the infantryman to be able to run 100 yards in 12 seconds (wearing heavy army shoes and clothing), doing 35 pushups and 10 chin-ups and completing an obstacle course within a prescribed time. Qualification also meant tests on the range

The Americans reinforced the small bridge that spans the entrance to the Boat Float, Dartmouth, to prevent it from collapsing due to the heavy military vehicles that were used.

using small arms weapons. Units of the 29th Division were involved in regular forced marches in all kinds of weather that consisted of road marches and cross-country runs to test the conditions of the troops. For example, C Company, 121 Engineer Combat Battalion, were involved in five-day marches that began on 5th July 1943 from a training area near the main Totnes-Plymouth Road. The following day the march continued that passed the Two Bridges hotel to Dartmeet then back to Gidley Bridge to Paignton. The first and last days of the march were on hard-surfaced roads, the other three days were over Dartmoor. where the weather varied from fair to chilly rain and mist.

In July 1943 the personnel of the American Army's 115th Field Hospital arrived at Plaster Down on the edge of Dartmoor, three miles from Tavistock. Here a modern 1500 bedded Hospital was built to serve American and British servicemen. By the end of 1943 10 000 in-patients and 16 000 out- patients had been treated. Other large American station hospitals in Devon included 316th Hospital, Stover Park, near Newton Abbot, 313th Station Hospital, Fremington near Barnstaple and the 36th Hospital (neuropsychiatric cases) near Exeter.

US 4TH INFANTRY DIVISION

The composition of the US 4th Infantry Division was made up of three regiments, the 8th, 12th, and 22nd Infantry. Each regiment was organised into three 870-man battalions, designated 1st, 2nd and 3rd; battalions that functioned as companies. Each battalion included a headquarters company. The men of the US 4th Infantry Division were known as the 'Ivy Boys', from the Division's Roman-numerical designation IV, subsequently pronounced 'IVY'. To symbolise this name four ivy leaves were entwined to produce the divisional sleeve shoulder patches. The Divisions slogan was 'Steadfast and Loyal'. The troops were a mix of men from the Southern states whose grandfathers had fought in the Civil War under Robert E. Lee; many of the men were farmer's sons.

The Commanding Officer of the 4th Infantry Division was the fifty-four-year-old Major General Raymond Barton described as "a very strict disciplinarian who commanded his division with an iron hand". His manner was firm and brisk. However, Barton commanded respect from his troops. On taking command of the 4th Infantry Division Barton told the men of the 22nd Infantry, "I am your leader, I want you to know what you think. In the not too distant future we will be in battle. When bullets start flying over your head your minds will freeze and you will act according to habit. In order that you develop the right habits, training and discipline must be strict. I know 90 percent of you want to cooperate. I will take care of the other 10 percent".

It was planned that the entire US 4th Infantry would be involved in the Invasion of Normandy with part of the follow up 90th Division, two airborne divisions and many specialized units. The 4th Division had sailed from New York on 18th January 1944 and arrived at Liverpool eleven days later. On disembarkation the troops immediately travelled

Troops of the US 4th Infantry Division line up in a muddy field for a meal in a large tented canteen somewhere in south-west Devon.

Troops of the US 4th Infantry Division embarking on to a landing craft. Notice the large painted letters that spells out 'Dartmouth' on the embankment wall that should have been deleted at the time of the expected invasion of England.

General Omar Bradley Commander of the US First Army speaking to officers in a field near Tavistock.

Troops of the US 4th Infantry Division being briefed by an officer 'somewhere in Devon'.

by train to Devon. The Divisional Headquarters were established at Collipriest, Tiverton. The troops were camped in villages and towns throughout the county. Before the Division had completed unloading its equipment and stores, the 8th Infantry Regiment of the US 4th Division at Heathfield Camp, Honiton, was visited by the Supreme Commander General Eisenhower and his deputy Air Marshal Sir Arthur Tedder. The 4th Division in Devon had arrived three weeks after the Slapton Battle Training Area opened. It had been chosen to assault Utah Beach on D-Day. In addition to the three regiments, the Division had 10 additional units attached to it. They included the Fourth Medical Battalion that had crossed the Atlantic in the liner *Capetown Castle*. The Battalion consisted of 40 Officers, 2 Warrant Officers and 492 enlisted men. Their headquarters was also at Tiverton. The Battalion's Company A command post was at Widworthy near Honiton.

Many of the assembly areas in Devon and Cornwall were located along the edge of roads and wooded areas that had turf surfaces, which once torn up by troops and vehicles quickly turn into quagmires. Because of this the areas were built around secondary paved roads in the shape of sausages, by which name they were known. These huge camping areas were barred to civilians. If it happened that people lived within the bounds of a 'sausage' encampment it made life very difficult for them. The strict security that was enforced forbid the civilian residents to be in personal contact with the American troops. For example, a civilian could be out in the front garden of her cottage with American soldiers on the other side of the gate, but no communication however informal was allowed. This posed a particular problem with children who persisted in hanging around the army's cookhouses.

The size of the American presence in Devon, that continued to increase up to the departure of the troops for D-Day, was bewildering. It sometimes seemed as if there was going to be insufficient space to accommodate them all. The 4th Infantry Division was camped across the county at Seaton in East Devon, and to the north-west as far as Holsworthy, close to the border of Cornwall. Small wooden huts were erected in the hedgerows of the Devon lanes for the storage of artillery shells. The 42nd Field Artillery Battalion was based at Broomhill Camp, Honiton; it was at this camp that a drunken US private killed a sergeant. He was found guilty of murder and executed at Shepton Mallet Prison.

The 44th Field Artillery was based at Denbury Camp (formerly Rawlinson Barracks) close to the village of Denbury near Newton Abbot. Immediately on arrival it lost its Commander in a fatal accident. The 704th Ordnance Company was based at the bypass camp in Exeter. At Tiverton, the headquarters of the US 4th Division, the divisional signals and cavalry reconnaissance troops were encamped).[11]

At Seaton, where the 2nd Battalion of the 8th Regiment of the 4th Infantry Division were stationed, Claridge House, a popular pre-war hotel, accommodated the headquarters company. Empty buildings, including the chalets of a holiday camp were used to provide places for the troops. Many of the US troops appreciated being based in Seaton and friendships developed with the local families. When away on exercise in North Devon and

An inside view of part of the huge stores set up by the Americans in Exeter in preparations for the forthcoming invasion of Normandy. This picture shows packing cases filled with rifles, bren guns and mortars.

An M7 tank of Battery B 42nd Field Artillery about to pass Coronation Park on its way to the hard by the higher ferry, Dartmouth.

confined to camp, some soldiers use to sneak away and return to Seaton to visit their 'adopted families'.[12] As D-Day drew closer, the troops based at Seaton were moved by truck to a tent city on the outskirts of Torquay. They realised this move was no manoeuvre as each day they were getting briefings.

Many of the GIs were nervous; everyone was on edge and eager to get going on their mission to the far shore.

The 12th Infantry Regiment of the 4th Infantry Division arrived at Exmouth in February 1944. The 1st Engineer Special Brigade and the 531 Engineer Shore Regiment had arrived in the town during December 1943. They had temporarily been relieved of combat duties after serving in North Africa. Tunisia, Sicily and Italy. The arrival of the GIs had an impact on the Exmouth community as their presence increased the morale of the townspeople by bringing a spirit of optimism.[13] The American troops were camped under tents on the Rugby Ground.

Troops of the 4th Infantry Division were kept occupied by training as shown by the abstracts from the three official unit reports. For example, the report of the 4th Ren Troop covering Ist February–29th February 1944 records that training in the following subjects has begun or had been accomplished:

1. Physical conditioning – 30 hours completed.
2. Observation – scouting and patrolling, including two days field problems.
3. Map reading – 14 hours mostly class work.
4. German language – Introduction to language and key military words.
5. Employment of cavalry weapons 17 hours, including two days of field problems.
6. First aid – 8 hours on most important phases.
7. Communications – radio operators school began and classes in message writing.
8. Chemical warfare – 6 hours covering all phases.
9. Periods of dismounted drill, orientation, military courtesy.

Opposite, top:
General Sir Bernard Montgomery addressing a large gathering of troops of the US 4th Infantry Division at Newton Abbot on 14 April 1944.

Opposite, bottom:
US troops exercising on Dartmoor. The machine gun crew seen in the front of the picture having dug a foxhole.

Training varied, for example, the same unit report covering I March 1944–31 March 1944 states, " The third week was spent on the Moors, there were problems with training ammunition". The following week two platoons were kept in an area near Tiverton engaged on reconnaissance against each other. From 27–31 March the unit participated in Exercise Beaver. The report then covers the period of April 1944. The first week of April was devoted to the maintenance of vehicles and equipment after Exercise Beaver. Radio classes continued as did drill. The unit strength in May 1944 was 8 Officers and 174 ranks. Time was spent waterproofing vehicles for Exercise Tiger. The unit participated in Exercise Tiger in which it was reported that many important things were learnt on communications, liaison and tactics. A footnote added to this report states there were factors beyond our control, which hampered the efficiency of our operation. These were the late date arrival of the necessary papers and information pertaining to the exercise in which they had participated.

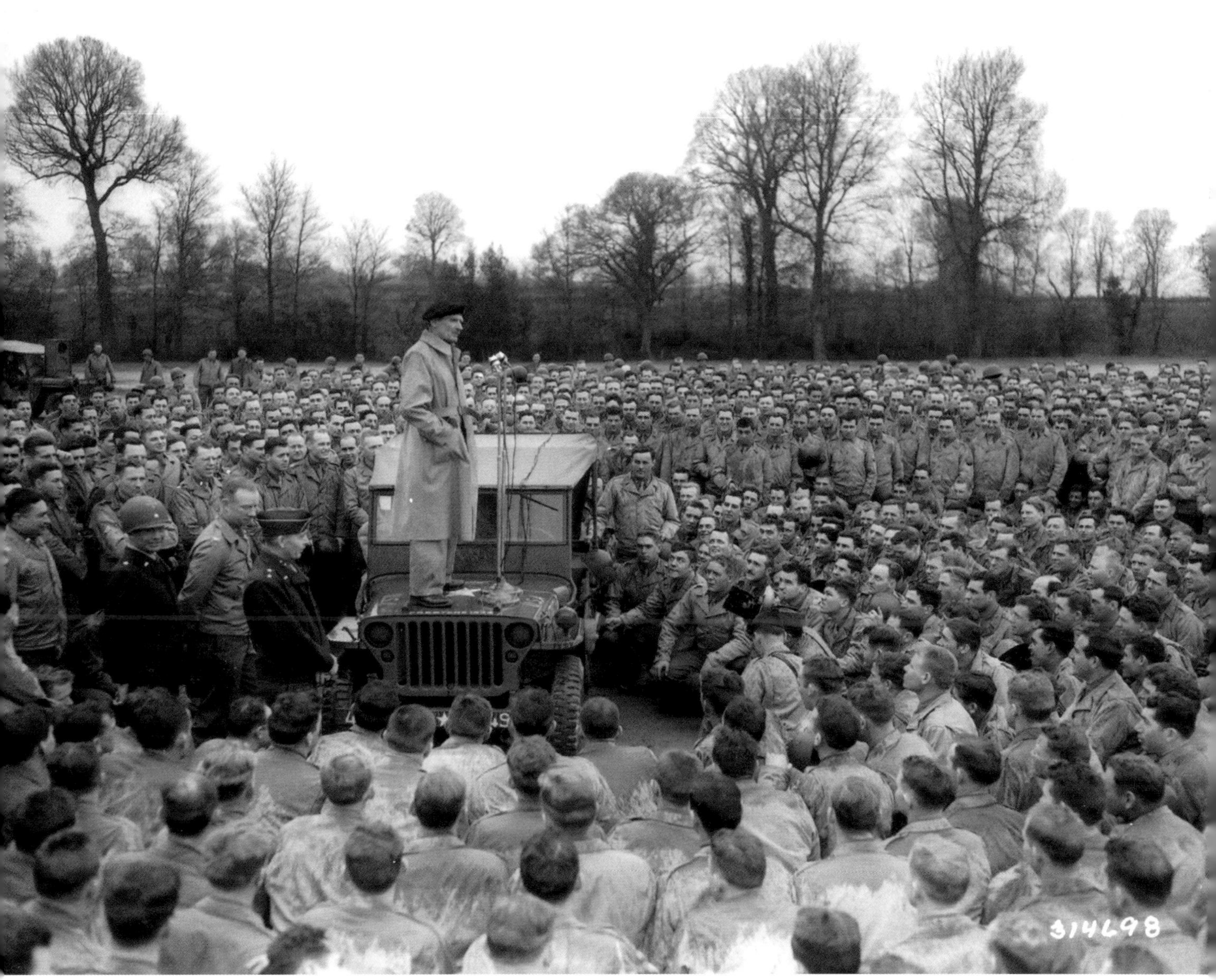
314698

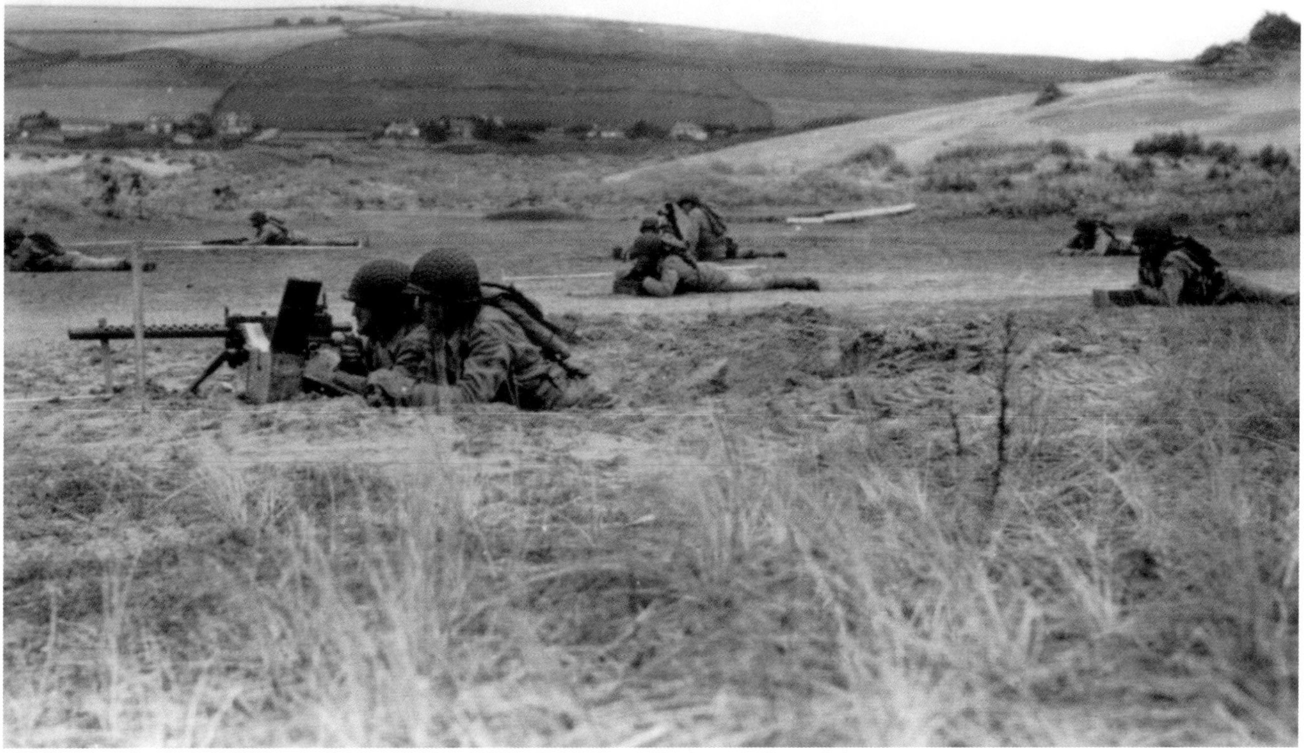

Soldiers on exercise crossing a rope bridge strung across the upper reaches of the River Dart come under fire of exploding ordnance.

US soldiers on Dartmoor washing in a cold moorland stream

---

1. *Exeter Express and Echo*, Exeter 18 January 1944.
2. Gardiner Juliet. *'Over Here' The GIs in wartime Britain* 1992 Collins and Brown, p.116.
3. Reynolds David, *Rich Relations, The American Occupation of Britain 1942-1945*. 1995 Harper Collings. pp.110-111.
4. Thomas David and Holmes Patrick, *Queen Mary and the Cruiser, The Curacoa Disaster* 1997 Leo Cooper pp. 92-95.
5. Butcher Harry, *Three Years with Eisenhower 1946*. Heinemann. p. 417.
6. Reynolds David, *Rich Relations, The American Occupation of Britain 1942- 1945*. 1995 Harper Collins. p123.
7. Reynolds David, p.123.
8. Slaughter John, *Omah Beach and Beyond. The long march of Sgt Bob Slaughter* 2009 Zenith Press. pp. 80-81.
9. Issaac Walter, *The Way Twas*. no date private publication. p.56.
10. Gardiner Juliet, *'Over Here' The GIs in Wartime Britain*, 1992, Collins and Brown. p.197.
11. *History of the US 4th Infantry Division*, IWM.
12. Longmate Arthur. *The G.I's. The Americans in Britain 1942-1945*. 1975, Hutchinson. p.29.
13. Cook Arthur, *Exmouth at War* 2010 Halsgrove, pp.136-139.

5 The Woolacombe Assault Training Centre

THE ATLANTIC WALL

GERMANY HAD IN the summer of 1940 occupied northern Europe. By the end of April 1941 the centre of Plymouth was in ruins caused by the intensive fire raids on the city. In the early summer of 1941 Germany had invaded Russia. Hitler had taken the offensive and placed a number of long-range guns on the French coast to bombard Dover, Folkestone and Allied shipping in the Channel. The enemy shelling caused many civilian casualties. On the 7 December 1941 the United States was at war with Japan who had made a devastating air attack on the US Pacific Naval Base at Pearl Harbor, Hawaii, destroying a large part of the American naval force. Four days later Hitler declared war on the United States resulting in a change in the conduct of the war.

After the Battle of Britain and the cancellation of the invasion of England, Hitler adopted a defensive policy along the English Channel coast because he was concerned about the possibility of Allied landings somewhere along the French coast. He believed that the British would attempt to land military forces on the shores of occupied Europe, but exactly where these landings would take place was not known. The Germans began to install coastal defences along the channel coastline from Holland to the north-west of France, as there was a belief that any attempted Allied landing would take place somewhere in this region. In December 1941 Hitler ordered the construction of the 'Atlantic Wall', a massive system of fortifications that would extend from Norway to Spain.[1] The German Todt organization was the principal constructor. General Feldmarschall von Rundstedt, who had been recalled to active service, was appointed Commander-in-Chief.

On the 28 March 1942 British Commandos departing from Falmouth surprised the Germans by mounting an amphibious attack on the heavily defended dry dock at St Nazaire on the north-west Atlantic coast of occupied France. The objective of the raid was to cause enough destruction to the dock to prevent any German warships from being repaired there.[2] The attack took place near to the scene of the SS *Lancastria* disaster of 17 June 1940 when the ship was bombed resulting in the loss of an estimated 4000 lives, double the number of lives lost on the *Titanic*.[3] Although the St Nazaire Raid achieved its objective, 169 Commandos were killed.

On 19 August 1942 an allied force attempted an amphibious landing on Dieppe's beach, the objective to prove it was possible to temporarily capture a major port and to obtain prisoners to gather intelligence. The Dieppe Raid involved 6000 troops, mainly from the Canadian 2nd Division and 50 US Rangers. The mission in spite of many acts of bravery was a disaster, as sixty percent of the Allied forces were captured, killed or wounded; likewise the RAF suffered the loss of many aircraft and the Royal Navy over 500 casualties. The part of the French coastal area that was attacked was not heavily fortified and it is thought the Germans had prior knowledge of the attempted landing, as it appeared not to surprise the defending forces. Severe lessons were learned by the Allies regarding attempting an amphibious

A map of northern Europe indicating the extent of the Atlantic Wall. It must be appreciated that not all the Atlantic Wall was heavily defended. The main defences were concentrated along the shores of northern France, Belgium and Holland.

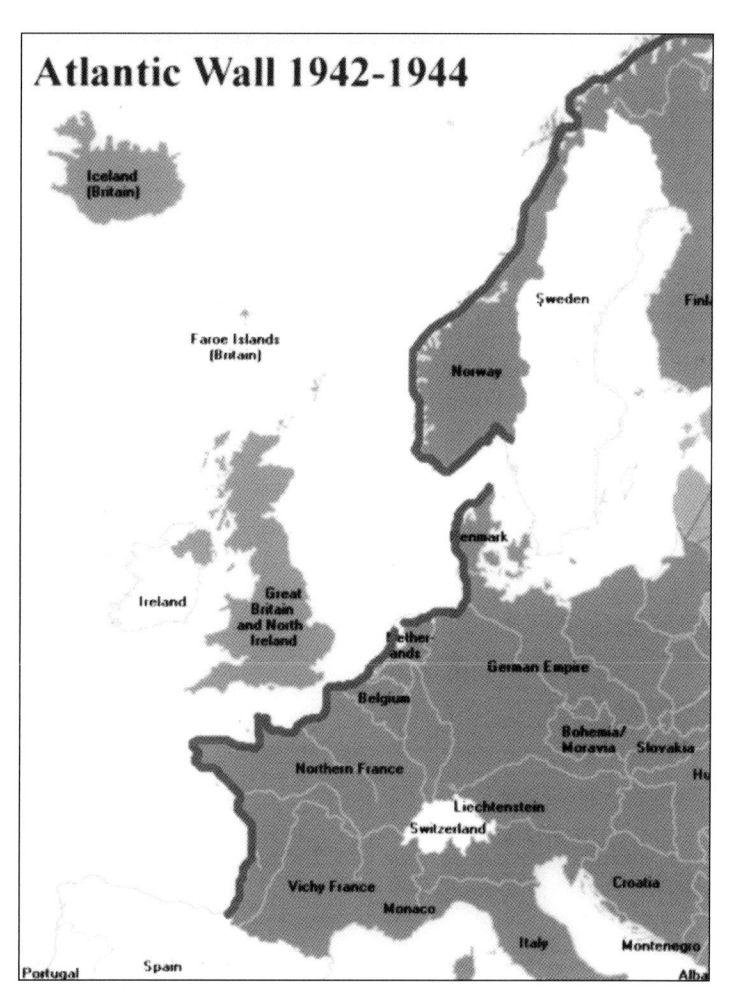

Clockwise from top left: This German propaganda poster referring to the expected Allied invasion is designed to remind the Allies what disaster befell them when they attempted a landing in the infamous Dieppe Raid of 1942.

A cartoon published in a German wartime newspaper conveying the strength of the Atlantic Wall. It shows Winston Churchill colliding with the European shield and the mighty sword of the German Armoured Divisions that would be used to throw the Allied invaders back into the sea.

A poster in Dutch exalting the strength of the Atlantic Wall. The brief message proclaims that 1943 will not be like 1918, the year the German Army was forced to sign the Armistice.

A British propaganda poster indicating the enemy is watching you.

A posed photograph intended to convey an image of fierceness by these Panzer troops that were part of the German defence in the west.

attack on the German channel defences. The consequences of the Allied attempted landing at Dieppe alerted the Germans to further attempted amphibious landings by the Allies. The raid confirmed Hitler's belief that the Atlantic Wall would be successful in defeating an Allied invasion and the Allies would launched an invasion at a place near a port that had flat sandy beaches.[4] Hitler ordered the construction of the Atlantic Wall to be speeded up, including the reinforcement of a massive system of fortifications and obstacles as a means of thwarting the Allies. The Atlantic Wall was never a totally coordinated defence system based on a master plan, the defences varied in length and strength. As the construction of the Wall continued so the existing defences were strengthened with concrete bunkers built to withstand heavy bombardment. Josef Goebbels, the German Minister of Propaganda, very cleverly published posters and other material suggesting that the Atlantic Wall was impregnable.

Hitler believed at first the Pas-de-Calais coast would be the place of a forthcoming invasion. An important contribution by the Allies related to preparing for D-Day was the success of the deception ploy, code named *Operation Fortitude*, used to deceive the German High Command into believing the Allied Invasion force would land in the Pas-de-Calais area. *Fortitude* was planned to draw attention away from the real invasion force accumulating on the south and south-west coast of England. Part of the deception was the Allied use of double agents to successfully transmit false information to the enemy. There is an interesting link with Plymouth and *Operation Fortitude* that is worth recording. On the 24 April 1942 Juan Pujol, code name Garbo, probably the most successful agent for the Allies, arrived at RAF Mount Batten, Plymouth, in a Sunderland flying boat and stayed in a hotel before travelling to London. Garbo became a double agent and played a key role in the success of *Operation Fortitude*. Pujol was later awarded a MBE for his services while the Germans presented him with the Iron Cross!

For the German forces the expected Allied invasion was a waiting game. This pictorial study shows a German sentry guarding a coastal gun looking towards England.

Some enemy machine gun units were protected by concrete casements that were sited close to the beaches where the American troops would land.

A post war photograph of part of the Longues-sur-Mer battery, showing a tiered concrete casement protecting a piece of artillery. Each casement was covered by machine guns, mine fields and barbed wire. This Battery posed particular dangers for Allied forces approaching the Gold and Omaha beaches.

Above left: Hitler had insisted on installing coastal batteries to deter Allied ships from navigating in the vicinity. The Mirus battery on Guernsey had been operational since the summer of 1942. The picture shows one of the huge guns being installed.

Above right: The Lindemann battery was the largest Atlantic Wall gun, as housed in a massive concrete casement. This picture taken in 1942 shows the inauguration ceremony.

A propaganda poster of one of the huge guns sited in the Pas-de-Calais area that bombarded Dover, inflicting casualties and damage to property.

Feldmarschall Von Rundstedt had submitted a report to Hitler that the coastal fortifications were inadequate, resulting in Feldmarschall Rommel, the 'Desert Fox' being appointed Inspector General of the Defences. In 1944 Rommel conducted a survey of the existing defences. His tour of inspection of the much-vaunted Atlantic Wall revealed to him that its impregnability was a myth, generated by Goebbels' propaganda machine.[5] He reported back to Hitler that the defences were not sufficient to repel an Allied invasion.

Hitler and Von Rundstedt, continued in their belief that the narrow stretches of the Pas-de-Calais would be the site of the expected forthcoming invasion whereas Rommel believed the most likely place of an attempted Allied landing would be on the Normandy beaches and that the German Army would have to defeat the Allied invasion force before it got off the beaches.

The Atlantic Wall, whatever its critics suggested, presented a formidable defence. The German weaponry, including high calibre guns and rapid firing anti-tank guns, by the end of 1943 comprised 2692 pieces of artillery. Among the largest were the 15cm guns of the Longues-sur-Mer battery, placed in thick concrete casements and sited to the north of Bayeux. These would be used to target the Allied invasion fleet up to 20 kilometres out to sea thus prevented attacking forces from reaching the beaches. There were large numbers of bunkers, gun emplacements, observation posts, machine gun posts and radar stations, and gun positions were placed to establish zones of cross fire on the beaches.

In 1944 a rapid development programme of the Atlantic Wall began. A considerable amount of the construction work was carried by over a thousand French companies that employed 200 000 French and French Colonial labourers; furthermore the Germans forced thousands of men from the occupied countries to construct the defences. Prior to D-Day 286 000 workers were involved in building the Atlantic Wall, while only 15 000 Germans were involved.[6]

Other than the mass of firepower that had been installed on or behind the beaches, overcoming the enemy obstacles and coastal fortifications that the Allied forces had not previously encountered presented a huge challenge. This led to the creation of special units to deal with the obstacles that would face the early waves of troops landing on the Normandy beaches. An array of thousands of different obstacles had been placed on the beaches to sink or rip open the hulls of the allied landing craft. Five million mines had been sown. Long wooden or metal stakes were driven into the beaches to which mines or other explosive devices were attached that would detonate if struck by a landing craft. Crossed steel girders were used as ant-tank obstacles. Gate like metal obstacles, seven feet high, known as 'Belgian gates' were secured on the beaches. More than a million wooden poles up to 16 feet high, known as 'Rommel's asparagus' were placed in the Normandy fields and coastal areas of Holland as obstacles to air landings.

A situation that American Intelligence failed to detect before D-Day was that since November 1943, the number of enemy troops on the Wall had increased from 46 to 58 Divisions, some of them composed of high quality troops that had served on the Russian front.

Top: A battery of German anti-aircraft guns sited close to a Normandy beach.

Centre left: Enemy gun emplacements were protected with landmines, barbed wire and small arms fire. The picture shows six infantrymen at the double responsible for defending the casement at the back of the picture.

Centre, right: A huge German searchlight hidden under the roof of a Normandy bar.

Bottom: Hitler gave Feldmarschall Rommel the task of inspecting the coastal defences of the Atlantic Wall. In April 1944 Rommel visited the Normandy beaches on a tour of inspection which resulted in the defences being strengthened. This picture shows the Feldmarschall inspecting beach obstacles. The tree trunks shown were 8 metres in length, dug into the beach sand and fitted with anti-tank mines and steel blades, 'Hemmbalken' (Hedgehogs) for destroying landing craft that came up against them.

An important part of the Atlantic Wall defences was the mass erection of concrete, metal, and wooden obstacles placed along the Normandy coast. They presented a challenge to the Allied forces to overcome on D-Day. This was one of the reasons for the establishment of the Woolacombe Assault Training Centre and the Slapton Battle Training Area. This picture shows rows of 'Czech hedgehogs' on a Normandy beach. They were embedded in concreted to prevent them from being moved by the force of the tide.

An artillery unit supplied with an anti-tank Pak37 that was most lethal against Allied tanks.

The Germans boasted of the Atlantic Wall as being 'Festung Europa (Fortress Europe), the most colossal fortification of all time'.

For the Allied forces to land in Europe and then advance into Germany they would first be required to mount a huge amphibious operation on this formidable coastal fortress that appeared to be an impregnable military defence. The challenge for the Allies was to overcome the Atlantic Wall defences and then hold their position from any expected enemy counterattacks. Landing on a hostile, heavily defended enemy shore required not only courage but new skills of warfare that would have to be learnt, tried, tested and believed in, before any major military operation could begin. Furthermore the Allied invading force needed to be assembled at specific departure points. The planners of the American forces had also to consider, alongside their own tasks, those of the Allied air forces and armies. The unique requirements of amphibious operations resulted in varying doctrinal conclusions and the need to produce and develop new strategies. This led to the appointment of the American, Lieutenant Colonel P. Thompson to establish the Woolacombe Assault Training Centre.

Hitler believed the Atlantic Wall was virtually impregnable and that his forces in France could easily defeat an invasion.[7] He recognised that the fighting would be fierce and ordered that his troops were to fight to the last man.[8] However he also knew that if after landing on the beaches the Allied forces established a bridgehead and forced a breakout this would have incalculable consequences for the Germans. Despite the military reverses by the Germans on the Russian Front, their preparations to counter an Allied invasion in north-west France was a menacing threat. The Allies were not at all certain of a successful landing.[9]

THE ASSAULT TRAINING CENTRE, WOOLACOMBE.

In recent years there has been an increasing amount of information revealed concerning the American Assault Training Centre, Woolacombe.[10] A social survey of Devon and Cornwall of the 1930s describes that the greater part of North Devon during the interwar period 'as a land of decaying towns and decaying countryside'. Agricultural wages were low and young workers were attracted to towns in other parts of the county. Only in the rural district of Barnstaple was there was a reversal in the trend of decreasing population due to the an influx of residents in the smaller resorts of North Devon, arriving to permanently settle there. Among the communities that rapidly grew were Instow, Mortehoe and Woolacombe.

The population of Braunton in the early 1930s was just over 3000, while the nearby village of Saunton had 400 residents. During the decade of the 1930s seasonable unemployment, particularly in the holiday industry, was prominent. Other areas of unemployment in the Barnstaple area at this period were in the textile trade, furniture making, clothing and agriculture.[11]

At the outbreak of the Second World War unemployment in Devon although prevalent had been reduced. The North Devon communities faced up to the many challenges on the Home Front. The trials and tribulations of the years 1940–1942 are well documented. The Luftwaffe dropped bombs in the region but there were no intensive air raids in the area. Mention is made that in November 1941 a German Junker 88 bomber aircraft landed by mistake at RAF Chivenor; all the crew were taken prisoner.

By 1943, the Allies had made their decision to invade Europe by a seaborne landing. This meant an amphibious assault, a direct frontal attack on the enemy's defences with the implicit dangers of a high casualty rate.[12] As part of overcoming the huge challenge faced by the Allies in preparing for D-Day, the American Assault Training Centre with its headquarters at Woolacombe had been established and became operational on the 1st September 1943. The primary mission of the ATC was to prepare the American troops selected to spearhead the assault on the Normandy beaches by teaching them how to overcome the numerous obstacles and fortified positions they would encounter. Among the military units who attended training courses at Woolacombe's ATC were the US 4th and 29th Infantry Divisions. The 116th Regimental Combat Team of the 29th Division was the first infantry unit to take and pass the course. General Gerhardt, Commanding Officer of the 29th Infantry, praised the facilities at Woolacombe as superb.

In charge of the Woolacombe ATC was Lieutenant Colonel Paul Thompson who had experienced problems in acquiring land for training purposes. He had wanted the civilian populations of Georgeham and Croyde to be evacuated, but this was refused. For some unexplained reason he could not obtain a compulsory evacuation order. What is known is that the local civilian population understandably objected to the idea of being evacuated.

The Third Reich battle flag.

'Victory will be ours'.

The main exercise area for American troops was at first centred around Woolacombe on the North Devon coast but later expanded to embrace Morte Point across to Westward Ho! a distance of ten miles.

During the early period of the training exercises there was a shortage of landing craft for troops to practise on. To overcome this problem dummy landing craft were constructed as shown by these American troops about to be disgorged on to Braunton Burrows.

DUKWs were versatile amphibious landing craft capable of being driven directly on to the land from the water. The picture shows one of them exercising among the sand dunes at Saunton Sands, c.1943.

Opposite, top:
A receding tide at Woolacombe Bay reveals three American tanks that were lost overboard when three landing craft capsized during an exercise. In the front of the picture can be seen observers and men, possibly survivors, scrambling up the rocks to safety. 18 December 1943.

Opposite, bottom:
Colonel Paul Thompson. Commanding Officer of the Assault Training Centre. In the front of the jeep is Lt-General Jacob Denvers.

American troops on Woolacombe Beach marching down to embark on a landing craft. A watercolour by the American artist Olin Dows.

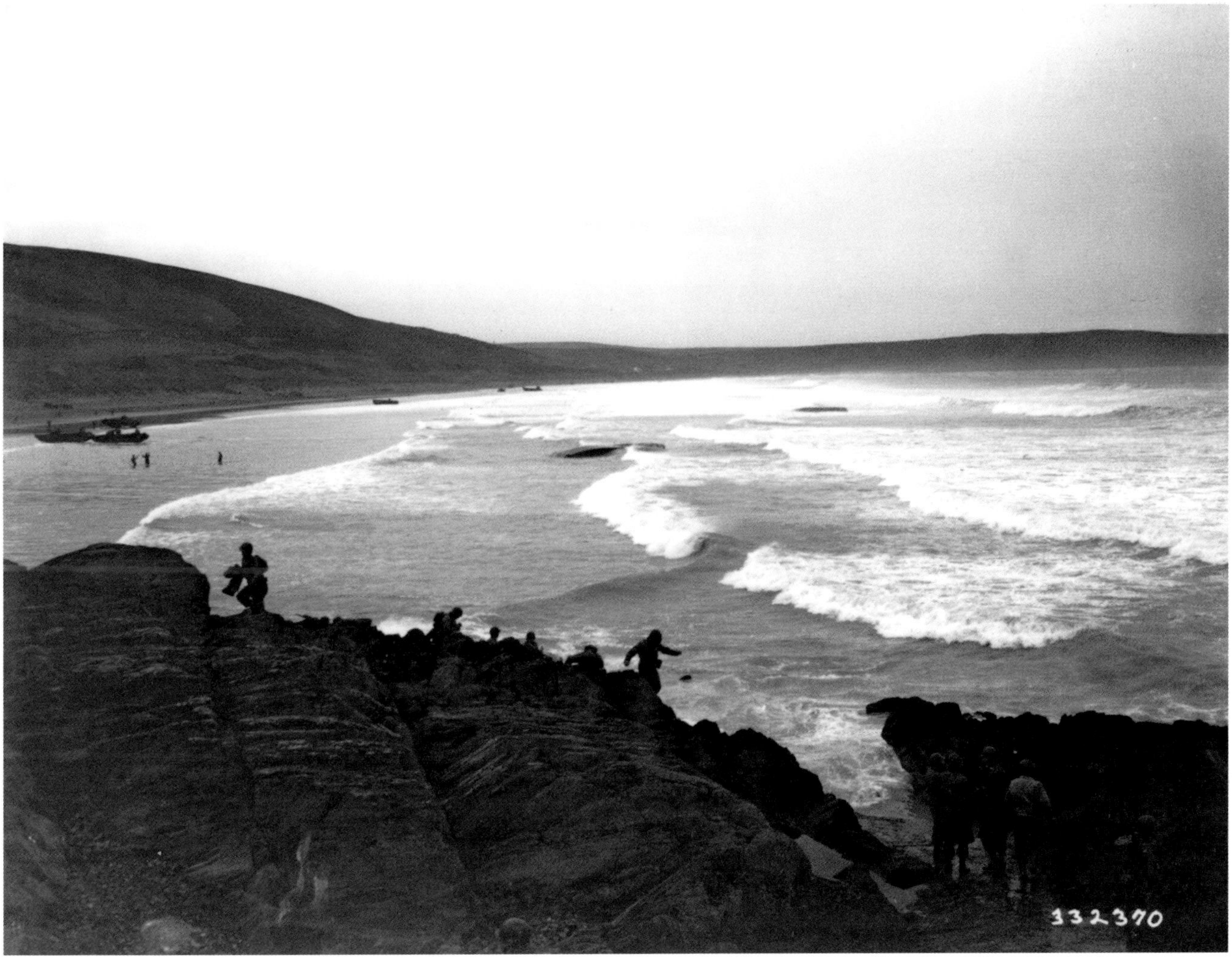
332370

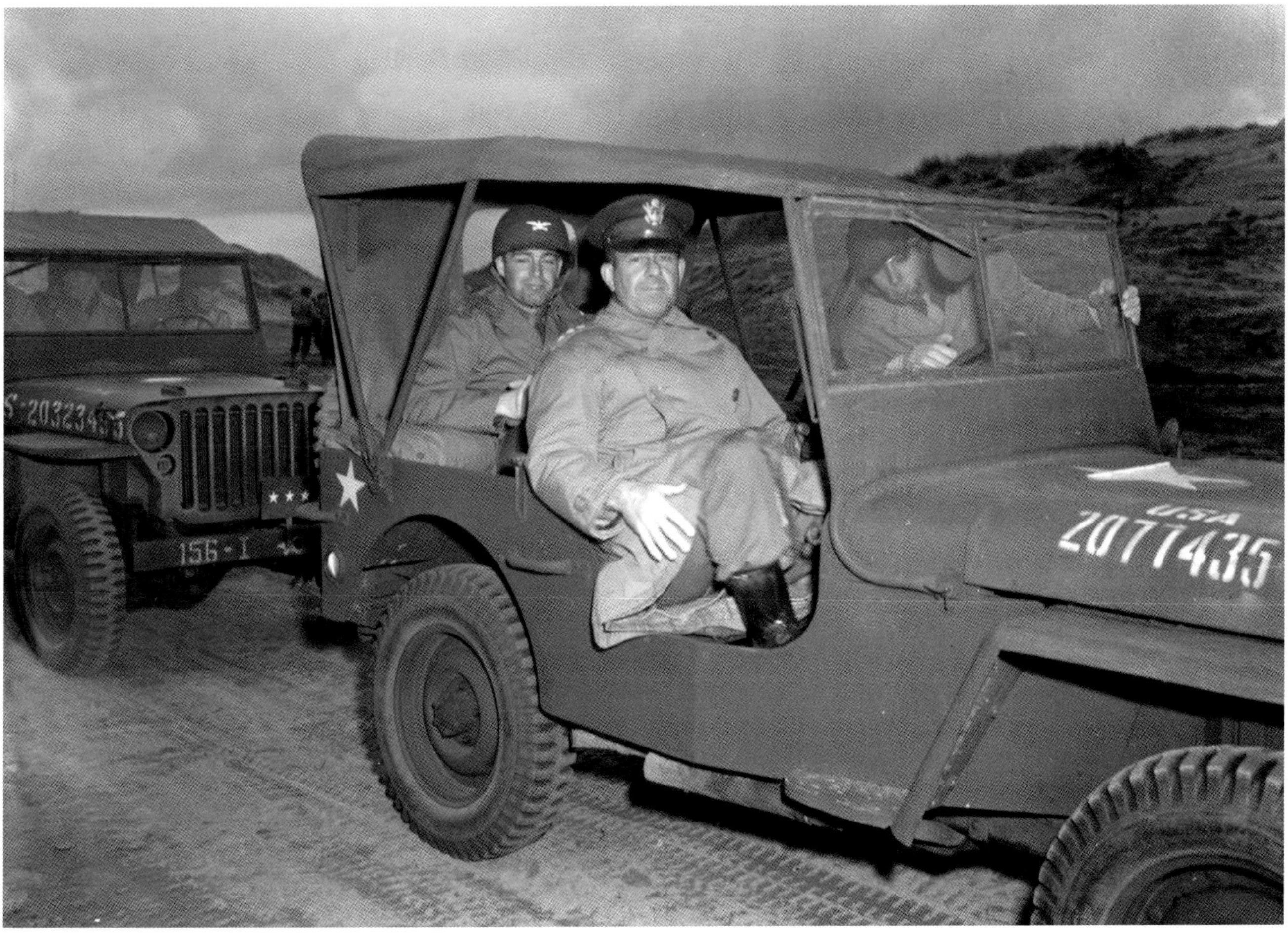
156-I
U.S.A
20771435

A recent photograph of Woolacombe Beach, a two-mile-long stretch of sand showing the expanse and layout that was used during the Second World War by the Americans. This coast is subject to the second largest rise and fall of tide in the world.

No evidence has been found in the records of The Interdepartmental Committee of Combined Training in Devon, Wales and Scotland 1943, that a formal request had been made by the Americans for permission to use part of North Devon as an assault training area. Requests for land to train on entailed negotiations with the War Office and the Ministry of Agriculture. Where large amounts of land were involved the request went to the British Cabinet.[13] Eventually 25 square miles of land and eight thousand yards of beach was released to the Americans.

Before the land could be used for training masses of barbed wire entanglements and land mines that had been laid three years before, at the time of the expected German invasion, had to be removed together with the wooden posts that had been dug into the beaches. Woolacombe Beach Hotel became the Headquarters for the Training Centre. Unlike the Slapton Battle Training Area with its imposed security, civilians could sit on Woolacombe Beach and watch the training exercises, with the main practice beaches at Woolacombe Sands, yet it must be assumed there were distinct perimeter notices and markers for safety

Beyond the stooks of corn can be seen the USS *President Warfield* moored in the River Torridge. The boat was used to accommodate US service personnel. Later it was deployed on the Normandy beaches.

Amphibious exercises on Woolacombe Beach. Troops emerging from the open bow of a landing craft, watched by observers to the left of the picture c.1943.

reasons.[14] The training area was spread out across the shores of part of North Devon. A key feature associated with the ATC was the rivers Taw and Torridge that merge at Appledore and flow into the Bristol Channel over the Bideford Bar. The USS *President Warfield*, accommodating US naval personnel, was moored on the Torridge between Bideford and Instow.

With the establishment of the ATC, the town of Ilfracombe swarmed with American servicemen who were the training staff at Woolacombe. Most of the town's hotel accommodation had been taken up by American officers. The town was full of US Army vehicles, as every US officer appeared to have his own jeep. Camps were built at Braunton and Saunton for the troops who attended the training courses. The ATC programs were organised in a way that certain beaches and land were allocated for particular training exercises. The Americans with considerable activity went about constructing fortifications and obstacles. Replication of the German coastal concrete defences were built that had been identified by allied reconnaissance aircraft.

The ATC started its training courses on the 1st September 1943 nearly three months before General Eisenhower had arrived in England to take up his post of Commander-in-Chief. By January 1944, the ATC was operating at its peak with a quick turn around. As one military unit completed its course, another arrived to be trained. Each combat unit spent a three-week extensive training period at the Centre; the emphasis was on amphibious operations. Training extended well beyond Woolacombe to places along the North Devon coast including Braunton, Saunton Sands, Croyde Bay and Mortehoe. A young American soldier describes his impression of this part of North Devon when he was stationed at Braunton. He describes the vast sand dunes, the sea-shore, the round hills, the deep green of the fields, the stone fences and hedges, the narrow streets of the villages and the neatly manicured gardens. "Everywhere were scenes that I had known only on picture postcards or on the movie screen."[15]

Training was carried out in designated sectors. Richard Bass describes ten training areas in North Devon used by the Americans.[16] For example, at Braunton, the Americans took over 10 000 acres of farmland. Although there was no mass evacuation of civilians, as there was in the South Hams, there were villagers in the Braunton area who were evicted from their homes.[17]

A US amphibious exercise at Woolacombe beach showing troops disgorging from the open bow of a landing craft and advancing into what appears to be a smoke screen. Baggy Point is seen in the distant background. c.1943.

One of the hardships the Americans troops endured was a shortage of water at Braunton. With the arrival of the Americans the town's water supply had dropped. This was a challenge that the Americans excelled in. They immediately when to work and built Braunton a completely new water system for which the local community were very grateful.[18]

It was at Braunton railway station that many of the troops who attended an ATC course arrived and were then driven to one of the 'tent cities'.

Braunton Burrows is the largest area of sand dunes in Britain, lying back along the three and half miles of Saunton beach. The Burrows was used for various training purposes including flame throwing, wire cutting and a challenging obstacle course. Scaffold towers were erected and draped with cargo nets for troops to practice their descent into a landing craft. Most of the live firing ranges were on Braunton Burrows.[19] The US Navy provided the landing craft that were based at Appledore and Instow. They would sail from Appledore across the estuaries of the Taw and Torridge to a small-secluded beach at Crow Point to embark troops, military vehicles, tanks and artillery. At Crow Point troops were trained to embark or disembark in landing craft using dummy versions of small landing craft.

The ATC made a vital contribution to amphibious doctrine by experimenting with new equipment, holding combined exercises and organising conferences on tactics to overcome the German coastal defences. The outcome improved tactical methods and modified tactical concepts. A memorandum from the Woolacombe ATC Centre to the European Theatre of Operations, US Army, dated 15 January 1944, discussed the subject of attacking a fortified beach.[20] It stated that preliminary air and naval bombardments would be employed to

Below left: A Sherman tank coming on to Instow beach. Some Sherman DD tanks were fitted with wading trunks, as seen in this picture, that allowed them to move ashore with water up to the top of the turret.

Below right: This 'desert like' image is part of Saunton Sands showing a line of DUKWs to the right of the picture and tractors to the left. The troops are possibly part of the column shown in the next picture.

A column of troops marching from Crow Point to embark at Broadsands.

US assault troops under live fire in a battle training exercise on Woolacombe beach.

Opposite: One of the exercise at the Assault Training Centre was for troops to practice using rope netting. This was to get the men used to transferring from their troop ships by climbing down the nets into small landing craft that would take them to their designated sector of a Normandy beach.

disrupt the field of fire and to provide craters for the assault sections to use as cover for their advance. Tanks would neutralise or destroy the defensive works by firing into all pillboxes embrasures and this would enable the assault infantry to advance. All aspects of amphibious warfare needed to be considered if the invasion of France was to be successful.

It was at the Woolacombe ATC that the idea of the self-contained boat team was introduced and perfected. This form of assault team did not exist in conventional US Army divisions. This new doctrine meant that adjustments had to be made to certain infantry divisions to form, if only temporarily, thirty-men boat teams with each boat equipped to fight independently with its own weapons if it became separated or lost its leader. Boat teams practiced as separate units on land, assaulting individual pillboxes using live ammunition. There was no guarantee that assault teams would land at the designated places on the beach that had been planned for. This was another reason that it was decided that each assault team had to be self contained and versatile.[21] Each infantry assault company was made up of six thirty-man sections, supported by two platoons of tanks. Each section had a leader (Officer), who was first out of the landing craft and an assistant leader (non commissioned officer), last out of the landing craft. The sections consisted of teams of infantrymen. The specialised team was comprised of eight riflemen, a four-man light machine gun team, a four-man mortar team, a four-man wire cutting team and a four-man rocketeer team. A two-man flamethrower team and a four-man demolition team completed the unit.[22]

The plan for the American landings at Normandy was to launch the Sherman (swimming) tanks offshore, then for them to move on to the beach and to commence firing at the pillboxes at H-Hour minus five minutes, to provide cover for the first wave of infantry teams which would land at H-Hour.[23]

The troops had worked on climbing nets and learned to scale the sea wall they expected to encounter. Men were trained in separate classes to improve their proficiency, these included bazooka teams, bangalore torpedo teams, machine gunners and mortar teams. The amphibious assault teams trained in close contact with machine gun fire using live bullets that were aimed a few inches above the men's head. Accidents and casualties were reported. Other skills that combat teams were taught was how to probe for land mines with bayonets, detect booby traps, dig foxholes and survive unarmed combat.[24] Among the units who attended the ATC was the US 2nd Ranger Battalion who in April 1944 travelled from Bude, Cornwall. For many of the Rangers it was the hardest training they had experienced working under British commando instructors.[25]

The final part of the training for the US Ranger Battalion was at Baggy Point, where a duplicated German fortification and trench system, as prepared on the French coast, had

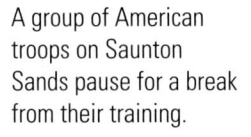

A group of American troops on Saunton Sands pause for a break from their training.

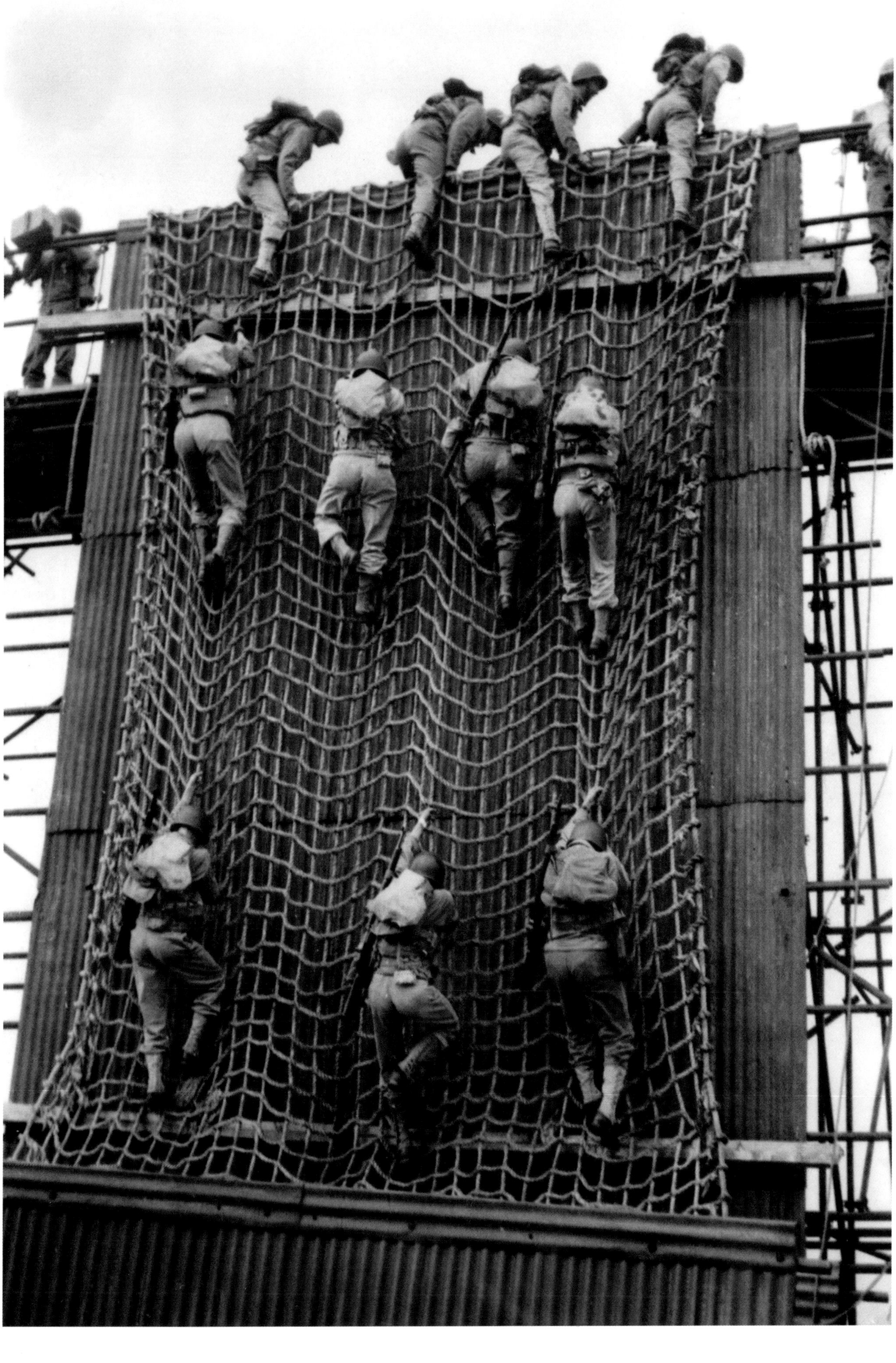

Cliff scaling training, Lee Bay, North Devon, 13 December 1943.

Opposite top:
US Assault troops training with a 'bangalore torpedo', used for blowing gaps in concertina defences (barbed wire) at the Assault Training Centre.

Opposite bottom:
A picture of the engineers' obstacle course at Crow Point. The troops had the challenge to work their way through the different sections of obstacles. The purpose of the exercise was to clear a path for a tank.

been constructed. The Rangers were also required to scale the cliffs, ascending them under fire, by free-rope climbs and then to eliminate the defences. This training continued when selected companies travelled to Swanage, there to practise on the high cliffs of Alum Bay and the Needles. These were the Rangers who on D-Day would scale the cliffs at Pointe du Hoc to destroy the massive German guns that threatened the Allied invasion force only to discover that the Germans had moved their artillery inland.

Prolonged and large-scale special amphibious training and experimental work was also carried out at the Advanced Amphibious Training Base at Appledore.[26] Its function was to train combat teams in landing craft operations and going ashore under realistic battle conditions. Problems arising from landing on a hostile beach were investigated and exercises carried out on the beaches of Instow and Westward Ho! American and British landing craft that had been damaged on exercise queued up to be repaired at Appledore. There had been

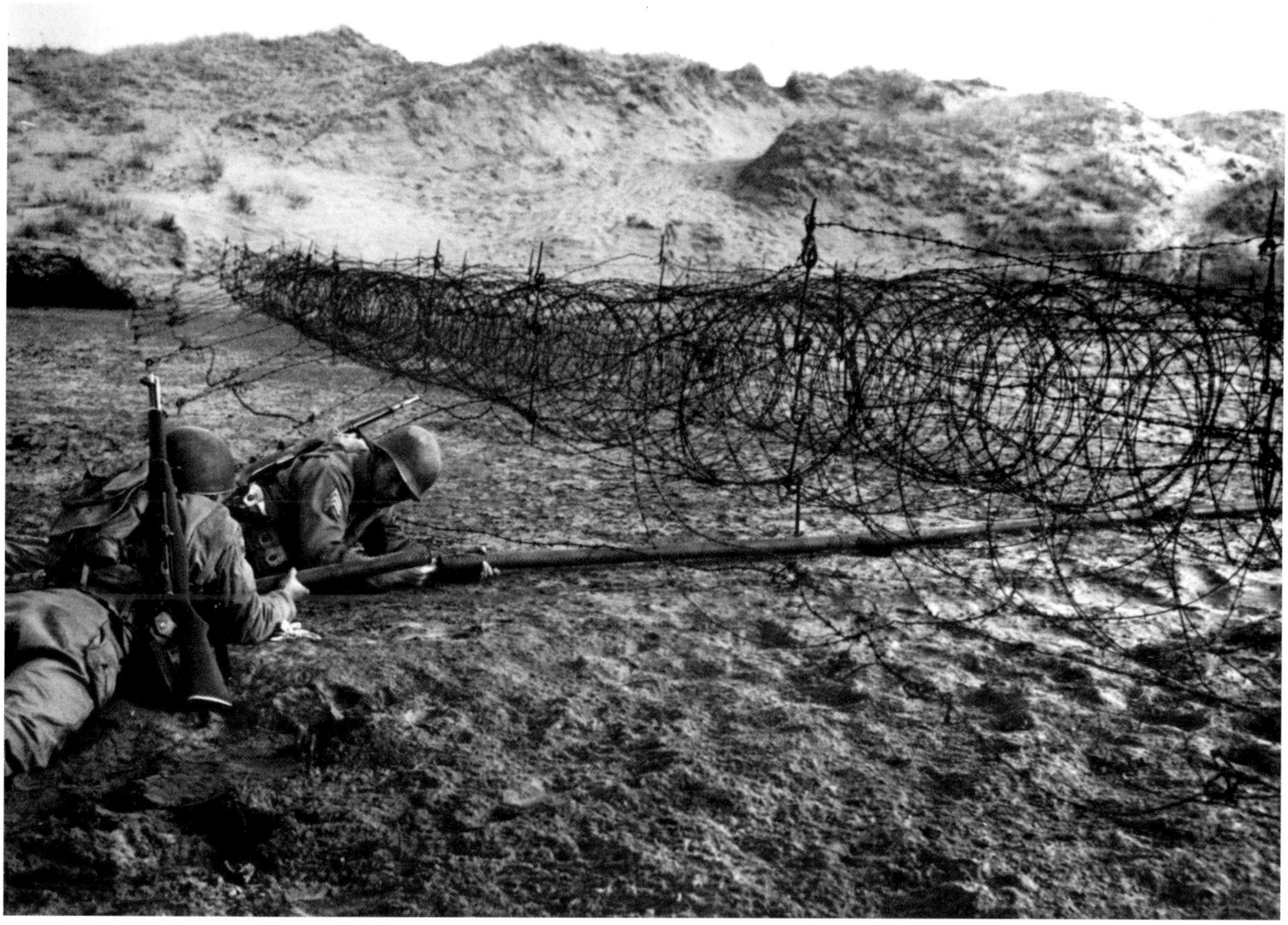

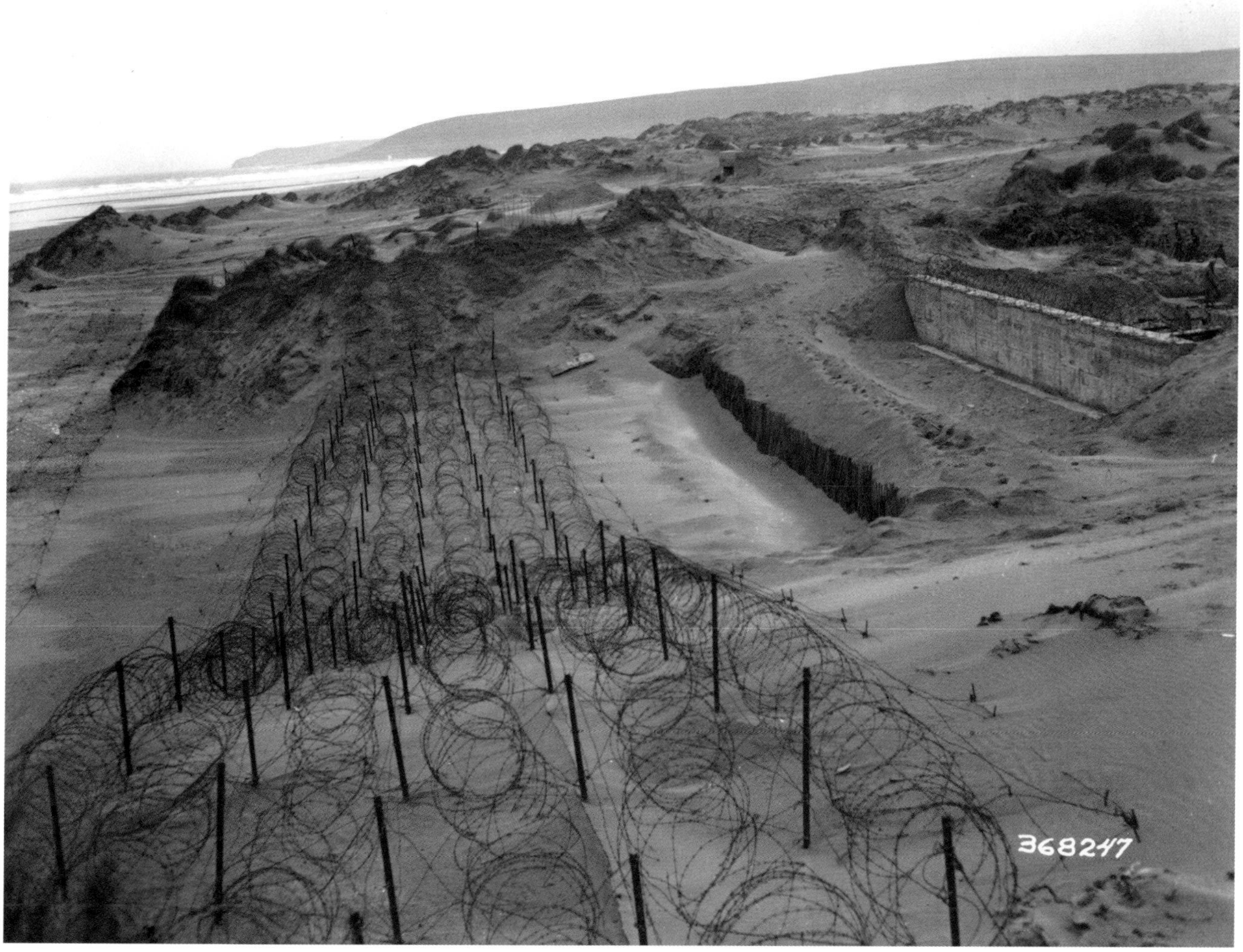
368247

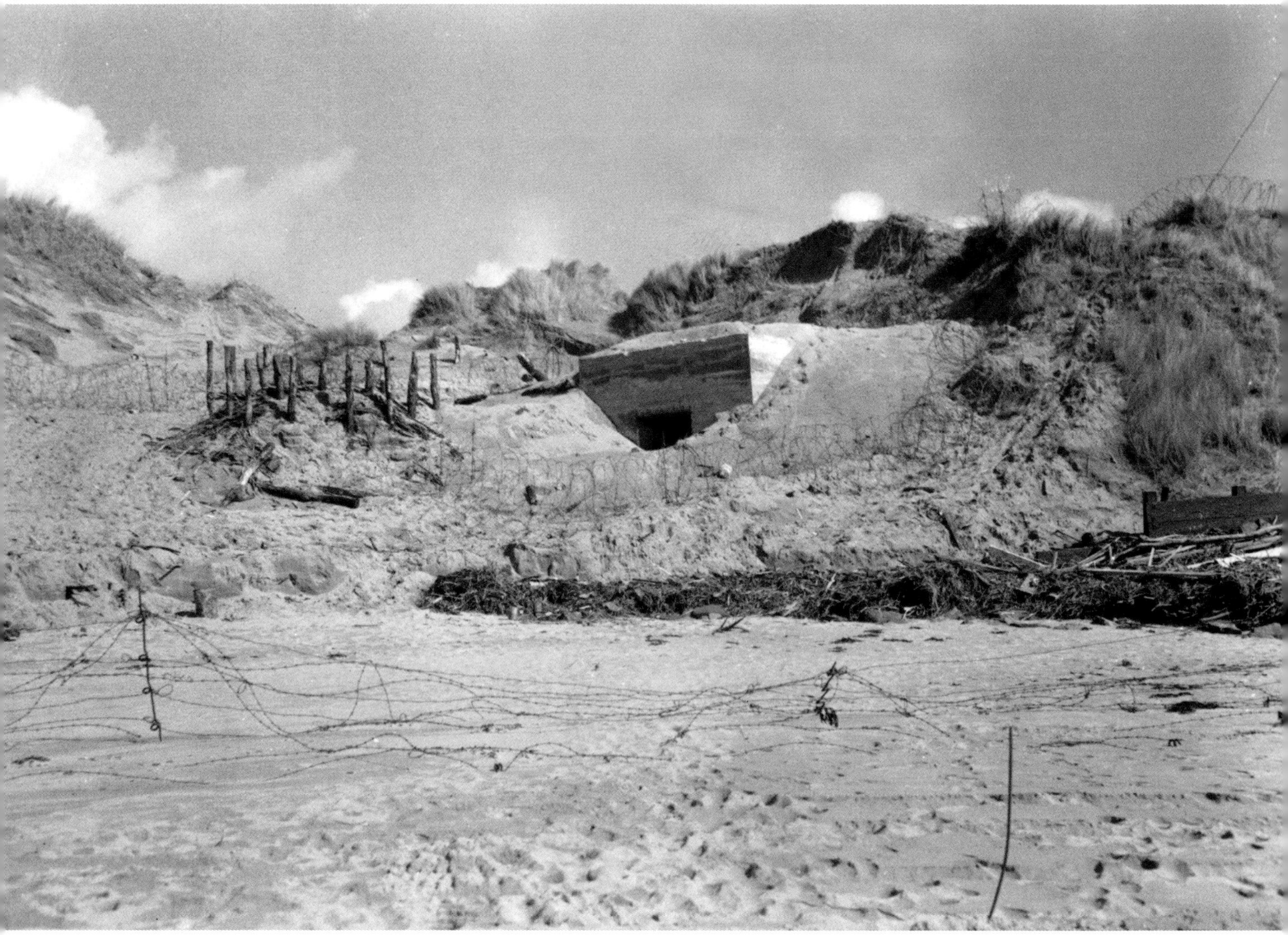

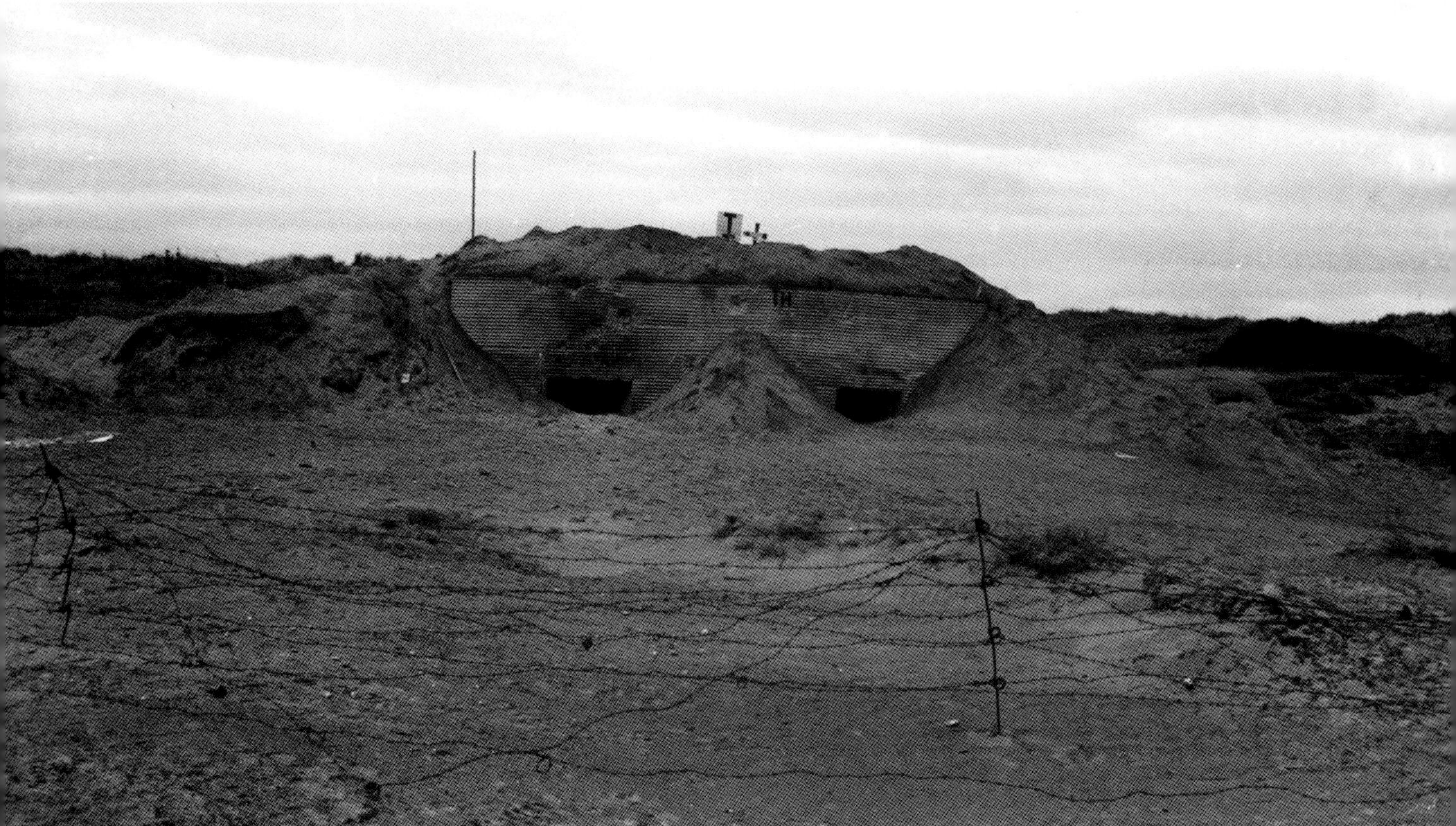

casualties during the ATC exercises, although there is no definitive figure. Many years ago a visitor records seeing a plaque commemorating the loss of 98 US servicemen who had drowned in Woolacombe Bay.

This huge challenge of amphibious beach assault confronting the American forces (and the rest of the Allies) fell on the young conscript servicemen many of them without any previous battle experience. It says a lot about their courage how they faced up to their training and then in combat. On the 26th May 1944 the Assault Training Centre was disbanded. Thereafter amphibious training and rehearsals continued on a much larger scale at the Battle Training Area in the Slapton region of South Hams.

It is important to mention the Combined Operation Experimental Establishment (COXE), at Appledore that was involved in developing various projects that made an important contribution during the Allied invasion of France. Their work included testing landing craft and devising methods of destroying underwater obstacles. One expert who would visit the establishment to discuss sand velocity was the famous racing driver Sir Malcolm Campbell associated with the then record breaking *Bluebird*.

The Allies knew much about the formidable Atlantic Wall defences along the French coast of the English Channel. For the Allied forces to land on the beaches and move inland would require the demolition of the huge bastions of reinforced concrete. A remarkable weapon of destruction that was not used was constructed of enormous steel wheels, ten feet in diameter with a concrete tread, connected by a drum-like axles containing high explosives. This monstrous device was driven by rockets with the intention that it would break through the enemy coastal defences. Named the 'Great Panjandrum' it was tested on Westward Ho! beach but it was never used against the enemy.

The British plan for landing on the Normandy beaches was to use Sherman DD tanks to destroy the pill boxes, then Sherman flail tanks to clear the beach of mines to breach the sea wall with high explosive charges, in order to allow the infantry and special teams to deal with bunkers, pillboxes and machine gun nests.

Opposite top: One of the many concrete pill-boxes built at the Assault Training Centre, The one in the picture was on (area B), Saunton Sands.

Opposite bottom: Two adjacent pill boxes on Saunton Sands, the one on the left having been damaged by live shells.

---

1. Saunders, Anthony. *Hitler's Atlantic Wall*, 2001. Sutton Publishing. p.2.
2. *The Raid on Saint-Nazaire*, 1988 number 59, Battle of Britain Prints International Ltd. pp. 1-25.
3. Fenby, John. *The Sinking of the Lancastria, Britain's Greatest Disaster and Churchill's Cover-up*, 2005 Simon & Schuster. p.8.
4. Saunders, Anthony. *Hitler's Atlantic Wall*, 2001. Sutton Publishing.
5. Saunders Anthony, p.5.
6. Saunders Anthony, p.83.
7. Beevor, Antony. *D-Day, the Battle for Normandy*, 2009. Viking page 31.
8 Saunders, Anthony *Hitlers Atlantic Wall* p.22.
9. Penrose, Jane (ed). *The D-Day Companion*, 2004. Osprey, p.18-19.
10. Bass, Richard. *Spirits of the Sand, The history of the US army Assault Training Centre*, 1991. Lee Publishing.
11. *Devon and Cornwall: A Preliminary Survey*, p.17.
12. Weigley, Russell. *Eisenhower's Lieutenants: The campaign of France and Germany, 1944-1945*, 1981. Indiana University Press, Bloomington, USA. p.77.
13. Reynolds, David. *Rich Relations, The American Occupation of Britain 1942-1945*, 1995. Harper Collins. p.125.
14. BBC 'The Peoples War', *Tales of Woolacombe at War*. Article ID: A1969194, p.10.
15. Bass, Richard. *Spirits of the Sand*. 1992. Lee Publishing. p.151.
16. Bass, Richard. *Spirits of the Sand*, Field Edition, 2005. pp.29-93.
17. Gaydon, Tina. *Braunton*, 1989. Badger Books. p.92.
18. Longate, Norman. *The G.Is The Americans in Britain 1942-1945*, 1975. Hutchinson p. 80.
19. Bass, Richard, *Spirits of the Sand*, Field Edition, 2005, p.18.
20. *Operation Neptune, Training Memorandum*. 15 January 1944. Assault Training Centre Report, RG 498. US National Archives, College Park, MD.
21. Bass, Richard,. *Spirits of the Sand*, 1992. Lee Publishing. p.48.
22. Bass, Richard. *Spirits of the Sands*, Field Edition. 2005. pp. 13-17.
23, Ambrose, Stephen. *D-Day. June 6, 1944: The Battle for the Normandy Beaches*, 2002. Simon & Schuster. p.256.
24. Slaughter, John. *Omaha Beach and Beyond*. 2009. Zenith Press. pp. 83-84.
25. Black, Col. Robert. *The Battalion. The Dramatic Storey of the 2nd Ranger Battalion in World War 11*, 2006. Stackpole Books. pp. 71-72.
26. Yung, Christopher, *Gators of Neptune*, 2006. Naval Institute Press USA. P.156.

6 The Evacuation of Villagers in the South Hams

Opposite: A previously unpublished map of the Slapton Battle Area showing the disputed Area B. The British Government wanted this area of rich fertile soil to be kept for farming as part of the war effort. However the US military insisted that Area B should not be separated from Area A to enable live shelling to take place.

WHATEVER THE BENEFITS of training and experimental development work carried out at the Woolacombe Assault Training Centre, a larger area was needed for the US task forces to be able to participate in full-scale amphibious rehearsals, as live shelling would be required to be used during the exercises. For this reason part of the area of South Hams that included Slapton Sands was chosen. This decision was announced at a meeting of the Devon County Emergency Committee on the 4 November 1943 from a message received from the Cabinet.[1]

According to British Cabinet records, during the preparation of *Overlord* there were 28 combined-operational training areas from the Wash on the east coast to Land's End; these included the Southwold beaches, Studland Bay and Start Bay. The United States military forces had established eight major training centres and numerous smaller bases in Britain including the Woolacombe Assault Training Centre and the Slapton Battle Training Area. To enable the US forces to carry out their major amphibious exercises called upon the evacuation of all the residents in many villages and hamlets in part of the South Hams. This was not the first time in Britain that people were forced to quit their homes. The concept of the Battle School was suggested by General F. Anderson, who at one time was C-in-C of Eastern Command. When the British military authorities ordered the evacuation of part of East Anglia there was a public outcry, with protests by the local council and newspapers, with questions raised in the House of Commons. Local people believed this area was where the Germans were expected to invade. It was in fact General Anderson's first Battle School, where live ammunition fired from machine guns and artillery shelling was all part of the training. Soon after other Battle Schools opened in other parts of the country. Across the Atlantic the Americans had realised the value of the 'live' battle course. But the use of live ammunition by the American forces for training was a political issue that the American public was very sensitive about.

In June 1943 the *Assault Training Areas Selection Committee*. (ATASC) consisting of representatives of all the armed services was set up to examine a number of inter-service assault training areas in certain parts of the coast of Britain.[2] The Admiralty had been made responsible for co-ordinating the requirements of the interested military forces who required both a stretch of practicable beach and depth of hinterland. There were few options left for the American forces. Other places around Britain that would have been suitable for full assault training had already been earmarked by other armed services.

Four possible assault-training areas were identified by ATASC that may have satisfied the Chiefs of Staff and the Supreme Commander of the Allied Forces. They were Slapton Sands, the Gower Peninsula, the Tarbat Peninsula and Culbin Sands. Of these four areas

Slapton Beach prior to its being use for amphibious exercises.

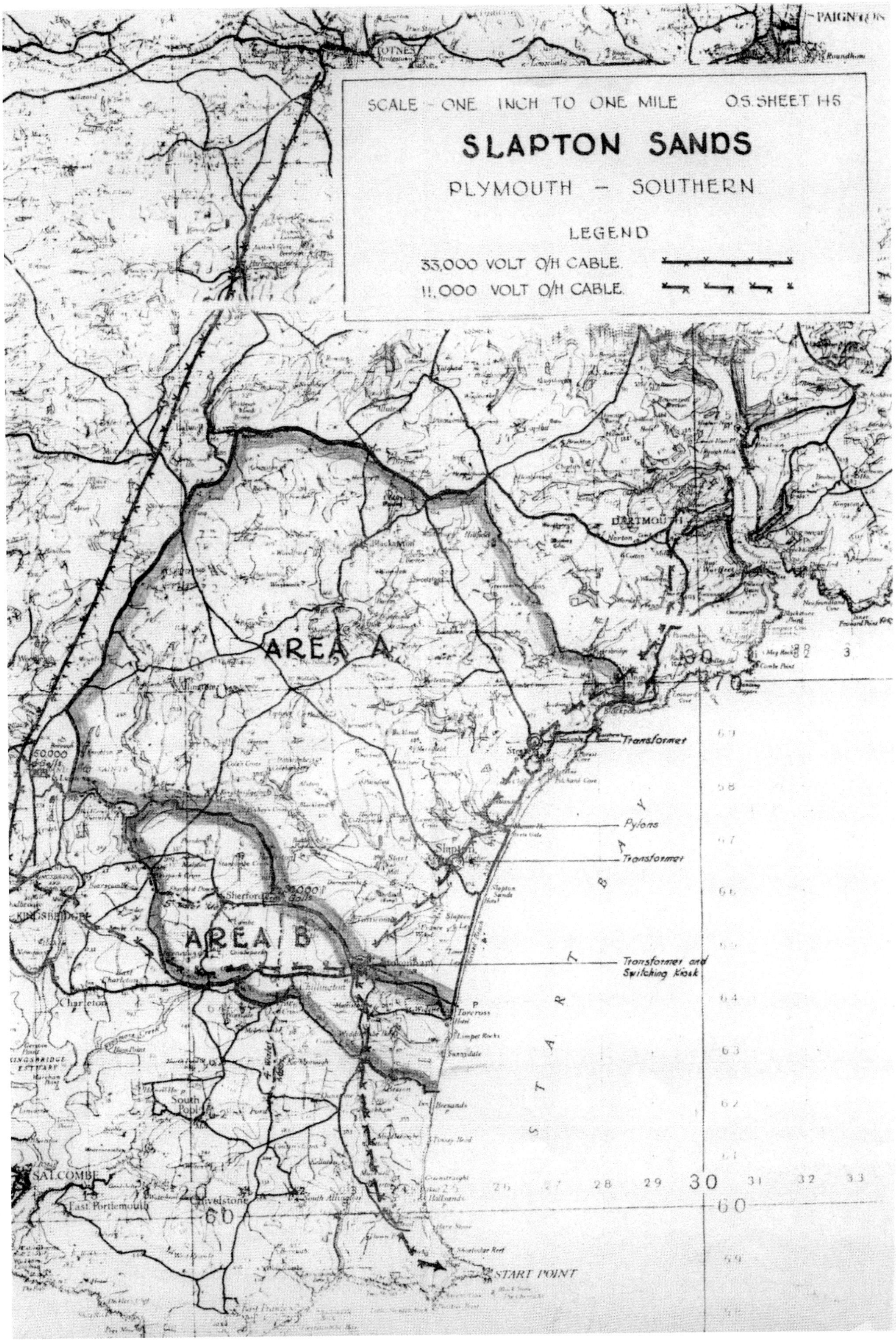
SCALE - ONE INCH TO ONE MILE O.S. SHEET 145
SLAPTON SANDS
PLYMOUTH - SOUTHERN
LEGEND
33,000 VOLT O/H CABLE
11,000 VOLT O/H CABLE
AREA A
AREA B
Transformer
Pylons
Transformer
Transformer and Switching Kiosk
START BAY
START POINT
DARTMOUTH
KINGSBRIDGE
SALCOMBE
Slapton
Sherford
Charleton
South Pool
East Portlemouth
PAIGNTON
TOTNES
50,000 Galls
30,000 Galls

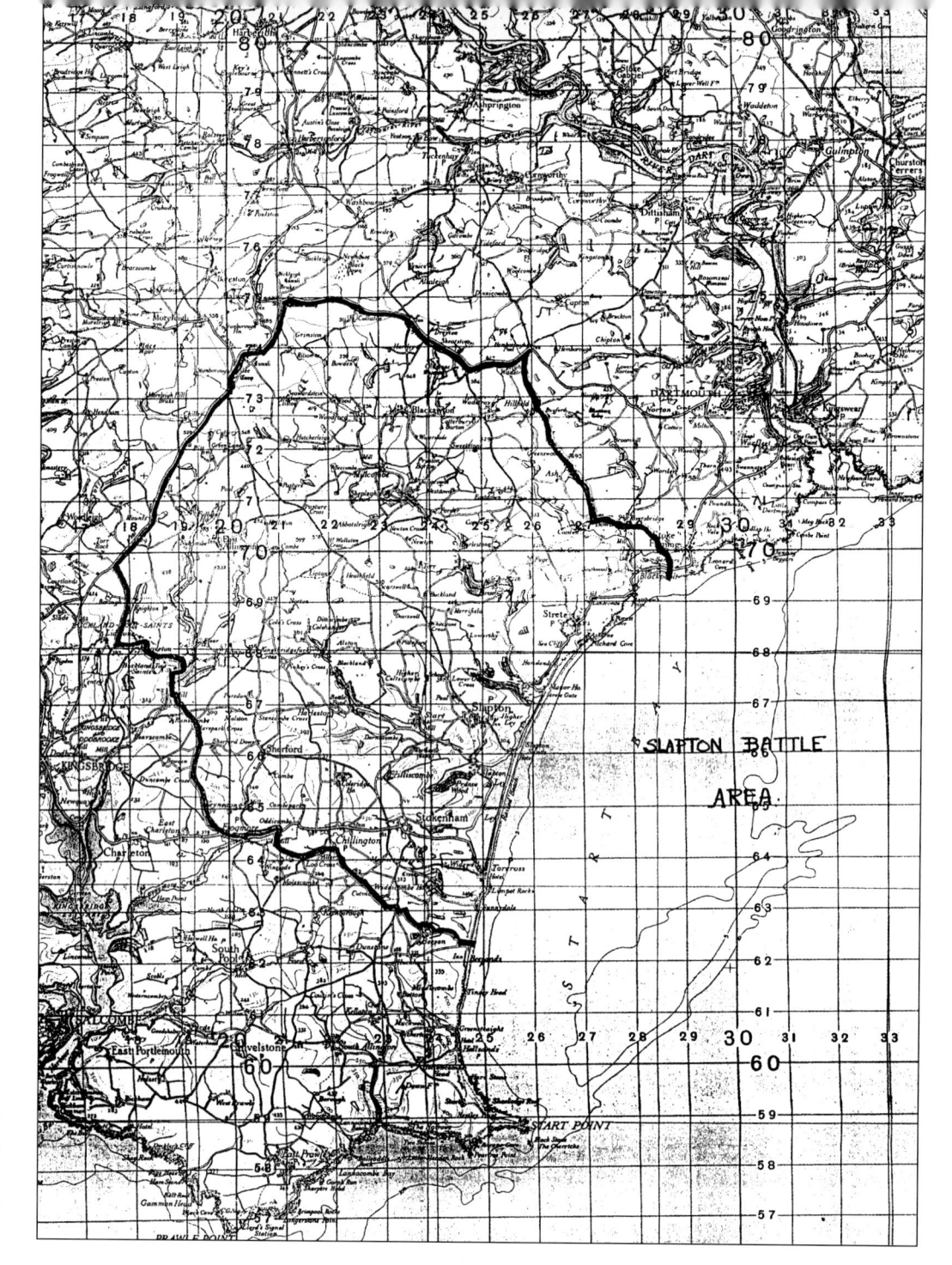

A copy of the official map of the Slapton Battle Training Area deposited at the National Archives.

only two would be available for full assault training. As regards Slapton Sands, this was an area of particular interest to the American Forces. However to use the land for military purposes required the compulsory requisition of part of the South Hams that had serious social and agricultural implications. Complete evacuation of the residents would be essential but this was fertile land excellent for farming and its loss would be accepted with great reluctance by the Ministry of Agriculture.

In the original plan of Slapton Sands Battle Training Area it had been proposed that it would consist of two sections. The smaller southern area to be used for landing troops and manoeuvring without any firing. If this had been approved, the evacuation of this southern area would not have been necessary. The planners had also considered including the village of Stoke Fleming in the battle training area.[3] But the US army representatives insisted if the training was to be effective, live shelling must be allowed to fire over the whole area.[4] The ATASC Committee decided that, as this part of the South Hams was the only available area large enough in the UK suitable for live shelling during battle training, it could be used by the Americans for amphibious exercises. It is a misconception that Slapton Sands was chosen because of its similarity to the Normandy landing beaches, this was a post-war explanation used by certain authors. For anyone visiting the Normandy D-Day beaches and hinterland, it is obvious that they bear little resemblance to the Slapton coastal regions of the South Hams.

American officers studying a large relief map of the Slapton Battle Training Area. Brigadier Bernard Montgomery employed his son to construct a similar relief map for the 1938 Slapton Sands amphibious exercise.

Early in the Second World War the shoreline around part of Slapton Bay was mined and extensive barbed wire entanglements erected as part of the defences that had been prepared for the expected invasion of England. War Office records reveal over a 1000 anti-personnel mines were laid on Slapton beach and 98 land mines were buried at Blackpool Sands. Two 4-inch guns had been installed at Torcross and Strete. In June 1943 the Royal Engineers cleared the Slapton Beach of Mines.

During the summer of 1943 the Kingsbridge Women Voluntary Service (WVS) began to organise teams of volunteers to prepare to cook and serve meals in the event they were needed, thus allowing the WVS to try out their emergency catering.

An early task was undertaken by Captain Buckley of the US Navy to survey the Slapton beach to ensue it's suitability for the proposed exercises. His aim was to identify and quantify the nature of the pebbles and rough shingle together with ascertaining tide levels and the beach gradient. During his survey the Captain was urgently called back to his base in Falmouth when it was discovered that not all the land mines had been removed from the beaches. It was not until October 1943 that the mines buried on nearby Blackpool Sands were removed.

On the 16 August 1943. The Royal Navy landed a small detachment of men from Headquarters Company of the US 175 Infantry Division on the beach. The men deployed on the beach where they lay down with their rifles at the firing position. This was a trial exercise to check how the surface of the shingle beach would withstand the movement of a body of troops as they came ashore.

By October 1943 the Committee of the Combined Training Areas had published their report to the Chiefs of Staff and had approved that Slapton Sands would be requisitioned under Defence Regulation 51. The report added that the complete evacuation of civilians and livestock area would be required. This decision involved the following:

Total area of land	18 500 acres
Number of Farms	300
Number of Cottages	350
Number of Houses	100
Number of Churches and Chapel	6
Number of Shops	25
Number of Inns	7
Number of School And other Buildings	20
Population to be expelled	3000

Date by which site has to be cleared, 30 December 1943 (Later changed to 20 December)
Source: The National Archives, Kew.

The Ministry of Works had listed a number of buildings of historic interest that were to be protected, they included: Area A: East Allington Church and Rectory; Blackawton Church; Slapton Church; the Chantry and Pool House, Slapton. Area B1: nil. Area B2: Stokenham Church; Sherford Church; Keynedon House, Sherford. In addition there were many substantial private country residences in the evacuation area that included Fallapit House, East Allington; Sheplegh Court, Blackawton; Hillfields, Blackawton; Stokely House, Stokenham; Bowden House, Stoke Fleming; Prospect House, Slapton; Blackpool Cottage, Stoke Fleming.

How did the owners or tenants of these buildings proceed to evacuate these buildings? Until the compulsory order of evacuation was served the residents of the villages had led a relatively quiet existence, but it would be naive to believe that they had been marginalised by the war. There were villagers who had been conscripted to serve in the armed forces while other local men served in the Home Guard, Civil Defence, or were employed in the vital occupation of agriculture. In Start Bay Allied merchant ships and warships had been engaged in enemy action, while nearby Dartmouth, Kingsbridge and Torcross had all suffered bombing and casualties.

By the autumn of 1943 villagers began to sense that something was amiss. There had been official-looking men not normally seen in the area walking around Blackawton calling at the Church and visiting the school. The same men were also seen at Stokenham, near Torcross. There were villagers who recognised these visitors as members of Devon County Council and Kingsbridge Rural District Council.[5] The recollection of the 1938 amphibious exercises by local residents and the current rumours of a Second Front at a time when masses of American servicemen were arriving in England gave the locals good reason to believe the area may again be used for military purposes, but perhaps not as they may have envisaged.

It was not enough for the Government to rely solely on goodwill and patriotism of the South Hams villagers to voluntary evacuate their homes, but to apply a policy of compulsion to ensure that residents left the area and, indeed, this was not the first time since the war began that a compulsion order had been served on some South Hams residents. In the summer of 1940 the Devon County War Agriculture Committee confiscated a number of farms to make them more productive.[6]

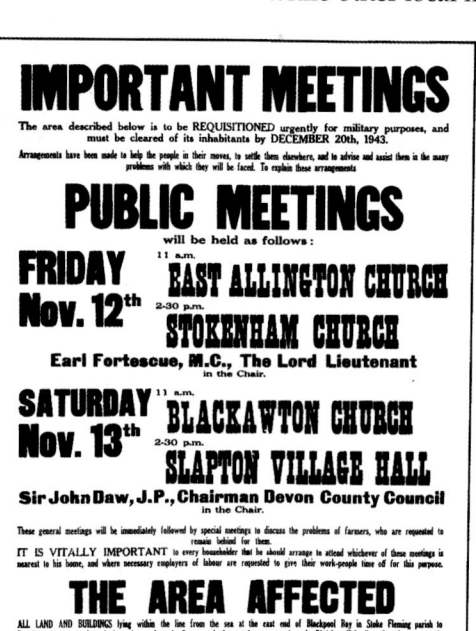

Whatever local rumours had been circulating about some South Hams villages that were to be evacuated, the first official news the villagers knew about their compulsory expulsion came through the posters requesting villagers to attend one of the four public meetings that had been arranged.

Two weeks before the 1943 notification of evacuation was published the worst disaster so far to befall the Royal Navy in the English Channel occurred. At the end of October 1943, Admiralty's Operation Intelligence had warned Admiral Leatham, Commander in Chief Plymouth, that an enemy blockade-runner, *Munsterland* was moving from the Bay of Biscay up the English Channel. During her passage from Brest to Cherbourg she was escorted by five German destroyers.[7] Admiral Leatham decided to implement Operation Tunnel, a naval plan to intercept and destroy enemy shipping in the English Channel. Among the British naval force of seven warships that set out on 22 October 1943 was the cruiser HMS *Charybdis* and the destroyer HMS *Limbourne*. Owing to the failure of communications between these two vessels, both were torpedoed and sunk off the French coast by the German destroyers. Only four officers and 103 ratings from a crew of 688 were saved.[8]

The villagers involved in the evacuation were summoned to attend public meetings to be held at East Allington Church or Stokenham Church on Friday 12 November 1944, or on the following day at Blackawton Church or Slapton Village Hall. At these meetings the villagers were told they were to leave their home with their chattels and find alternative accommodation by the end of December 1944. At the same time the notice of compulsory expulsion had been served on the Devon villagers, a similar demand had been made on the people of Tyneham, Dorset. These villagers were notified on 11 November 1944 by the receipt of a letter, that they were to vacate their homes by the 19th of December 1944, as the area was to be taken over by the War Office for training purposes.[9] The villagers of Tyneham were never allowed to return to repossess their homes.

The official South Hams evacuation order was carried out by the Admiralty Land Agent at Dittisham Court Hotel. The villagers, and those who assisted in the exodus, were not given much time to complete the evacuation. The evacuation was required to be completed within six weeks; the target day for complete clearance was the 20 December 1943. Success depended largely on the co-operation of the villagers, who by being compulsorily expelled,

Above left: A copy of a rare newspaper picture taken at the Blackawton Information Centre showing a villager being interviewed. The lady wearing a hat in the front of the picture was a member of the Women Voluntary Services.

Above right: Families started packing up their personal and household effects. Some villagers decided not to take certain items and store them, in the belief they would still be there when they eventually returned to their home. This picture shows Mrs Mitchelmore's son helping his mother to pack items into a suitcase.

Below left: It is of interest to note that on 16 November 1943, the day the requisition of the South Hams villages took effect, was also the date the villagers in the area of East Holme, Dorset, were officially told that the British Army, Southern Command required the area for training purposes and the villagers would have to go. They were not told at the time that they would never return to their homes.

Below right: To assist in the evacuation each household in the South Hams was given a form to complete that was collected by an official.

SOUTHERN COMMAND

TRAINING AREA, EAST HOLME, Nr. LULWORTH

IN order to give our troops the fullest opportunity to perfect their training in the use of modern weapons of war, the Army must have an area of land particularly suited to their special needs and in which they can use live shells. For this reason you will realise the chosen area must be cleared of all civilians.

The most careful search has been made to find an area suitable for the Army's purpose and which, at the same time, will involve the smallest number of persons and property. The area decided on, after the most careful study and consultation between all the Government Authorities concerned, lies roughly inside of the square formed by EAST LULWORTH—EAST STOKE—EAST HOLME—KIMMERIDGE BAY.

It is regretted that, in the National Interest, it is necessary to move you from your homes, and everything possible will be done to help you, both by payment of compensation, and by finding other accommodation for you if you are unable to do so yourself.

The date on which the Military will take over this area is the 19th December next, and all civilians must be out of the area by that date.

A special office will be opened at Westport House, WAREHAM, on Wednesday the 17th November, and you will be able to get advice between the hours of 10 a.m. and 7 p.m. from there on your personal problems and difficulties. Any letters should be sent to that address also for the present.

The Government appreciate that this is no small sacrifice which you are asked to make, but they are sure that you will give this further help towards winning the war with a good heart.

C. H. MILLER,
Major-General i/c Administration,
Southern Command.

16th November, 1943.

had no choice but to go. At first the residents were expected to find their own accommodation and they were cajoled into packing up their homes and moving. Whatever rumours had previously been circulating around the villages, many villagers were deeply shocked, bewildered and confused once the reality of the situation dawned on them. It made no sense for many of them that they had to give up their homes, and some their livelihood, and move away. For those who worked on the land, producing vital food supplies demanded by the Ministry of Agriculture, it was a blow from which some never recovered.

It was well enough for the authorities to applaud the patriotic sacrifice made by these people, stating that the evacuation would surely shorten the war, but where were evacuees to obtain accommodation? At this time few people had a telephone to make enquires and not all villagers would be conversant in using a telephone. The duties undertaken by the WVS in helping residents during the evacuation are well documented.[10]

The American forces were intent on using the South Hams area for their major amphibious exercises, for without training facilities of this nature the success of the *Overlord* operations would be jeopardized. To achieve their aim of total freedom for live firing, including naval and aerial bombardment, they enlisted the American Ambassador to personally influence Winston Churchill in agreeing to the take over of the land.[11] No evidence has come to light that the Americans agreed a payment to the British Government for the facilities they were given, although the villagers were told they would receive compensation, the amount governed by the Compensation (Defence) Act of 1939. The Act permitted the payment of compensation rent for buildings requisitioned and for the cost of damage done and not repaired. It did not permit any payment to compensate an evacuated person for the loss of his or her employment if, for example, a farmer could not be resettled and lost his income from his farm. The same applied if a shopkeeper lost the income from his shop. There were other people too, including elderly women who ran lodging houses in the villages and provided bed and breakfast accommodation who were left entirely without resources. Mr and Mrs Trout of Strete who ran the village Post Office were able to find a flat in nearby Stoke Fleming, but their furniture was stored in a farm near Bovey Tracy. They received only ten pounds in compensation for all the months they were away from their home.[12]

Perhaps because of political implications involved, the author's searches of official records fail find any mention of villagers being told their homes may be used in mock battle,, bombarded with live shells and that American servicemen would use their homes as billets. The local newspapers limited their reports of the evacuation to mentioning the exodus of the people and expressed their concern about the possible plight of the old and infirm.

Before the people finally left their homes there was a considerable amount of work to do. There was not enough local accommodation to rehouse all the people and this meant there were villagers who had to look further afield for somewhere to live. For some it was a case of having to find alternative employment. Farmers had to arrange to sell their cattle at Kingsbridge market or find a co-operative farmer outside the training area to accommodate their stock. A farmer with no farm had no income, unless he found other employment. To compound their misery, the period of evacuation was hampered by heavy rain and an influenza outbreak among the populace.

The Ministry of Agriculture reported to the ATASC that the area of South Hams being evacuated was above the average fertility of land in the county. The Ministry released figures of the crops grown in the area during 1943, including 6200 acres of corn, 600 acres of potatoes and 1560 acres of root and other crops. Livestock on the 4 June 1943 included 1620 dairy cows, 3800 other cattle, 11 000 sheep, 830 pigs, 16 000 poultry and 580 horses all of which were to be disposed of by sale, or slaughtered.[13]

The number of local people associated with agriculture was less than a third of the total number that were evacuated. Out of the total population of 3000 expelled, 625 were farmers, their wives, housekeepers and whole-time agricultural workers.

The removal of the anti-invasion defences along the coast weakened the local defence measures. At the village of Strete the important secret coastal intercept station whose function was to monitor and identify enemy navigation signals and pass this information on to headquarters at Kingsdown, Kent, was closed down.[14]

From the start of the evacuation the Regional authority turned to the WVS for help in a task for which there was no other obvious agency. The WVS was the largest voluntary organisation on the Home Front throughout the Second World War. It was a remarkable organisation formed by Lady Reading in 1938 at the direct request of the Government to provide a channel through which women could enrol and serve the Air Raid Precautions Service in a variety of different way, for example post raid social work. Lady Reading had been married to a former Viceroy of India and spent much of her time as a high society hostess. In this elevated social position she had raised funds to provide clothes for the unemployed, demonstrating that along with being a socialite she was capable of holding important positions in charities and women's organisations. The WVS leadership was based on an autocratic style of management of upper-middle class women, the leaders predominately those with social standing who were seen to be capable for the required tasks. The pre-war lives of WVS members often revolved around the attendances of luncheon clubs, whist drives, and organising garden fetes and flag days for their local hospitals.

This philanthropy was to provide such middle class women with the confidence to achieve the authority and leadership skills that they now displayed on the Home Front in the Second World War.[15] Members were expected to pay out of their own pocket for the WVS uniform, this acted as a deterrent for working class women to join the WVS. The tailored made-to-measure uniform symbolised the class status of a disciplined auxiliary service raised on very different principles to other established voluntary organisations. According to Lady Reading being a member of the WVS was 'a payment for the privilege of living in the best country in the world'.

According to the social historian Professor Arthur Marwick, the WVS was as least as important and probably considerably more in evidence than the Home Guard.[16] Without these middle and upper class ladies, the wartime social services would have been considerable poorer.

The evacuation of South Hams was undertaken by 156 members of the WVS, many of whom travelled many miles to report at Blackawton or Stokenham. Other than the services rendered by the WVS, there were Ministry clerks, naval ratings and American soldiers involved in the evacuation. The local MP sometimes intervened to help the plight of the villagers but, considering the large number of residents involved in the exodus, no evidence has been discovered of any local leader having emerged from one of the villages to represent the interests of the communities. The question arises did any organisations, for example, trade unions, charitable organisations, church guilds come forward with the offer of help and support for the villagers, or were such offers suppressed? Some of the treatment meted out to the evacuees was disgraceful. Many of the villagers were poor and did not possess any cases in which to pack their belongings. They were offered cardboard boxes that they were expected to pay for. Arguably these people were paying out of their own pocket to be expelled from their homes!

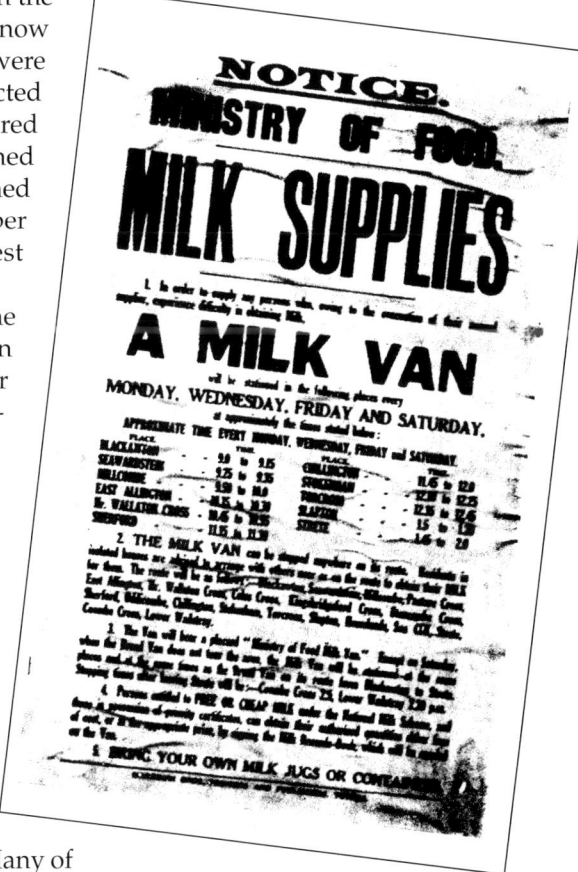

The Ministry of Food displayed notices in the evacuated villages that milk would be delivered four days a week to the remaining residents.

Miss Martin, the WVS lady in charge of the Information Centre at Blackawton, recalls in her report on the evacuation to Lady Reading how on a bitterly cold day in the middle of November 1943, forty members of the WVS met at the Victory Hall, Stokenham, listening to the Regional Commissioner's representative explaining to them what was likely to happen and what was expected of them. This meeting was held a day before the public meeting that had been arranged to take place at St Michael Church Blackawton, to inform the residents what had been planned and how it would affect them. The WVS members were told there would be two public information centres, one at Stokenham, the other at Blackawton.[17] To get to Blackawton had meant having to drive or walk through a maze of narrow lanes. It seemed impossible to reach the village without someone who knew the local countryside. The Blackawton Information Centre, was based in the village school close to the Norman church. On 13 November 1943, Blackawton Church was filled to capacity, probably a bigger congregation than it had ever seen. Sitting with their backs to the historic rood screen was the Bishop of Exeter, the Regional Commissioner, the Chairman of Devon County Council, an American General and a senior naval officer. The meeting began with a prayer and finished with the people singing God Save the King. The villagers were told what was to happen, praised for the greatness of their sacrifice, and advised of the amount of help that would be given. The meeting was an example of different social classes coming together for a common purpose in time of urgent circumstances. Yet for the villagers it was a bewildering experience.

On 27 November 1943, the first week of the South Hams evacuation, a major disaster involving American servicemen took place in the Mediterranean, an event the American

Government suppressed details of for decades. The reason for touching upon the disaster here is that it has certain similarities with the Exercise Tiger tragedy in Lyme Bay that was to take place only five months later. The British ship the HMT *Rohna* was one of a convoy of four ships destined for Port Said, Egypt. The *Rohna* with a crew of 195 men was carrying 1889 American troops and seven Red Cross personnel when a German glider bomb sank it. Engulfed in flames she sank in the darkness and hundreds of the men perished in the water of the Mediterranean. The casualty list included the death of 1015 US servicemen. Over 800 bodies were never recovered. Furthermore 120-crew members and three Red Cross personnel died.[18]

Both of the information centres were kept busy helping people trying to resolve their numerous problems, including arranging transport to their new destination. The villagers' homes were dispersed over a wide area. One lady, who never returned to the South Hams, was evacuated to Scotland. Blackawton's village postman was the first villager to be helped by the Information Centre. He was taken with his family by car to Wadebridge, Cornwall; to view a cottage that he knew was vacant. The visit was successful and eventually he settled in Cornwall.

The busiest time at the Centre according to Miss Martin was during the late morning when the Strete bus arrived in Blackawton bringing in people requiring help. This was a difficult period for everyone as the weather changed and became very cold, followed by heavy rain that resulted in the constant flow of traffic churning up the mud in the country lanes creating bog-like conditions. This was particularly unpleasant for the Land Army girls and sailors who worked in the fields helping to harvest what crops remained. Other than assisting with people, there was the problem of finding homes for animals.

As the evacuation proceeded so more transport arrived in the villages. For example Blackawton became blocked with traffic that continued to arrive and depart. As the furniture vans became loaded and drove away, so lorries piled up with harvested crops made their exodus from the farms. An indication of the increasing exodus of people away from

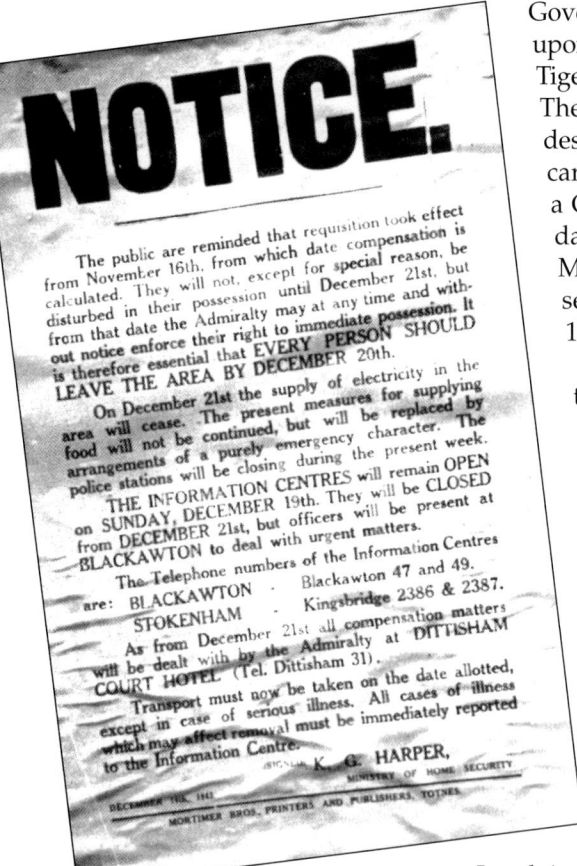

A Home Security public notice displayed around the communities was to remind the villagers that every person should leave their home by the 20 December 1944

Removal day for the family at Stenthill Farm, Slapton village, December 1943.

the villages was that the smoke from the chimneys grew less and less. Arrangements had been made to remove the sacred and historic contents from the local churches that were taken to Ashburton, Brixham, Totnes and Widecombe to be stored.[19] Reports claim how in spite of the difficulties faced by the villagers being expelled the evacuation proceeded in a spirit of good will. Many of the post-war recollections of the evacuations are testimonies given by people who were children at the time. A recent film of the evacuation was released with interviews of people from three of the villages recalling their memories.[20] What is known is that villagers on leaving were given a print of the King and Queen. It would have

As time went by, an increasing number of vehicles, as shown by the congestion at Blackawton, arrived in the villages to transport the villagers and their goods to new homes.

Other than the harvesting of the crops that remained in the fields, farming implements had to be moved. Alan Jarvis is seen in this picture driving his steam tractor and threshing machine away from the evacuation area, December 1943.

One householder displays his picture of Queen Victoria before it was packed.

As the local village stores began to close emergency meals were provided by a Ministry of Food flying squad. This picture shows volunteers preparing a hot meal in the communal kitchen, Strete.

Washing up the pots after the volunteers had prepared a meal for the remaining residents at Strete.

Valuable and historic items from buildings, particularly churches, were required to be moved away to a place of safety. This picture shows part of the ancient rood screen of Blackawton Church being packed into a wooden crate, assisted by two American soldiers. During the last weeks of 1943, American soldiers had arrived and were called upon to help the villagers in packing.

As the Admiralty could not guarantee the safety of the church treasures, arrangements were made to remove those that were portable to a place of safety. The picture shows the removal of a large decorative armorial board from Slapton Church. Treasures that could not be removed were sandbagged to protect them from being damaged.

Packing the font cover of Blackawton church to be taken away for safe keeping.

The King's Arms, Strete. Last orders before final closure!

Eventually the time had come for everyone to go. The last drinks were served. The picture shows villagers with two American soldiers drinking 'last orders' at the Queens Arms, Slapton.

been interesting to know if any villagers had left a Union Flag for the royal couple in their front window as a patriotic gesture!

As the deadline of 20th December 1943 came closer. Local deliveries of food to the village stores was stopped. Emergency bread and milk deliveries were made, the milkman stopping in each village for 15 minutes. The village public houses served their last drinks and then closed. When the last inhabitants had gone, there remained a strange silence in the empty villages that was remarked upon by the remaining volunteers. On 20 December 1944 the area was officially handed over to the Americans.

However there is another side to the history of the evacuation that is not revealed in the propaganda and popular accounts of this wartime exodus. The historian Angus Calder refers to the Home Front during the Second World War as 'The People's War' and that the British people were protagonists in their own history in a fashion never known before. But there is no evidence that the villagers had a champion in their midst. The treatment by the

It was left to a dog to view the desolate scene of the empty village of Chillington.

Sergeant Burgoyne of the Home Guard with his wife and daughter. It is reputed they were the last people to be evacuated from East Allington.

Government of the residents expelled from the South Hams villages, despite the efforts of the WVS, was arguably one of the most shameful episodes in the history on the Home Front during the Second World War – a tragedy in which the villagers can justifiably be considered casualties. Although it is reported the villagers accepted the decision of compulsory evacuation in principle, the US Consul in Plymouth reported there had been much criticism of the Government's 'autocratic and undemocratic methods' while implementing the exodus, particularly the pressure exerted on the villagers by the speed of the evacuation. On the 15th December 1944, the US Consul noted 'Unofficial but reliable information about a fair number of suicides among civilians about to be evacuated'.[21]

The British authorities were concerned by the possibility of public reaction that would require the removal of some villagers by force. Monitoring the situation was Sir Hugh Elles, the Regional Commissioner, one-time Commanding Officer of Bovington Army Camp, Dorset. Whenever there had been an awkward person to deal with at the Blackawton Information Centre the WVS turned to the staff of the Regional Commissioner to deal with the situation. Miss Martin records a list was made of 'awkward people'.[22] It is reasonable to assume that many of these people were not 'awkward' but naturally simply very worried.

The American army wasted no time in moving into the area of the evacuated villages. Their first act was to erect barriers across the roads at Frogmore and Strete. The defence of the evacuated area was shared; in the daytime the Americans patrolled the outer perimeter roads and at night the 11th South Hams Battalion of the Home Guard carried out regular motor patrols. One company would proceed at a speed of 10mph along the roadway from Frogmore–Stokenham–Torcross–Strete–Blackpool–Stoke Fleming while another patrol, using the same route, set out in the reverse direction from Stoke Fleming and proceeded to Frogmore. The area was patrolled four times nightly.

American servicemen were supposedly not allowed to use evacuated homes as billets, but they did. For example, at Hillfields, near Blackawton, American officers used the large eighteenth century villa. Troops also used the villagers' cottages. The deserted Slapton beach

No sooner had the villagers moved out, than the American troops moved in. The picture shows them unloading bedding from their trucks, January 1944.

US troops set up a machine-gun post in the Chancelry at Slapton, January 1944.

With the villagers gone, Slapton Church was with the rest of the places of worship, out of bounds to the American troops. A wide strip of white paint on the church roof was used as an identification marker to prevent the church being used as a target for shelling, December 1943.

An American soldier stops to read a gravestone in Slapton churchyard.

During the early autumn of 1944, although the enemy still had to be defeated, the war situation allowed some villagers who had been evacuated to return to their home. However Mr F.H. Herd of Strete had to wait longer. He received his official letter informing his cottage had been released from requisition one year after he was compelled to be evacuated.

```
Tel. Nos. Dittisham 31 & 41.            ADMIRALTY LANDS OFFICE,
                                        DITTISHAM COURT HOTEL,
                                        DITTISHAM,
                                            DARTMOUTH,
In reply please quote:-                     SOUTH DEVON.

Slapton No...368..                      10th January 1945....194.

Dear Sir,

                re 4 Turnpike Cottages, Strete.

        I hereby give you formal notice that the above-named property
is released from requisition as from.12th January 1945. and that the
payment of any periodical compensation you may have received from
the Admiralty since its requisition will cease as from that date as
will all other liability that may have devolved on the Admiralty in
respect of the property during the period of requisition.

2.      Compensation in respect of any damage that may have occurred to
the property during the period of Admiralty occupation is payable
to the owner of the property and a separate communication has been
sent to him.

3.      If you have any claim to make under Section 2 (1)(d) of the
Compensation (Defence) Act, 1939, in respect of expenses, such as
the cost of transporting yourself and your belongings back to the
property, you should forward to this office a list of the expenses
for which you claim to be paid.  Arrangements will then be made as
soon as possible to effect a settlement of your claim.

4.      If you want a payment on account of compensation properly pay-
able to you this will be arranged on receipt of your request, and
if there is any other information you desire I shall be pleased to
supply it.

                                        Yours faithfully,

Mr.F.H.Head,
4 Turnpike Cottages,
Strete.
                                        SURVEYOR OF LANDS.

95Dd-TRB
```

and parts of the countryside within the Battle Training Area were installed with different types of obstacles and fortifications. This form of military set-up at Slapton Battle Training Area could be described as a giant stage of a theatre, as the scenery of obstacles and fortifications were moved around, with guns mounted on movable vehicles, the stage setting depending on the nature of the exercise that was taking place.

The personal situation of the expelled villagers varied after leaving their village. There were those who quickly settled into their new homes. But all was not well. One person describes, "That there is a growing discontent and unrest among the evacuated people of South Devon, on accounts of damage to their property by US forces and the failure of the US and the Admiralty to implement the promises made concerning the evacuation of the population". The text of one letter stated "it may not be generally known that the underground discontent and unrest is reaching serious proportions and wherever one goes among the evacuees one is met with bitter curses against the authority for failing to implement their promises and a truly embittered feeling against the American troops who have done so much willful damage to their homes." The letter continues, "news of such damages is leaking out of the evacuated area and this is intensifying the bitterness. The compulsory exodus has been a source of embitterment to the villagers and the cause of the breakdown in morale."

Compensation for the evacuees was governed by an Act of 1939 that permitted the payment of compensation for buildings requisitioned and the defrayment of expenses incurred in the move. A serious accusation by some villagers was that local officials dealing with the question of what was clearly inadequate compensation took every advantage of any loopholes in the Compensation Act to deprive evacuees of fair or reasonable recompense. One third of the village households had suffered significant financial hardship.[23] The British Government much to their dishonour ignored the plight of these villagers. The Americans made a contribution of £6000, a donation of £2 for each evacuated villager to relieve their financial hardship.

How much damage had been done to the South Hams villagers' property? Many published photographs of the American forces are of small amphibious craft disgorging troops on Slapton beach and do not truly reflect the thousands of American troops on exercise who moved from the beach inland into the Slapton Battle Training Area. American Staff

Whatever promise had been made by the Admiralty to assure villagers that their homes would not be used by the American troops for accommodation, this photograph shows the beds of the American forces stacked up outside properties they had occupied.

The remains of the thatched-roof buildings at Strete that were burnt out when an exploding shell set the properties on fire. One of the buildings was used by the local Women's institute.

Another view of the ruined and burnt out properties that were never rebuilt. The ground is now used as a car park.

The destruction by shell fire of the Manor House Hotel, Strete gate.

Sergeant Bernard Klein states in his autobiography, "we attacked that (Devon) village for two weeks from the land and the sea. We blew up houses, tore down boundary walls, threw grenades and activated booby traps to see their deadly effects. Then an order came down from Division for us to take it easy. When the request was read to us at the beginning of another wet run, we really tore up the place. The order came to late, the damage had been done".[24] In an official letter to a Mr Picket from the Admiralty, dated 21 July 1944, it is stated the training at Slapton had been more continuous and on an even larger scale than was anticipated with the inevitable result that the damage to property had been considerable.[25]

At the end of the Summer of 1945, the first sign that some villagers who had been evacuated were allowed to return to their homes after the American occupation was when smoke was seen coming out of the chimneys. There was no welcome home present for the evacuees, for example a gift box of Ministry of Food emergency rations, bottled beer and a ration of cigarettes. Instead they were presented with a heavy-duty broom, a bucket and cleaning material to clean up the mess that the Americans had made. Patriotism and self-sacrifice it appeared was not enough.

According to the testimonies of some villagers the evacuation caused the break-up of the pre-war communities as so many people did not return.[26] To be able to return to one's home, a villager required a letter of permission from the Admiralty. The bomb squads had already been to clear the area of unexploded shells and other dangerous ordnance that had been left and was required to be made safe and removed. How well the squads had done their job is open to question. Brian Tucker whose family were tenants of Coombe Farm,

The misdirected shelling caused damage not only to property, but the trees and walls. This picture shows the destruction of part of stone wall and the remains of some trees with Slapton beach in the background.

With the road between Torcross and Street Gate re-opened to the public, to venture on to Slapton Beach was, as this warning notice conveys, a risk fraught with danger.

Evidence of damage caused by a shell at the Church House Inn during the American occupation.

Blackawton, recalls on returning to their farm thousands of rounds of live bullets were found in the hayricks.[27]

A Land Army girl recalls on going back to the farm were she worked up to the time of the evacuation, that the cows each went to their old stall at milking time as though nothing had changed.

---

1. Bradbeer, Grace. *The Evacuation of the South Hams.* The Devonshire Association, Vol.100, 1968. pp, 231-232.
2. *Assault Training Areas, Lands Branch Arrangements.* ADM 116/ 5080. National Archives.
3. Report to the Chiefs of Staff, October 1943. *The Interdepartmental Committee of Combined Training Areas in Devon, Wales and Scotland.* ADM 116/ 5080. p. 4.
4. ADM 116 5080. NA.
5. Bradbeer, Grace. *The Land Changed its Face. The Evacuation of Devons South Hams 1943-1944*, 1972. David & Charles. pp. 44-45.
6. Oswald Neville. *Life in the South Hams in World War 2.* Trans Devon . Ass. Advmt Sci;120, December 1988. p, 105.
7. Beesley, Patrick. *Very Special Intelligence, The Story of the Admiralty's Operational Intelligence Centre 1939-1945*, 2006. Chatham Publishing. p.227.
8. Smith, Peter. *Naval Warfare in the English Channel 1939-1945*, 2007 Pen & Sword p.222.
9. Wright, Patrick. *The Village that died for England*, 2002. Faber & Faber. p.36.
10. Martin, Nancy. *Blackawton Information Centre. Report on the evacuation*, December 1943. pp 1-7. Kingsbridge Heritage Centre. (KHC).
11. Reynolds, David. *Rich Relations: The American Occupation of Britain 1942-1945.* 1995, Harper Collins, p. 392.
12. 'Villagers who gave their all'. The *Western Morning News*, 21 August 1984, page 163.
13. *Interdepartmental Committee of Combined Training Areas in Devon, Wales and Scotland* Report to the Chiefs of Staff. October 1943. p. 4. ADM 116/ 5080. NA.
14. Clayton, Aileen. *The Enemy is Listening : The story of the Y service*, 1980. Hutchinson, p.131
15. Hinton, James, Women, *Social Leadership and the Second World War : Continuities of Class.* 2002, Oxford University Press, p.39.
16. Marwick Arthur, *The Home Front: The British and the Second World War,* 1976. Thames & Hudson, p.78.
17. Martin Nancy. *Report of the evacuation 1943.* December 1943. p.1. Kingsbridge Heritage Centre.
18. Bennet, James. *The Rohna Disaster: World War 2's Secret Tragedy*, 1999. Xlibris Corporation.
19. Bradbeer Grace, *The Evacuation of the South Hams.* The Devonshire Association, volume 100, 1968. p.237.
20. *Evacuation: A tale of three villages.* 2012. South Devon Coastal Local Action Group.
21. Reynolds, David. *Rich Relations: The American Occupation of Britain 1942-1945.* 1995, Harper Collins, p.126.
22. Martin, Nancy, *Report of the evacuation 1943.* December 1943. p.4. KHC.
23. Letter d. 29 June 1944 from Mr F. Picket (late of Chillington) to Colonel Rayner, MP. p.2. Adm 116/5081.
24. Krien, Bernhardt, *Once around the Block,* 2011. Author House USA. pp.160-61.
25. Letter dated 21 July 1944 from my Lords Commissioners of the Admiralty to Mr Picket Adm 116/ 5081. NA.
26. *Evacuation: A tale of three villages.* 2012. South Devon Coastal Local Action Group.
27. Rose-Price, Robin and Parnell, Jean. *The Land we left behind : A pictorial history and memories of the war years in the South Hams,* 2004. Orchard Publications, p.76.

7 The Major Amphibious Exercises

AN AMPHIBIOUS OPERATION was often the prelude to a large land military campaign. The amphibious assault landings on the Normandy coast on D-Day were planned to establish a bridgehead, a position held in advance of the main force and as a basis for further advance. The doctrine of amphibious warfare had developed to the extent that it was acknowledged such forces should consist of a naval force, support ships and a land force, supported from the air. It was recognised that special craft were needed to land combat units together with artillery, tanks, other vehicles and essential stores. It was also recognised that aircraft were required to play an essential role in supporting the landing force. Historian's debate which was the first country or service to invent amphibious war? Christopher Yung, a senior US naval researcher cites the authors, Isley and Crowl, who argue it was the creation of the US Marine Corps and the US Navy. What is known is that the first British motorised landing craft was designed in 1922, four years after the First World War. By 1930 three of these craft had been built. Furthermore a British interservice training and development centre had been established that reported directly to the Chiefs of Staff. Until the early 1940s the American Army had not focused on amphibious operations, but had concentrated on land warfare. The early German victories of the Second World War resulting in their occupation of northern Europe and the construction of the Atlantic wall. A massive military effort would be required to plan and organise large-scale amphibious operations against enemy occupied Europe.

When America entered the Second World War, whatever plans and development concerning amphibious operations had so far been decided, the major debate among the politicians and Allied commanders was to decide where to deploy the major US military forces, in the European or the Pacific theatre of war? Their decision to first invade Europe resulted in the US and British developing their doctrines of amphibious warfare. The first part of the training program for *Neptune* was the establishment of Woolacombe Assault

Before the Slapton Sands amphibious exercises commenced the beach had been surveyed and tested for its suitability for military training. This famous photograph is not a record of one of the major amphibious exercises but of US troops, during August 1943, in co-operation with the Royal Navy going through test procedures on Slapton beach.

```
KNOWN UNITS AT SLAPTON SANDS

GROUPS, ARMY, AND CORPS        COLONEL PAUL W. THOMPSON
1ST U.S. ARMY CORPS            COSSAC
1ST U.S. ARMY
V CORPS
VII CORPS

DIVISIONS
1ST INF
4TH INF
29TH INF
82ND A/B
83RD INF
101ST A/B

1ST ENGINEER SPECIAL BRIGADE
6TH ENGINEER SPECIAL BRIGADE

REGIMENT
8TH INF T
12TH INF
16TH INF
22ND INF
188TH FIELD ARTILLERY GROUP
501ST PARACHUTE INFANTRY
502ND PARACHUTE INFANTRY
505TH PARACHUTE INFANTRY
506TH PARACHUTE INFANTRY
1106TH ENGINEER COMBAT GROUP
327TH GLIDER INFANTRY REGIMENT

BATTALIONS, SQUADRONS, COMPANY
4TH CAVALRY SQUDRON            57TH QM RAILHEAD CO
4TH MEDICAL BN T               363RD QM SERVICE CO
70TH TANK BN T                 440TH ENGINEER CO T
87TH ARMORED F A BN            462ND AMPHIBIOUS TRUCK CO T
203RD ENGINEER COMBAT BN       556TH QM RAILHEAD CO T
261ST MEDICAL BN               557TH QM RAILHEAD CO T
321ST GLIDER F A BN            562ND QM RAILHEAD CO T
326TH A/B ENGINEER BN          3206TH QM SERVICE CO T
377TH PARACHUTE F A BN         3891ST QM TRUCK CO T
746TH TANK BN                  478TH AMPHIBIOUS TRUCK CO T
907TH F A BN
33RD CHEMICAL COMPANY T
```

Details of Exercises at Slapton Battle Training Area

1 DUCK   31 December to 3 January 1944
   Bombardment by 4 British Hunt class destroyers
   British reports state that Green Beach not used until exercise Tiger.
   War diaries of LST 400 shows she landed on the beach.

2 FOX   10 to 12 March 1944
   Bombardment by 2 cruisers and 8 destroyers.

3 MUSKRAT   24 to 27 March 1944
   Bombardmemt by 2 cruisers and USS *Bayfield*.
   LST 400 loaded troops at Dartmouth and sailed straight to assembly area.

4 BEAVER   29 to 31 March 1944
   Bombardment by 2 cruisers and 8 destroyers.
   LST 46 landed on green beach.

5 TROUSERS   11 to 13 April 1944
   Details not known.

6 TIGER   26 to 29 April 1944 (U Force)
   Bombardment by 2 cruisers, one of which was HMS *Enterprise* and 7 destroyers.
   Not all vessels sailed the long convoy route. These included the USS's *Bayfield* and *Joseph T Dickman* and HMS *Empire Gauntlet* and some LST's, including LST 50, yet LST 46 which took the long route passed the enemy action position some 12 hours before the attack.

7 Fabius   3 to 6 May 1944 (O Force)
   Bombardment by USS *Augusta* and HMS *Glasgow* and 9 US destroyers.
   A number of LST's sailed from Dartmouth to the beaches at the end of the exercise. They collected the troops and took them back to Dartmouth.

When D Day arrived O Force would be landed at Omaha Beach, and U Force at Utah Beach. The former sailing from Southampton to Portland and the latter from Portland to Falmouth. Back up forces sailed from Scotland, N Ireland, Wales and the Bristol Channel ports.

Above left: A list of American army units that were involved in amphibious exercises at Slapton Sands, from the National Archives, Kew.

Above right: A list of the major amphibious exercises obtained from the National Archives, Kew. Although useful, it gives limited details of the exercises.

Training Centre. The second phase was the major amphibious exercises. These amphibious training exercises held in Devon during 1943–44 were part of the vital military precursors that were to ensure the success of the Allied assault on the Normandy beaches on D-Day 1944. Without this practical indoctrination the D-Day landings would not have been possible. The Second World War amphibious exercises are of key importance in the history of the conflict. The military forces that participated in the exercises involved thousands of men, and vast numbers of vehicles and military equipment. Likewise the naval contribution included warships of different size and power, landing craft flotillas, naval construction battalions, beach battalions, demolition combat units, beach jumpers and supporting units including medical, communication and radar services.

The amphibious exercises were held to give the different units experience in the type of tasks they would be expected to perform. They had been planned as building-up exercises, from platoon to company, company to battalion, battalion to brigade, brigade to division, division to corps. All the major amphibious exercises at Slapton were planned to be preceded by a naval bombardment. The use of live ammunition, including machine gun and rifle fire, introduced realism into the exercises as had been ordered by the Supreme Commander, General Eisenhower, who believed troops in training they should undergo the experience of being under fire.

Throughout the first six months of 1944, the Slapton Battle Training Area was a continuous hive of activity involving thousands of troops. Other than the named large-scale amphibious exercises and rehearsals conducted, there were smaller, some unnamed, exercises carried out on Slapton beach, or on other beaches along the south-west coast of Devon and Cornwall. For example, at Salcombe, the 6th and 7th Beach Battalion who were based in a hutted camp above the town were designated to act as Beach Masters on the far shore.[1] They practiced landings from small amphibious craft in Kingsbridge estuary at Fisherman Cove. The US 6th Engineers Special Brigade stationed at Paignton carried out training exercises at nearby Goodrington Sands, Broadsands and Elberry Cove. At Dartmouth large numbers of small craft tied up in rows along the embankment ready to participate in practice runs or small scale exercises. These would start early in the morning with the appearance of trainee sailors, many of them from the Royal Navy, who were directed to a particular craft that would take on American troops and sail out of the River Dart making their way towards Slapton beach.[2]

The exercises or rehearsals described below were part of a great plan that unfolded from January 1944. From that time the tempo of the exercises quickened. The British Vice Admiral Leatham wrote to the American, Rear Admiral Hall, the Commander of the 11th Amphibious Force, whose role was to plan, oversee and train the force for the forthcoming assault on the shores of Normandy. Leatham's communication was to clarify the responsibilities concerning the American and British navies during the naval training activities. Leatham wrote, "From the time of leaving Falmouth, the port of embarkation for the exercises, the American Commander involved would be in charge of his forces, including all the British vessels that formed the close escort. Should I have any information of enemy attack by E boats, submarine or air, it will be passed to you to take such action as you may think fit." He ended his letter by stating he would retain full control of the covering forces through the operation. What appeared, as a straightforward document was far from clear for within four months this communication was to have important consequences concerning the officers of the American and British navy involved in Exercise Tiger.

The public were not spectators to these amphibious exercises but there was sufficient evidence for them to realise that important military operations were being carried out. People had seen the LSTs laden with troops and vehicles, or the convoys of trucks pulling

The five-star General Eisenhower, supreme Commander Allied Forces, later President of the United States of America,

Evidence that American troops were participating in exercises in the Westcountry as early as August 1943. It is surprising that details of the deaths of American Troops in an unnamed river while on an operational exercise was allowed to be published. From the *Western Morning News*, 7 August 1943.

A post war aerial photograph showing the Dartmouth and Kingswear hards constructed near the higher chain ferry that were used by the American forces. To the right of the Dartmouth hards can been seen the remains of the US Navy depot in Coronation Park.

There were small scale exercise landings on other beaches in Devon and Cornwall. This picture shows the 7th Beach Battalion, based at Salcombe, practising a landing at Fisherman's Cove, Salcombe.

Small scale landing exercises were carried out at St Mary's beach and other beaches near Brixham. The picture records landing craft 599 (LCP 599) and Assault Craft A43 (AC A43) disgorging US troops on to St Mary's beach. Sharkham Point is in the background.

howitzers travelling towards the hards. The actual amphibious exercises echoed with a whole range of noises heard along the seashores of the Westcountry and far inland. The boom of the bombardment from the warships' guns firing live shells on to the Slapton Battle Training Area, or the continuous short bursts of rifle or machine gun fire intermingled with the thump of the tank or anti-tank guns, all added to the cacophony of an exercise. Second Lieutenant John Good of the Royal Marines was undergoing training at Thurlestone, a few miles from Salcombe. For some reason that he never understood, his course officer arranged for Good to observe one of the amphibious exercises by standing on high ground at the south-east end of Slapton Beach, (probably in the area of Strete Gate). John Good gives a rare description of what he saw: "It was absolutely amazing. I remember so clearly all our diagrams, learned in the classroom becoming reality. You look down on to the bay and there it all was, in front of your very eyes, that included the fire support guns, rockets, the full works. And as the exercise progressed I was able to watch the big LSTs coming in and beach. I think I learned more from those few hours about amphibious operations than any amount of classroom work could ever have taught me".[3]

A familiar sight seen in the South Hams skies during the exercises and over other parts of Devon were the US Piper cub liaison aircraft. These small lightweight aircraft had a cruis-

A posed but interesting picture taken from the Stoke Fleming side of the perimeter of the training area showing a US armed guard. In the background landing craft can just be seen at Blackpool Sands.

Opposite: Blackpool Sands close to Slapton beach was also use by the US forces. Behind the beach was a small camp and parking area. On the hillside at the back of Blackpool Sands were boundary markers that identified the perimeter of the Slapton Battle Training Area adjacent to Stoke Fleming, Civilians are known to have come to the wooded hillside area to watch the military beach activities.

ing speed of 75 mph and their flying range was 190 miles. The aircraft were painted in drab green with a large white star on the fuselage. Accommodation was limited to a pilot and an observer. Their function was to carry American Army personnel to attend meetings or as transport couriers. They were also used as visual reconnaissance. Both the 4th and 29th Infantry divisions were supplied with these aircraft. The Piper Club did not require an airfield to operate, it was able to land and take off from any small strip of land that was reasonably level. Examples of the location of the numerous airstrips used by these small aircraft in Devon are:

Blackawton: Strete
Slapton Sands: Ivybridge
Paignton: Tavistock
Barnstaple: Tiverton
Torquay: Okehampton
Great Torrington: Walkhampton

As there was radio equipment in the aircraft, navigation depended on visual control. A major hazard were barrage balloons one of which was the cause of an accident over Dartmouth where balloons were flown from the large landing craft anchored in the river. On 8 April 1944, a Piper Cub had taken off from the airstrip near Paignton sea front to fly to Slapton Sands in connection with an amphibious exercise. As the pilot approached the River Dart the visibility deteriorated and the aircraft struck a balloon cable causing the aircraft to crash into Dartmouth Harbour. Luckily the pilot was rescued and escaped with minor injuries.[4]

SLAPTON ASSAULT TRAINING AREA

The Admiralty delegated the administration of the Slapton assault training area to the Commander-in-Chief, Plymouth. The Range Commandant was a US Army Colonel who worked with an appointed British Naval Liaison Officer and a range party. The training area was approximately five square miles extended from East Allington to Blackawton and down to the coast between the villages of Torcross and Strete.[6] It also included Slapton Ley, Slapton Beach and Blackpool beach. The inland battlefield training area consisted mainly of hilly countryside with narrow country roads or lanes. High hedges bound many of the fields and the American made gaps in the hedgerows to allow their troops and transport to enter and cross the fields. During the exercises troops would meet up at designated assem-

An exercise in logistics being carried out at Blackpool Sands.

THE MAJOR AMPHIBIOUS EXERCISES

American infantry disembark from a landing craft No 90 (LCI) at Slapton Sands.

Troops assemble on the Kingswear hard alongside the River Dart to participate in Operation Duck.

bly areas, For example the assembly area for Exercise Trousers was in an area near Sherford Village. The range boundaries were marked by large red flags and signs 'Admiralty, Danger, Keep Out, Battle Range'. In the impact area for guns ashore there were signs that read 'no firing in this area'. For guns afloat the impact area was marked on the shore and were visible from the sea.

The first act of the Americans after the training area had been formally handed over to them was to erect barriers across the relevant roads to prevent the entry of civilians. One barrier was erected outside the village of Chillington, on the approach to Frogmore. The battle area boundaries were defined by miles of barbed wire that was patrolled by security troops. Vacated properties within the battlefield training area perimeter were soon installed with bunks to accommodate the range staff. Captain Buckley of the US Navy had completed his survey of the gradients of the beach to confirm its suitability as a training area. Slapton Beach had been cleared of the mines that the British had laid in 1940.[5]

The Americans lost no time in introducing their major amphibious training exercises. On the last day of 1943, the US 29th Infantry Division were at Slapton Sands taking part in Exercise Duck. This was the first of six amphibious exercises conducted at Corps level. These practice landings were held under considerable secrecy. In the first six months of 1944 the Luftwaffe flew 32 daytime reconnaissance flights over the UK, not all over southern England.[6] The RAF had introduced continuous flying patrols to preventing the enemy flying space over the area. An incident occurred when men of the 4th Infantry Division shot down a German aircraft on reconnaissance over Slapton Sands and captured the enemy pilot. This was the US 4th Infantry Division's first prisoner of war.

A number of assembly areas were established in Cornwall and Devon to bring together the relevant military forces that were to be involved in one of the amphibious exercises. These were large camps where the forces assembled before making their way to the embarkation points (some being 13 miles away). For example, assembly area K-Torquay consisted of camps at K1-South Brent; camps at K2-Dartington; camps at K3- and K4-Totnes. The camps at K2-Dartington were located at Dartington, Staverton Bridge, Hood Manor, Kingston House.

EXERCISE DUCK

Exercise Duck I had been discussed in mid summer 1943. It was initiated by the 11th Amphibious Force and was the first major exercise held at Slapton Sands, lasting from 31 December–2 January 1944. This was followed by Duck II (February) and Duck III (23 February–1 March). Duck I was the first of a series of exercises involving practice landings. The purpose of Duck I was to give troops experience with LSTs and LCTs working together as an Assault Force and embarking and landing assault combat troops on the far shore.[7] The troops involved in Duck I were from the 29th Infantry Division that camped in the vicinity of Plymouth, Taunton, Barnstaple and Land's End. They had embarked from Falmouth and Dartmouth. The scale of the exercise was enormous; it involved 553 officers, 9600 other ranks and 1096 vehicles. Five camps areas were set aside, for the exercise, four of them in Cornwall, the other at Lupton House, Churston, near Brixham. The assault convoy was made up of 219 landing craft guarded by four Royal Navy destroyers, three landing craft tanks equipped with 105m howitzers and several other fire-support vessels. The exercise was held in the vicinity of Manor House nearby Strete Gate. The observation post stood on a hill south-west of Torcross.

A secondary assault exercise was held at Coleton Heights to contain enemy forces in the Brixham peninsula. At the end of the exercise rockets were fired on to Slapton Beach. Whatever the criticisms of Duck I, and there were many, it was probably the most important of the exercises, as the flaws that were shown up were corrected for the exercises that followed. After the Duck exercises, a series of smaller exercises involving the US 4th Infantry Division were carried to get the troops accustomed to the realities of amphibious warfare. These lesser-known exercises were named, Teal, Mallard, Mink, Otter and Gull.

The Government had been increasingly concerned about security regarding the preparation for D-Day. They pursued a policy of using posters and propaganda films encouraging people not to gossip or spread rumours. However many civilians did not keep their counsel. Evidence as to the extent of the references made in civilian letters to the 'invasion exercises' in Devon was revealed in a wartime census taken in South Devon. From a sample of 24 000 letters intercepted by the censors, eighty per cent of them referred to the preparation for the Allied invasion. At midnight on the 17–18 April, ten days before Exercise Tiger, the War Cabinet imposed a ban on visitors throughout the coastal area from the Wash on the east coast of England down to Cornwall covering the coastline ten miles deep.[8] Anyone who had arrived in a prohibited area without permission was escorted back to their transport by the police. Train passengers' credentials were checked to confirm if they were allowed to continue their journey. A father who had travelled from London to visit his evacuated son at Brixham was refused permission at first to leave Paignton railway station. Explaining to the police the purpose of his visit he was eventually allowed to continue his journey to Brixham on condition he returned to London later that same day.

A Cabinet note dated 3 March 1944, that draws attention to the lax security detected in civilian letters from the Torquay, Dartmouth, Brixham and Totnes areas referring to the preparation of the predicted Allied invasion.

US army troops using a signalling lamp to transmit messages out to a Rhino out in Slapton Bay.

Troops disembark from a Landing Craft Infantry No.84. Note the small gun on the bow of the craft.

American Troops coming ashore at Slapton using small Higgins boats, but hundred of other soldiers disembarked from larger landing craft.

EXERCISE FOX

Exercise Fox, held at Slapton Sands on 9–10 March 1944, was the largest of the amphibious exercises prior to Tiger and Fabius I. Admiral Hall as Commander of Force 'O' was in charge of the operation. The exercise plan was based on the operations for the Omaha Beach assault involving the 16th Regimental Combat Team of the 1st Infantry Division, 116th Regimental Combat Team of the 29th Infantry Division and other Battalions that included DUKW companies, medical and signal detachments quartermaster troops and port troops. The marshalling areas were in Dorset. Over 16 000 troops and 1908 vehicles embarked at Dartmouth, Plymouth, Portland and Weymouth. The task force that departed for Slapton Sands was escorted by five Royal Navy destroyers and air cover was provided by the US 9th Air Force. The convoy consisted of over a 100 craft, including 21 Landing Ship Tanks and 49 Landing Craft Tanks. The beach landings were supported by naval gunfire using live ammunition.

EXERCISE MUSKRAT I

Muskrat I was not associated with Slapton Sands. The 12th US Infantry Regiment that embarked at Plymouth and sailed to the Firth of Clyde, Scotland, to participate in battalion landing team exercises, held it on 13–23 March 1944. On 24–26 March the landing exercises designated Muskrat II continued, with the reinforcement of the 1st Engineer Special Brigade detachment.

EXERCISE BEAVER

This exercise held at Slapton Sands took place during 27–30 March by the 8th and 22nd Infantry Regiment combat teams and was reinforced by a detachment of a 1st Engineer Special Brigade and the 502st Paratroop Infantry. Marshalling and embarkation was at Brixham and Plymouth. Part of the 11th Amphibious Force protected the assault convoy.

At least six LCIs have arrived at Slapton Sands and appear to have unloaded their troops.

A rare picture of two landing craft tied up on Slapton beach. US 495 appears to be in the process of unloading.

Two landing craft infantry beached on Slapton Sands in the area close to Strete Gate.

THE MAJOR AMPHIBIOUS EXERCISES

A close-up of the open bow of a landing craft disgorging a Sherman tank to participate in an exercise.

The same Sherman tank clear of the LST, making its way on Slapton Sands.

Activity on Slapton Sands, showing a DD Sherman 'swimming' tank in the foreground with its skirting down.

Troops coming ashore at Slapton Sands from a landing craft Infantry (LCI). The white stripe on the back of a helmet denotes an officer.

This picture conveys the magnitude of an amphibious exercise. It gives a good side view of a loaded LST and also shows that larger tanks as well as the smaller Sherman tanks were involved at Slapton Sands.

THE MAJOR AMPHIBIOUS EXERCISES

Top left: A long column of American vehicles, the leading half tracks armed with anti-aircraft guns, halt on the road by Slapton Sands close to the village of Torcross.

Top right: US Troops passing the ruins of the Royal Sands Hotel with Slapton Ley in the background.

Centre left: Troops coming ashore at Slapton Sands. Part of the skirting of a DD Sherman 'swimming' tank is seen to the left of the picture.

Bottom left: One of the machine gun emplacements on Slapton Sands.

Troops laying on the beach near Strete Gate contemplating how they are to overcome the barbed wire entanglements, while higher up men are preparing to negotiate climbing the hill.

EXERCISE TROUSERS

An exception to the American presence at Slapton Sand was that of the Canadian force which participated in Exercise Trousers that took place on 18 April 1944. This was a full-scale practice for D-Day. The force rehearsed the passage, approach and assault landing on to the beach. The Canadians also practised signal communication and fire support. While the exercise itself was a serious undertaking, some signals that were used in the exercise appear to be deliberately comical. For example, 'Trousers Down' was the signal for 'start loading in accordance with detailed orders'. Loading for Exercise Trousers took place at Southampton and Stanswood Hards. The large force sailed without incident from their assembly positions in the Spithead and Solent area across Lyme Bay to Slapton Sands. The Naval Force consisted of a bombardment force of two cruisers, four destroyers and three minesweeper flotillas. The armada included 166 landing ships and landing craft. There were also four Rhino ferries and two tugs. The military force comprised 20 000 men from the HQ 3 Canadian Infantry Division. RAF fighter squadrons and coastal aircraft were present to protect the Canadian force against any air or E boat activity. Particular attention

Among officers who were present at Slapton to observe Operation Trousers was Field Marshall Bernard Montgomery seen here on Slapton Beach in discussion with Allied Officers.

THE MAJOR AMPHIBIOUS EXERCISES

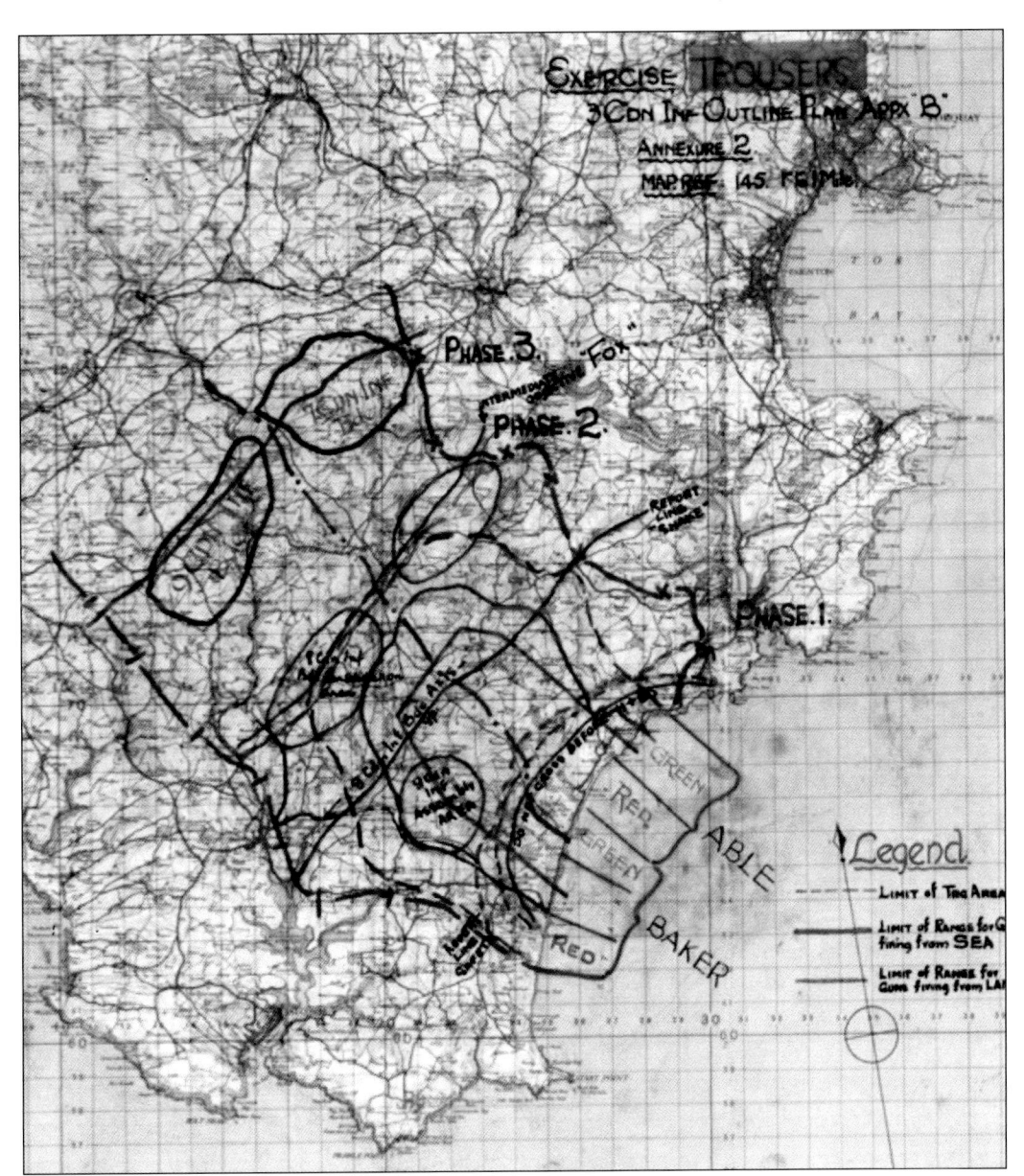

The Exercise Trousers plan shows the proposed movement of troops in the training area, the Canadian Force having advanced from Slapton Beach. It reveals that most of the Slapton Battle Training Area was planned to be utilized by the Canadians.

Below: Exercise Trousers involved units of the Canadian Army, and was the last major amphibious exercise before the ill-fated Lyme Bay disaster. Holding the exercise at Slapton Battle Training Area meant transporting a large military force across the potentially dangerous waters of Lyme Bay and Slapton Bay.

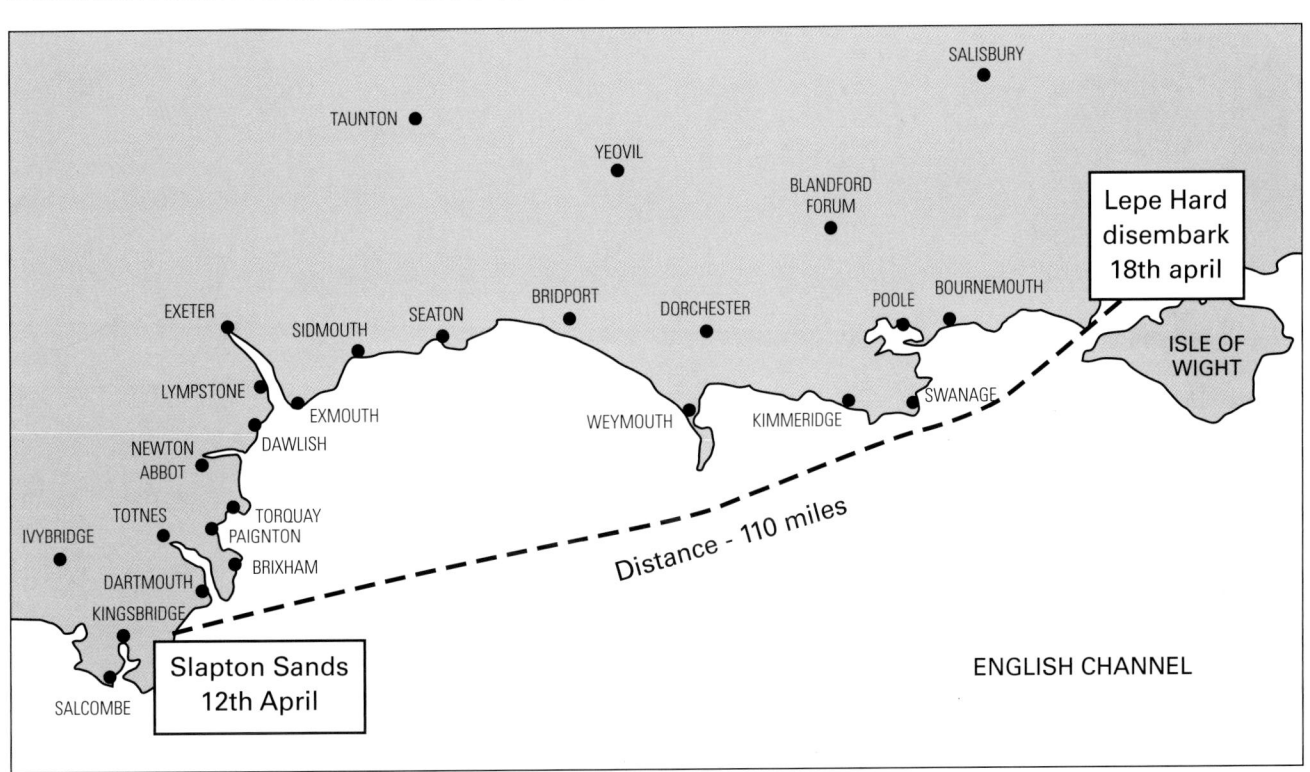

Serial	Signal	Meaning
1.	Trousers Down	Start loading in accordance with detailed orders, or resume loading if serials 2, 3 or 4 have been made
2.	Trousers Open	Start of loading postponed 24 hrs
3.	Trousers Up	Stop loading LST and LCT craft already loaded are not to unload. Unladen craft in groups actually loading are to be loaded.
4.	Trousers Torn	Stop loading LCI. Troops already loaded in LCI are to disembark and all are to return to concentration area.
5.	Trousers Button	Exercise "TROUSERS" will take place with D day as indicated.
6.	Trousers Wet	Exercise postponed 24 hrs. Craft which have sailed to return by reverse route. Craft which have not sailed to remain at berth.
7.	Trousers Utility	Exercise "TROUSERS" cancelled.
8.	TROUSERS Split	Cease landing. No further loads to be disembarked. Minor craft return to parent ship forthwith.
9.	Trousers Tight	There will be no air support

Exercise Trousers: A table of important signals used by the Canadian Army at Slapton Sands.

General Bernard Montgomery at Kingsbridge station, c.1944.

was paid by the Commanding Officers of all the ships and craft to the degree of AA readiness in anticipation of the force being exposed to enemy air action as was previously experienced in exercises in the vicinity of Portsmouth.

Several miles from Slapton Beach a fleet of landing craft had been packed with troops that had been transferred from the large troop ships. Aboard one of the LCTs was Nevil Shute, acclaimed for his novels such as *A Town Like Alice*. He describes the craft was loaded with Sherman tanks and 'Priest Guns', these were 105mm self-propelled guns mounted on a tank chassis. Shute describes how his LCT went in to bombard part of the Slapton coast a place he knew well and where in peacetime he had anchored his yacht. Using field glasses he watched the shells bursting inland.[9]

An observation post was provided in the vicinity of Torcross and among the large party of official observers was General Montgomery, General Miles Dempsey, Commander of the British Second Army and Canadian Forces on D-Day, Admiral Ramsay and Admiral Ralph Leatham. The exercise was considered satisfactory although there were vehicles and tanks that got stuck in the shingle of Slapton beach. Nevil Shute describes leaving Slapton Sands as 'the assaulted and devastated coast'.

As the amphibious exercises continued during the Spring, of 1944, so increasing numbers of American servicemen arrived in Devon (and in other southwestern regions of England) as part of the build up for D-Day. By the end of April 1944 there were a total of 124 024 US troops in Devon and Cornwall.[10] These figures do not reflect the distribution of US troops throughout Britain at this period of time. This influx of troops was accompanied by vast quantities of equipment, stores and munitions. Furthermore ships and landing craft continued to assemble at the departure ports in Devon and Cornwall.

EXERCISE TIGER
27 APRIL- 29 APRIL 1944 (see Chapter Eight)

EXERCISE FABIUS

Exercise Fabius was the final amphibious rehearsal before D-Day; its purpose was to give the troops experience in their allotted tasks and to give the invasion machinery a chance to function as a whole. Fabius was a combination of six separate major exercises designated Fabius I–VI carried out on the south-south-west coasts of Britain between the 3 May–6 May 1944. This was the largest amphibious exercise of the Second World War and involved all the Allied invasion assault and build-up forces that were planned to land on the Normandy beaches. Fabius I was the rehearsal for Force 'O', under the Command of Major General Huebner, USA. This force comprised troops of the US 1st Infantry Division, the US 29th Infantry Division and the Provisional Engineer Special Brigade Group that was destined to assault Omaha Beach, Normandy. Assault Force 'O' was assembled at Portland, Dorset. Fabius I involved the participation of 25 000 troops.

The troops taking part in Fabius I practised their amphibious landings at Slapton Sands with hundreds of vehicles including tanks, and then advanced inland into the Battle Training Area. At H Hour, two battalions of Sherman DD tanks, some 3000 yards from shore landed on Slapton beach and made their way to Torcross. At H plus 3 hrs another tank team of 18 tanks landed and join the other tank teams in an attack inland on the Slapton Battle Training Area.[11] This would have been an awesome sight for the evacuated villagers, to see tanks manoeuvre over ground they were familiar with. Three US Ranger Companies landed at Blackpool Sands, their mission to destroy mock enemy artillery installations; it was these special troops that would land at Point de Hoc on D-Day.

Richard Bass refers to an incident at Blackpool Sands when an unknown number of disembarking US Rangers, believing they were ashore, were drowned.[12] Admiral Ramsay

A sector of Slapton Sands just to the east of Strete Gate showing a Canadian unit setting up a radio communication point.

Exercise Trousers; a Canadian tank stuck in the shingle near Street Gate, Slapton Sands.

who had observed Fabius III was favourably impressed with the exercise. However he records in his diary that on 4 May at about four o'clock in the morning Allied twin-engine fighter-bombers attacked Allied motor torpedo boats, 'many casualties were inflicted'.[13]

The Lyme Bay E boat attack and the huge loss of US servicemen lives was known to Hitler. The Germans were looking for evidence regarding the timing of D-Day and where the Allied forces intended to land. It was impossible to hide from the enemy the fact that preparations for an Allied amphibious assault were underway. The German intelligence had used shore-based radar to monitored the major amphibious exercises, but they were

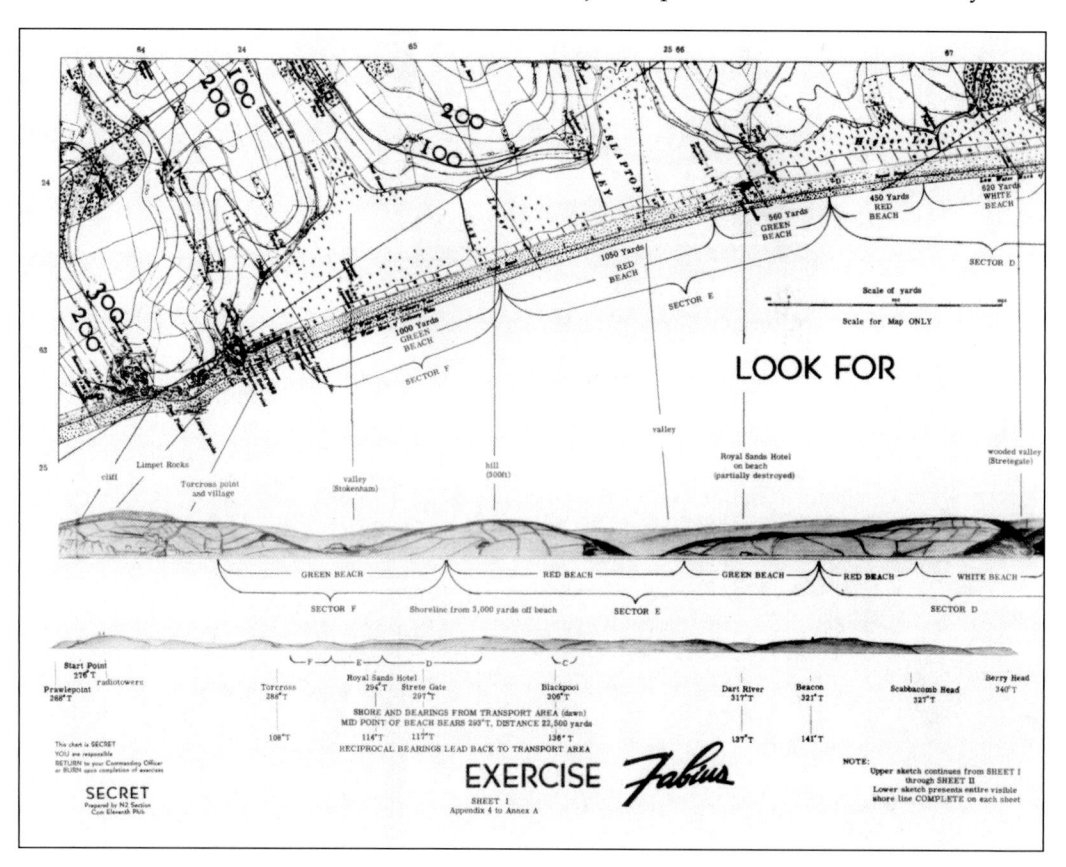

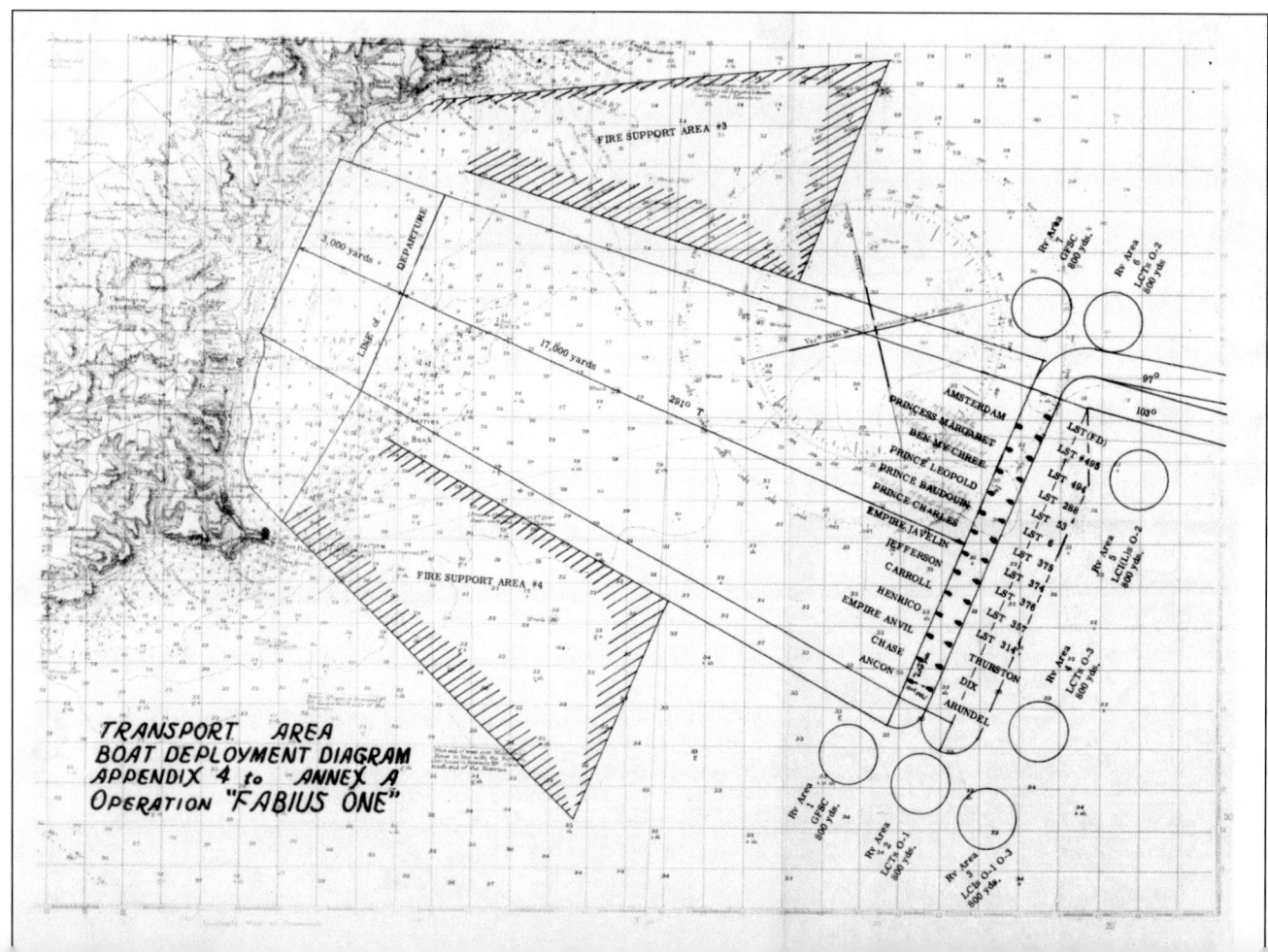

Below right: The beach plan for Exercise Fabius I showing the various areas of Slapton Beach that were involved in the exercise.

Below: Exercise Fabius I was part of the last major amphibious exercises held at Slapton Sands. This diagram illustrates the exercise in another dimension. It shows the large boat deployment in the transport area and reveals the huge scale of the exercise. The plan shows at a glance the placement of the armada of ships and other vessels that were involved. The ships were stationed 12 miles offshore from Slapton beach. Here in the transport area thousands of troops were transferred to smaller craft that then made their way to the beach.

A large crater caused by an exploding naval shell close to the ruins of the Royal Sands Hotel.

It was the practice for the small craft laden with troops, after leaving their mother ship, to move in a circle while waiting for other craft to join them, before receiving an order to head together for their destination.

A scene of activity of the shores of Slapton beach during Fabius I, with an interesting view of a DUKW about to come on to the beach.

At sunset, vessels in Slapton Bay participating in Exercise Fabius I.

unsure whether what they saw on their radar screens was just another exercise or the actual Allied invasion. In an attempt to convince the German High Command that the Allies intended to land their main forces at the Pas de Calais. The Allies had used the deception plan *Operation Fortitude*. This involved assembling imaginary concentrations of troops, fake wireless broadcasts, dummy tanks and aircraft and other forms of deception in the region of south-east England. Part of the deception involved using double agents that included Juan Pujol, alias Garbo, the famous double agent, who transmitted false information to his German masters concerning the movement of Canadian troops participating in Fabius III. The plan was to make *Operation Neptune*, the allied naval operation which was to follow Fabius, difficult for the enemy to distinguish from an elaborate amphibious exercise.[14]

OTHER FABIUS EXERCISES THAT WERE NOT HELD AT SLAPTON SANDS.
Fabius II was the rehearsal of units of the British 50 Infantry Division for Assault Force G destined to land on Gold Beach. They embarked from Southampton and Lymington and landed at Hayling Island.

An aerial view of Slapton Sands after an exercise.

Dwight Shepler's watercolour impression of an amphibious exercise at Slapton Sands, with Sherman tanks emerging from the sea to climb the gradient of the beach.

Fabius III involved elements of the Canadian 3rd Infantry Division that was to assault Juno Beach on D-Day. The Fabius III force embarked from Southampton and Gosport and landed at Bracklesham Bay.

Fabius IV was a marshalling exercise for British troops who would be involved in the initial build up forces for Gold, Juno and Sword beaches, departing from the Thames Estuary and east coast ports.

Fabius V was an American and British marshalling exercise for units departing from southern ports. The Americans forces used Portland and Weymouth. The British force marshalled at Southampton.

With D-Day only a month away, the units that had participated in Tiger and Fabius returned to their marshalling areas, not to their base camps, to await departure for the actual invasion of Normandy.

---

1. Murch, Muriel and David. *American and British Naval Forces at Salcombe and Slapton 1943-1945*, 1994. Phantom Publishing p.10.
2. Freeman, Ray. *We Remember D-Day*, 1994. Dartmouth History Research Group. p.11.
3. Bruce, Colin, *Invaders: British and American Experience of Seaborne Landings 1939-1945*, 1999. Chatham Publishing, p.122.
4. Wakefield, Kenneth. *The Fighting Grasshoppers*, 1990. Midland Publishing, p.58.
5. Oswald, Neville. *Life in the South Hams in World War II*, Trans, Devon. Ass, 120. December 1988. p.109.
6. Hinsley, F. (ed). *British Intelligence in the Second World War*, Vol 3 part 2. p.43. 1988 HMSO.
7. Yung, Christopher. *Gators of Neptune*, 2006. Naval Institute Press, Maryland. USA. p.157.
8. *Visitors' Ban*. HO 186 2260. The National Archives.
9. Anderson, John. *Nevil Shute: Exercise Trousers*, 2006. private publication pp1-3.
10. Reynolds David. *Rich Relations: The American Occupation of Britain 1942-1945*, 1995. Harper Collins. pp, 110-111.
11. Jones, Lt. Clifford. *Neptune Training: The Administrative and Logistical History of the European Theatre of Operations, 1946*. US Army Center of Military History. p.267.
12. Bass, Richard. *Exercise Tiger*, 2008 Tommies Guides pp,143-144.
13. Love, Robert and John, Major (eds). *The Year of D-Day: The 1944 Diary of Admiral Sir Bertram Ramsay*. p.63.
14. Taltry, Stephan. *Agent Garbo*, 2012. Houghton Harcourt, Boston pp.187- 189.

8 Exercise Tiger: 26 April–28 April 1944

This picture was taken on a fine sunny day from Bayards Cove. It records LST 283 loaded with troops, military equipment and small landing craft (suspended on davits), sailing out of Dartmouth Harbour to participate in Exercise Tiger. Across the river to the left of the Kingswear pontoon are three Free French MTBs that operated from Kingswear involved in clandestine operations across the English Channel.

OF ALL THE MAJOR amphibious rehearsals associated with D-Day that were held in the south-west of England during the Second World War, Exercise Tiger, with its tragic consequences, continues to excite interest because of the myths and unanswered questions that still remain. The accounts of the E boat attack on the US T4 Convoy in Lyme Bay has over the years attracted considerable publicity and has given rise to the misleading impression that the loss of so many American servicemen during this phase of the exercise is the only tragedy to befall the US troops. In recent years information has come to light that what happened off the Dorset coast on 28 April 1944 was but one of several incidents which over the course of months saw hundreds of deaths, in particular those who died on Slapton Sands the morning before, on 27 April.

Exercise Tiger, involved the participation of 25 000 troops and 2750 vehicles, was a formal rehearsal for units of the US 4th Infantry Division to simulate on Slapton Sands a far shore landing on a beach that was held and fortified by the enemy.[1] Preparations for the exercise began when the participating troops entered the marshalling areas on 22 April. A report by one officiating inspector reveals there was considerable delay in distributing the plans and orders before the exercise got underway. For example, in some cases orders had to be hurriedly rewritten. Furthermore many of the naval craft arrived late resulting in further confusion. The exercise was scheduled to take place in four phases during the last week of April 1944.

Phase 1: 26 April 1944
Complete embarkation and sail. Embarkation from Dartmouth, Brixham, Torquay and Plymouth.

Phase 2: 27 April 1944
Exercise Tiger D-Day

The plan for Phase 2 was that military activities would commence by an air attack on Slapton beach followed by a naval bombardment. Then combat units of the US 4th Division that had disembarked from their ships some 12 miles from Slapton Beach and had transferred into small landing craft would assault the enemy defences at Slapton Sands. The landing beach areas were designated 'Green Beach' and 'Red Beach'. This would be followed by a tactical exercise based on a Force 'U' assault plan for *Operation Overlord* as closely as the area permitted. A top-secret order stated service ammunition would be fired.

Phase 3: 28 April 1944
Complete concentration of forces at Slapton Sands. Return consolidation and extension of the beachhead line. Concentration of forces involved in preparation for return movement to home stations or marshalling areas

Phase 4: 29 April 1944
Complete unloading and operations of beach maintenance. Completion of unloading and continuation of operation of beach maintenance area.

Among the observers during the Phase 2 stage of the Exercise was General Eisenhower who had arrived by train at Dartmouth (Kingswear). At 6am on 27th April he boarded a landing craft infantry (LCI).[2] Other senior officer present included General Montgomery, General Bradly, Air Marshall Tedder, Admiral Ramsay and Admiral Wilkes. These officers embarked in two separate LCIs for security reasons. The two LCIs sailed out from the River Dart to Slapton Bay to take up a position to view the exercise. It was during the morning that Captain Harry Butcher, General Eisenhower's aide, describes the sinking of a Sherman tank. The tank crew was rescued and there were no casualties. This was the Sherman tank the late Ken Small retrieved and is displayed at Torcross.[3] Another Sherman tank that sank offshore, was retrieved and taken away by the Americans.

During the second phase of the Exercise it was planned for assault teams of the 4th Infantry Division to land on Slapton Beach early in the morning. (This was also an important day for the people of Plymouth as Professor Abercrombie's 'Plan for Plymouth' was to be published giving details of the rebuilding of the devastated city). During the early morning period of Exercise Tiger operations started to go wrong. For example, the US Air Force bombers scheduled to participate in the exercise never turned up. This was to be followed by a bombardment of live shells from British naval warships stationed 12 miles out in the English Channel. The shells were supposed to land and explode in designated fire support areas, before the American troops came ashore from their landing craft.

A major error occurred during this early stage of the exercise when the American Admiral Moon on board his flagship USS *Bayfield* ceded to a request from the Commander of Green Beach Assault Group for a delay of H-hour because some of his landing craft were behind schedule.[4] Another report states some of Force 'U' was out of position when the time came to lower landing craft into the water and Moon agreed to a delay in the landing until the ships were in their scheduled location. Moon wanted to consult with General Collins, Commanding General US Army V11 Corps (Admiral Moon's counterpart in the Army) about the request, but Collins had left the *Bayfield* and had gone ashore at Slapton beach. Admiral Moon therefore decided to delay the exercise for one hour. One of the consequences was that not all the participants in the exercise received the order to delay their activities. The order to stop the naval bombardment came too late to prevent many soldiers on the beach from being killed. This was to serve as a major lesson for the allied navies when D-Day itself arrived.[5]

Those troops who suffered under the naval bombardment were two companies of the US 4th Division that failed to receive the order to cease operations and had proceeded to land on Slapton Beach as planned. It was during this period of delay that the troops landing on the beach were greeted with a hail of bullets from 'defenders'; causing numerous casualties. One of the witnesses, and there were others to this slaughter, was Private Jim Curry,

Landing Craft Tank 975, setting out from the River Dart to participate in Exercise Tiger having been loaded at the Kingswear Hard.

LST 507, One of the ships sunk in the Lyme Bay disaster is shown crossing the Atlantic on her way to Britain from the USA where she was built.

The USS *Bayfield* was Admiral Moon's command ship. It is shown here on 25 April 1944 anchored in the Hamoaze, Plymouth, being loaded with a jeep in preparation for Exercise Tiger.

who after the war became a Cornwall County Councillor.[6] Curry, an army driver, was with his officer who was acting as an official observer, described his experience of watching the exercise from an observation area on a hillside close to Street Gate. He noticed how many of the American troops as they were coming ashore off their landing craft were collapsing on the beach and realised they were not feigning death but were being cut down by their own countrymen lined up on the hillside behind Slapton Higher Ley, firing rifle and machine guns. Curry and his Officer looked around but could not at first see an American officer to order a ceasefire. Eventually an officer was located and the firing stopped. Curry remembers counting at least 120 dead soldiers on the beach, but he confirmed there were many other corpses. Eventually his own officer ordered him away from their observation point and they drove back to their Churston headquarters. The historian Richard Bass records that the Slapton Beach deaths on the early morning of 27 April were caused by units of the US Ist Infantry Division.[7] However, it is possible another unit of the American Army may have been implicated in the 'massacre' that took place at Slapton Beach.

On the morning of the 27th April 1944, troops of Easy Company, 101 Airborne Regiment, the unit associated with the television series *The Band of Brothers*, had been camping at Torquay and had travelled in trucks to Slapton Sands. Here they acted as part of the enemy defence force and were positioned at the back of Slapton Higher Ley, between the bridge at Slapton and Strete Gate. Private Webster, a member of Easy Company, kept a record of his army service. He records watching men of the 4th Infantry Division come up from the beach and pass through Easy Company's position, noting that they were 'sweating, cursing, panting'. Webster records that the officers told the men of Easy Company, "we cannot write about our Torquay excursion".[8] Did this order to maintain silence refer to what the men of Easy Company saw or did at Slapton Higher Ley?

One official observer of the exercise had noted a large number of soldiers had not dug foxholes but were sleeping on Slapton Beach, not something sensible people would do on a sloping tidal beach; could these men have been dead soldiers?[9]

Watching this exercise were high ranking officers that included General Eisenhower who does not refer to this incident, or the Lyme Bay disaster, in his wartime diaries or autobiography. The incident is mentioned by Kay Summbersby in her biography *Eisenhower Was My Boss*. Summersby was General Eisenhower's driver during the Second World War and accompanied him on his journey to Dartmouth. While she would not have been allowed on one of the LCI's, Summersby describes Eisenhower's visit to Slapton Bay on 27 April:

Vice Admiral Don Moon who was in charge of Exercise Tiger. After the Lyme Bay disaster he came under criticism by some of his colleagues for what had happened. He was not officially reprimanded, yet later in August 1944 he committed suicide.

Dwight Shepler's painting showing the interior of an LST being loaded.

Two pages from General Eisenhower's desk diary in which he records his arrival at Dartmouth to observe the first day of Exercise Tiger at Slapton Sands.

Major General Lawton Collins, who was responsible for the US Army forces involved in Exercise Tiger. Collins was on Slapton Beach at the time Admiral Moon fatally decided to delay the exercise for one hour.

"He viewed the (US) 4th Division's amphibious landing exercises on beaches near Dartmouth; special units fouled up everything from timing to orders, casualties numbering several hundreds."[10] But did Summersby confuse this incident with the disaster on the following day at Lyme Bay?

General Eisenhower returned from Slapton to Dartmouth at 11.30am and proceeded by train to Taunton. His diary entry, 27 April 1944, briefly records, "the 4th Division landing exercise, the timing was bad. The exercise was delayed one hour. The bombers did not drop any bombs, neither did the rockets go off."[11]

Admiral Ramsay and General Montgomery had also watched the Tiger Exercise at Slapton Sands that day. They had previously breakfasted at 4.20am and left their train to travel by car to Stoke Fleming (a village near Slapton Sands), then drove on to Slapton Sands. They waited four hours for the beach assault to start. Ramsay wrote in his diary that the exercise was "a flop", with much to criticise. He makes no mention of the Slapton Sands or Lyme bay disasters, but records in his diary the important brief statement that, "putting off (the exercise) was a fatal error.[12] Captain Harry Butcher records, " I came away from the exercise feeling depressed."[13]

Staff Sergeant Bernhardt Krein of the 8th Battalion, 4th Infantry Division, records in his autobiography his experiences at Slapton during the early hours of 27th April 1944.[14] Although not a witness to the massacre, his recollection of that morning suggests that a serious incident did occur. Krein writes in a manner that suggests he knew more than he was prepared to publically state because of the fear of being court martialed. He records that in April 1944 he was involved in a full-scale exercise at Slapton. The plan was for one-third of his battalion, including Company C, would go over the side into their LCIs and head for Slapton beach. This was two hours before the planned main landing was to take place. Krien's task for his men was to gain a foothold on the beach and place lamps facing the sea to guide the assault crafts to their points of beaching. Krien and his men then waited for the light of dawn when the invasion was planned to start. He records the exercise had been going smoothly and as the sky began to show signs of light he and his men moved on through a village [Blackawton?] to a meadow that was two and a half miles inland where they dug in to await the main body of troops. He records shooting started, large bombs [naval shells?] were bursting and machine gunfire sounded that lasted for fifteen minutes.

Krein waited with his men expecting to join up with the main force. They waited for an hour; Krein wondered what was holding them up. Two hours passed and an uneasy feeling began to take hold. After three hours he knew something was amiss. A message came over the field telephone after four hours (up until then there had been no response on the phone), with the order "All troops are to stay in their foxholes, no one is to leave their area". Everyone began to relax when a line of two-and-a-half-ton trucks arrived and stopped in the field. What struck Krein was there was no 100-foot interval between each truck; he states that under normal circumstances drivers are brainwashed to maintain this distance.

Later, Krein and his men were taken from their base camp and tents and field kitchens were brought in. The only explanation they were given regarding the missing two-thirds of the battalion were the men were being trained as thirty-man assault teams. Weeks went by and none of the missing men were ever seen again. New faces arrived to build up the battalion.

The French historian Dominique Francois suggests that 750 American soldiers were killed at Slapton by friendly fire on the morning of 27 April 1944.[15] In correspondence he told the author that possibly even more were gunned down.

Another friendly fire incident linked with Devon, described as the 'Minesweeper Massacre', involved British Forces.[16] On 27 August 1944, Hawker Typhoon fighter-bomber aircraft of 263 Squadron RAF, stationed at RAF Harrowbeer, Yelverton, located on the edge of Dartmoor, had, along with 266 Squadron, been ordered to attack a flotilla of German minesweepers off the French coast. However the Royal Navy had failed to notify the RAF of the change of plan to move a British Minesweeping Flotilla that had been engaged in clearing magnetic mines. The Wing Commander leading the attack questioned his orders, as he was sure the ships were British, but the shore staff insisted on a rocket attack in the belief that these minesweepers were enemy vessels. As the attack commenced, recognition flares were fired by all the British ships and White Ensigns spread out on the decks but this failed to deflect the Typhoon aircraft from their orders. HMS *Britomark* and HMS *Hussar* were sunk and HMS *Salamander* was severely damaged beyond repair. The attack killed 117 sailors and wounded 153. The Royal Navy tried to hush up the affair and, as with the Tiger incident, the survivors were separated and sent to different ships with orders not to discuss the incident. Although recorded by Admiral Ramsay in his diary, the 'Minesweeper Massacre' was covered up by the British Government whose records were made subject to a 100-year secrecy order, lifted in 1994.

A Board of Enquiry recommended that no disciplinary action should be taken, but Admiral Sir Bertram Ramsay overruled the Board and advised that three naval officers should be court martialed. One of the officers was Lt Commander Robert Franks who was acquitted; five months later he was awarded the Distinguished Service Cross for guiding an amphibious landing against German fortifications. In the post-war years Captain Robert Franks CBE DSO DSC RN, became a well known and respected figure in Dartmouth.

*   *   *

Before describing the events of the Lyme Bay disaster on 28 April 1944, we look at German E boat operations and their sorties in the English Channel between January and April 1944. During this period the number of E boats operating in the Channel had increased from 18 to 24. These boats were 35 metres in length and each had a crew of 21. They were fast, some with a top speed of 45 knots. Other than torpedo operations their task was mine laying, was a major threat to Allied shipping.

When an E boat force was in pursuit of its prey it normally separated into small groups, and it was unusual for an Allied force to make contact with all the E boats in a flotilla. The success of British naval intelligence significantly reduced E boat attacks against Allied shipping through the introduction of improved radar technology and strong surface forces patrolling from Plymouth. This allowed the Allied naval forces to intercept the enemy on all but one occasion. During March 1944, prior to Exercise Tiger, E boats carried out 8 operations involving 74 sorties in the Channel.[17] The E boat attacks were now being seriously challenged by the Royal Navy but they continued to be seen by the Allies as a threat. During the planning of Exercise Tiger emphasis had been made on the need for security and ships' officers were warned to be vigilant for the presence of these enemy forces.

Although the German Navy still had considerable numbers of U boats, they had suffered a severe defeat in the Battle of the Atlantic. The Allies were now able to run large convoys of ships between North America and Britain. By April 1944 the Luftwaffe's presence over the English Channel was considerably reduced as the mastery of the air had been won by the allied air forces. However from 26 April 1944 the German Air Force had increased its daily reconnaissance between Dover and Land's End. One Luftwaffe report gave details of a large concentration of warships and assault shipping at Plymouth.

A recent photograph shows the area of Slapton beach where on the morning o 27 April 1944 US troops of the 4th Infantry Division on coming ashore from their landing craft were massacred by friendly fire.

HMS *Scimitar*, the destroyer that was allocated to escort convoy T4 but was withdrawn because of damage sustained that could not be immediately repaired at Devonport dockyard.

An historic official photograph of smoke caused from a bomb that exploded in Devonport on 29 April 1944, the day Plymouth experienced its last air raid of the war. Under the smoke can be seen three ships, the nearest one being the controversial HMS *Scimitar*.

A picture of the type of E boat that attacked the US convoy T4 in Lyme Bay, off the Dorset Coast that sunk two LSTs, damaged another and caused the deaths of 741 US Servicemen.

However the main Allied concern continued to be the enemy E boats. The Allies knew that the German navy had a number of E boat flotillas based in the enemy occupied Channel ports, with the 5th and 9th Flotilla operated from Cherbourg, northern France.

As the second phase of Exercise Tiger continued at Slapton Beach on the 27 April, six convoys of ships departed from Westcountry ports as part of the Exercise. Convoy T4 that began from Plymouth was joined by four LSTs that had sailed from Brixham. The ships were loaded with troops and military equipment. One of the LSTs towed two pontoons and was the cause of the very slow progress of the convoy. Time management was an important factor in the Exercise and the convoy was under orders to follow a defined route from Start Bay, and then sail across Lyme Bay to a point 13 miles from Portland Bill before returning to Slapton. The purpose of the voyage was to cover the same sea mileage that the LSTs would undertake when crossing the English Channel to France on D-Day. The T4 convoy was scheduled to arrive off Slapton Sands at 7.30am on 28th April, where it was planned to disembark men, vehicles and stores on Slapton Beach.

Convoy T4 consisted of eight LSTs, there should have been nine, but there is a question about LST 508 not having sailed because it had been damaged. An outer defensive ring of Allied warships had been placed closer to the French coast by Plymouth Command to prevent the intervention of the Cherbourg E boats. The T4 convoy's close escorts were the destroyer HMS *Scimitar* and the corvette HMS *Azalea*. Misfortune soon came to convoy T4 when HMS *Scimitar* collided with an American landing craft and had to return to Devonport. It was not possible to repair the damaged destroyer until the following morning. This was not the first time the *Scimitar* had been withdrawn from service; during the evacuation of Dunkirk in 1940, the First World War destroyer had collided with HMS *Icarus* and was ordered back to port. The decision by Plymouth Command to take HMS *Scimitar* out of service was not reported to the American Admiral in charge of Exercise Tiger. A replacement escort vessel, the destroyer HMS *Saladin* was ordered to join the convoy, but much valuable time had been lost. Furthermore the number one boiler of the *Saladin* was not working properly. Her Captain, Lieutenant Commander P.E. King, ordered a limit to her speed of twenty-three knots, only to be increased if they were pursing E boats.[18] The officers and men of convoy T4 out in the English Channel would not have been aware that they were sailing through dangerous waters almost unprotected. The *Saladin* eventually drew closer to the slow moving convoy but arrived only after one of the LSTs had been torpedoed.

At 1.30 am on 28 April 1944 convoy T4, including LST 531 carrying the 1st Engineer Special Brigade and VII Corps headquarters staff, was making its way across Lyme Bay when it was attacked. LST 531 was set on fire off Portland, Dorset, by E boats of the 5th and 9th Flotilla who then torpedoed and sank LST 507. The stern of LST 289 was also severely damaged by a torpedo. Admiral Moon was sleeping in his command ship, USS *Bayfield*, at the time the attack happened. When he was woken and told of the E Boat attack and the sinking of the two LSTs it was too late for him to take any effective action against the enemy force.

The history of the fate of the LST 289 is interesting. The ship managed to make its way into Dartmouth harbour with the assistance of a tug. Here the casualties were transferred to the Royal Naval College hospital. The stricken craft was then moved up the River Dart to the Noss shipyard where it underwent temporary repairs. Later, an evacuee, John Harding, who was out fishing, happened by chance to see the LST 289 being towed up the River Fal, Cornwall to the King Harry reaches. On seeing the damaged vessel he decided to sketch it.[19] LST 289 was eventually repaired and US Navy records state it was involved in the Normandy landings (not on D-Day) and after the war it was transferred and commissioned into the Royal Navy as HMS LST-289. It was later resold back to the American navy and eventually scrapped.

The American servicemen who had died or were missing due to the Lyme Bay E boat were victims of an act of war. There was also the loss of a vast amount of valuable military equipment that would have been used on D-Day. The testimony of survivors telling how their comrades lost their lives is appalling. Hundreds of men died of exposure in the cold water of the English Channel. Many men died because they had not fitted their life jackets correctly, others were killed by friendly fire when some crewmen of one LST, perhaps through panic, started firing machine guns indiscriminately.

The explosion caused by the torpedo that hit the LST 507, caused the fuel tanks that were full of gasolene to ignite resulting in a raging fire that threatened to spread to the stern of the ship. An officer, knowing that there were men trapped on the tank deck below but who were beyond saving, took the decision to close the hatches to prevent the fire from spreading through the ship.[20]

The 1st Engineer Special Brigade suffered 413 dead and 16 wounded. The 3206th Quartermaster Service Company was virtually wiped out and the 557th Quartermaster Railhead Company sustained heavy losses. Both Companies had to be replaced for the invasion of Normandy. Eventually, after the enemy left the scene, the hundreds of floating dead servicemen in Lyme Bay were collected up by naval vessels stationed at Portland. Other bodies had drifted with the tide on to Chesil beach, Dorset. Post-mortem examination showed evidence of bullet wounds, but most of the men taken from the water had died of hypothermia through exposure in the cold water. The survivors were treated in emergency tented casualty units or taken to hospital.

Many of the dead US servicemen were taken overnight to Brookwood (private) cemetery in Surrey where they were temporarily interred, each coffin covered with the Stars and Stripes. Other victims were buried at the US cemetery, Cambridge. Eventually many of the were reburied in the United States.

The survivors were sworn to secrecy on the threat of being court martialed if they revealed any information about the incident. Secret arrangements were quickly made to take the dead bodies, loaded in a convoy of trucks and driven through the night, to Brookwood private cemetery, Surrey.[21] Here they were identified and buried in a mass grave, each coffin draped with a flag of the United States. Other bodies were interred at the American forces cemetery in Cambridge. Later the bodies buried at Brookwood were reburied in the American cemetery, Cambridge, or sent back for reburial in America. The survivors of the Lyme Bay incident were taken to 'survivor camps' that had been set up to rehabilitate them, but to what extent the morale of the officers and ranks involved in the disaster been affected by the incident is open to speculation. US troops were aware there were gaps in their ranks due to those men who had been killed, injured, or were missing.

The deterioration of relationships between some of the American and British naval commanders after the Lyme Bay disaster did little to maintain the Allied cause. But, because of the imminence of D-Day, a call from the Allied Forces Executive was for the Americans and British to close ranks and maintain unity. Prompted by the E boat attack, Admiral Ramsay received a letter from the US Admiral Kirk, requesting a naval bombardment of

EXERCISE TIGER: 26 APRIL - 28 APRIL 1944

LST 289, escorted by a tug, arriving in the port of Dartmouth after being torpedoed in the stern at Lyme Bay. Although strict security had been imposed on the US servicemen involved in the disaster at the threat of being court martialed no such conditions appeared to have been imposed on photographing the crippled boat.

Damaged LST 289 temporarily docked alongside the Dartmouth embankment.

A close up rear view of the damaged LST 289 caused by the torpedo.

Above left: The LST289 tied up alongside a cat walk to transfer the casualties into waiting ambulances parked nearby in the road.

Above right: Stretcher bearers carrying the injured men to the ambulances that would take them to the nearby hospital in the Royal Naval College.

the E boats that were docked in their Cherbourg pens. Ramsay replied that although he took the E boat threat seriously, he believed it would be a mistake to overestimate it.[22] The 'E boat letter' became a controversy as Admiral Kirk's letter had been shown to General Eisenhower before it was received by Admiral Ramsay. The fact that Admiral Kirk's letter had been seen by Eisenhower upset Ramsay; it was in his opinion an act of insubordination and a violation of the chain of command.[23] However nothing more became of this situation. Ramsay thought Kirk was hysterical and noted in his diary that Kirk had lost his sense of proportion and was offensively rude; such was the relationship between two senior Allied naval commanders, just a few weeks before D-Day.

The testimonies of naval personnel in the aftermath of the Lyme Bay disaster revealed the disorganisation that had become apparent in the planning and operations of Exercise Tiger, but they produced more questions than answers to the origins of the disaster. The Americans diplomatically blamed the British; they believed the Plymouth Command had failed in their responsibility to provide protection for the US Navy ships operating in the waters of the Home Command.[24] Likewise the British blamed the Americans. The exchanges between some of the American and British Commanders regarding the Tiger disaster were taking their toll on the Supreme Commander, General Eisenhower.[25]

Whatever subsequent reports were published about the Lyme Bay disaster, no high ranking Allied officer was formally accused of negligence with the exception Colonel Eugene Caffey. For some unexplained reason General Omar Bradley did not at first receive a full report of the loss of the LSTs in Lyme Bay from Colonel Caffey. From the information that Bradley did receive he concluded the damage that had been inflicted was slight.

According to what was described as 'a poor show' by the 1st Engineer Special Brigade, General Bradley concluded it was due to a breakdown in command, and consequently the highly respected Colonel Caffey was relieved of his command.[26] But his military career in high office was not over as ten years later he was appointed Judge Advocate General of the United States Army.

The debate of who was responsible for the Tiger disaster at Lyme Bay continued in America at least until 1962, that is 18 years after the incident, when US Rear Admiral Alan Kirk, Commander, Western Naval Task Force gave his oral testimony. He told interviewers at the Columbia Oral History project that remained very cross that the British Admiralty was unwilling to take responsibility for 'Slapton Sands'.[27]

As for the American and British public, at the time they were not aware of this fateful disaster, as no information about the incident was published in the press. However it would be naive to believe that news would not eventually leak out about what happened in the early hours of 28 April 1944 at Lyme Bay. In 1944, the late John Harding, when he was living in Falmouth, was given details about this E boat attack by an American sailor.[28] Harding records, "We hadn't seen the sailors and their landing craft for some time and so when we saw them heading our way, all the gang was waiting. However the mood on the shore that night was more subdued than on their previous visits; the flamboyance and laughter from the US sailors had gone and now there were only four of them. Mary and June sat side by side with their special friends; there were long spells of silence. Johnny was alone offshore in his landing craft, another Johnny (Johnny Johnson) said. 'Somebody has to know' we have been through hell. After a pause he continued, (and I clearly remember his every word). Ships were sinking, men in the water on fire, screaming. There was nothing we could do to help."

Each death, or man missing in action, that occurred in Exercise Tiger represents the tragic loss for a particular American family or fiancée. But were there any British men on the ill-fated convoy? Rodney Legg, the Dorset historian, records there were fatalities among members of the Royal Artillery who manned the anti-aircraft guns on board some of the LSTs in Lyme Bay.[29] One civilian, known to be on board one of the ships in the Channel on this fateful night was the late Cecil Inder of Lower Broad Park, Dartmouth. Cecil was a Senior Draughtsman employed by Phillip & Co., shipbuilders in Dartmouth.

With all the publicity and speculation concerning the events of Exercise Tiger scant attention has been made of the heroes of this violent incident. On 27 May 1944 five enlisted men of the Headquarters Fourth Medical Battalion who were on LST 289 when it was torpedoed were awarded the Bronze Star and citations for their heroism and meritorious services at the time of the E boat attacks. Brigadier Theodore Roosevelt of the 4th Infantry Division presented the medals in a ceremony that took place in a field on the outskirts of Totnes. These were the first of a number of gallantry awards presented to enlisted men of the 4th Battalion and the USA 4th Infantry Division in the Second World War. The men were stationed at the Battalion headquarters in Tiverton. There were other men who were also decorated for their bravery during the Tiger incident but the men awarded the Bronze Star at Totnes were :

Corporal George Zest – Company A
Private Arrest Fortune – Company B
Private Albert E. Judd – Company C
Private Saul Stewart – Company C

Within hours of the Lyme Bay Tiger disaster there were more Allied casualties in the English Channel, off the Isle de Bas, Brittany. On the 28–29 April the destroyers HMS *Athabaskan* and HMS *Haida*, part of the outer defence force for Exercise Tiger, had been in action against a German flotilla of destroyers and had inflicted damage on two of the enemy ships. The destroyers were chasing the enemy towards Brest and eventually caught up with them. However the Germans employing their usual tactic, fired a salvo of 12 torpedoes scoring a devastating direct hit on the *Athabaskan* that caused the destroyer to explode and eventually sink, there were survivors, but 128 of the crew lost their lives.

At the end of this eventful and fateful week, the German air force on 30 April 1944, two days after the Lyme Bay disaster, avoided Allied air patrols and attacked Devonport dockyard. Their main target was a King George V class battleship. This attack was part of

The British Vice Admiral Sir Ralph Leatham, the Commander in Chief Plymouth, who admitted his failure in not providing adequate protection for the ill-fated T4 convoy.

Reports of the aftermath of the Tiger disaster indicate the survivors were dispersed to different rehabilitation camps before going on leave or posted to a new unit. This picture shows a small group of Tiger survivors who were sent to Plymouth.

Operation Steinbock, a retaliation bombing campaign by the Germans that began on the 21 January 1944. At first the main targets were directed against London and South East England, but the enemy decided to switched its attack to targets in the West of England.[31] The Steinbock attack on Devonport was different from all the previous enemy raids over Britain as they planned to use the Fritz X armour-piercing radio-controlled bombs delivered by a modified Dornier 217 K3 aircraft with extended wings. The attack failed, primarily due to poor visibility and the existence of a smoke screen that was used to hide the battleship. The attack caused civilian casualties at the village of Oreston where 18 people were killed when two air raid shelters were hit by bombs. Nearby at Prince Rock, Plymouth, nine people also lost their lives when another bomb exploded at the bus depot. One Dornier 217 K3 was shot down by an RAF Typhoon fighter and crashed at (evacuated) Pasture Farm, Blackawton. Another enemy aircraft crashed into the sea at Whitsand, south-west Devon, and two of the German airman that were captured had come ashore in a dinghy at Whitsand beach.

The Lyme Bay E boat incident that cost the lives of 749 American servicemens has been called an 'heroic' disaster. That some good came out of the catastrophe is no more than wishful thinking. What the incident did show, was what could happen if an E boat force got in among Allied landing craft on D-Day. The E Boat attack on Convoy T4 was carried out with ruthless efficiency. The ease with which the enemy flotilla appeared and attacked the convoy was surprising, more so when during the previous months the E Boats had not been successful in their Channel sorties because of the increasing operational efficiency of the Royal Navy. On could speculate the enemy have been tipped off and the American author Edwin Hoyt, states enemy radio and radar in France detected the movement of Convoy T4 and, before midnight, Kapitan Rudolf Petersen's headquarters had the news that the convoy was out in Lyme Bay and were able to locate its position.[32]

There is evidence that lessons had not been learned concerning the Tiger Lyme Bay disaster. It could be argued they were ignored when placed in context of the Channel war, for there followed further catastrophes involving American troops before the end of the year. Only four days before Christmas Eve 1944, the troopship *Empire Javelin*, that had transported the ill fated Bedford Boys (116th Infantry) to Normandy on D-Day, had sailed from Portsmouth with 583 US servicemen and was sunk off the Isle of Wight. There were casualties but fortunately most of the servicemen were rescued. On Christmas Eve 1944, a major disaster occurred when the SS *Leopoldville*, sailing from Southampton with 2200 troops of the US 66th infantry division aboard, was sunk in the English Channel off Cherbourg, resulting in the deaths of 802 troops and six of the crewmen. Because of the disorganized boarding procedure no official records were kept. None of the troops on board had received instruction in lifeboat drill or had been shown how to fasten their lifebelts.[33] It was eleven years before the *Leopoldville* disaster was declassified.

The sinking of the SS *Rhonda*, the friendly fire massacre at Slapton beach, the Lyme Bay Tiger disaster and the loss of SS *Leopoldville* all happened within twelve months. They are closely linked, not only by the huge loss of life of US servicemen, but by a lack of information or misleading information issued by the American Government concerning these catastrophes. Richard Bass, argues that an American naval officer, Commodore Vigil E. Korns, was employed to tamper with the Tiger records in an attempt to distort the facts.[34] Some historians have taken a philosophical approach to the disaster as a means to play down the 28 April Tiger incident by stating that fewer casualties were suffered by the American servicemen who went ashore on Utah beach on D-Day compared to the Lyme Bay incident. The low casualty rate of the US 4th Infantry Division on D-Day was due to the fact that the first wave of assault troops accidently landed on the wrong beach that was not so heavily defended as the beach that they were originally intended to assault. However many of the US troops of the 4th Infantry Division who had been based in Devon and had departed from the ports of Devon were very soon to become casualties, resulting in the decimation of the 4th Infantry Division. Major General Barton officially confirmed the situation: "We no longer have the division we bought ashore". The US 4th Infantry Division that landed on Utah beach on D-Day had within 5 week suffered the loss of 5400 men, with Barton recording: "The division was temporarily taken out of the line and kept in reserve".[35]

The tragedy of the Lyme Bay disaster was first referred to in the public domain two years after the incident occurred by Captain Butcher.[36] For many years after the Second World War the archival records of the Tiger incident in Lyme Bay lay dormant in the United States and Britain's national archives. Eventually further information was released concerning this tragedy. Dale Rodman, a survivor of the German E boat attack, compiled an important source of information regarding the Tiger casualties. He had taken on the role as a one-man unofficial investigator and published a list of men killed or missing in the disaster. This list has been used as a basis as an unofficial record by some authors.

It is recognised that the late Ken Small overcame many challenges to recover a sunken DD Sherman tank that is now used as a memorial at Torcross, Devon. However his book *The Forgotten Dead*, in which he describes the Lyme Bay incident, is unfortunately ambiguous, although he claims when he was in America he was given all the records of the 'Tiger Incident'.[37] For some reason in his account of the Lyme Bay disaster he has transposed parts of the incident as though they happened off Slapton Sands. One example, of this change of location is his statement that "it is an ironic fact while almost 1000 men lost their lives at Slapton...".[38] This startling error is equivalent to describing an incident that occurred in Exeter, but reporting that it happened 38 miles away in Plymouth. Later, Ken admitted to the press that mistakes had been made in his book but unfortunately the damage had been done as many people believed, and still believe, the Tiger disaster of the 28 April 1944 occurred off Slapton Sands. It is emphasised here that the ill-fated T4 convoy when it departed from Plymouth was *not* attacked by E boats off Slapton Sands on the 28 April 1944.

Furthermore both American and British news media fuelled gossip concerning the bodies of American servicemen who were buried in graves somewhere in the vicinity of the Slapton Battle Training Area as possible victims of the Lyme Bay disaster. One of the earliest realistic reports to offer an explanation of these reported graves was by Nigel Lewis who in his book *Channel Firing* suggested that these graves, if they did exist, could have been the result of a previous wartime incident. The location of these graves held a morbid fascination for some, and with the information that is now available, it is thought possible that the graves were those of US servicemen that were killed as the result of the friendly fire massacre of the 27 April 1944, as described earlier in this book.

But as rumour and an excited press continued to focus on a possible cover-up of the events and casualties, Charles Macdonald, a former deputy chief historian of the US Army's Center of Military History

The certificate of appreciation presented to author Ken Small. Unfortunately it records the wrong date and place of the tragedy. Were all the families listed on the certificate ever told that the information was not correct?

publishing an article the journal *Army*, titled 'Slapton Sands: The Cover-Up that Never Was'. MacDonald argued that there had never been a cover up, other than the brief veil of secrecy restrictions to avoid compromising D-Day, but he made no mention in his article of the friendly fire massacre.[39] As mentioned previously in this text there is an accumulating amount of evidence from witnesses that indicates that on Slapton Sands on the morning of 27 April 1944 a massacre occurred of hundreds of men of the 4th US Infantry Division, killed by shell fire from Royal Navy warships and by US troops using live ammunition, slaughtering their own country men.

The final reckoning of blame of the Lyme Bay disaster was directed against the British Naval Command at Plymouth. Admiral Leatham admitted responsibility and said he was sorry, but he did not resign, nor was he court martialed. Two years later Admiral Leatham was appointed Governor of Bermuda.

A copy of a Tiger disaster survivor's special pass issued while at the US Vicarage Road Camp, Plymouth.

Historians record that lessons were learned from the Lyme Bay disaster but within eight months of the tragedy the converted troopship *Leopoldville*, sailing from Southampton, was torpedoed by a German U boat in the English Channel. 763 American soldiers of the 66th Infantry Division were lost. The bodies of 493 soldiers were never found. The American Government covered up the incident for many years.

Kapitan Rudolf Petersen for his part in the Lyme Bay Tiger incident was awarded a set of oak leaves to his Iron Cross. But what was the position of Admiral Don Moon in charge of Exercise Tiger who ordered the fatal delay in the landing operations at Slapton on the morning of 27 April? On 16 June 1944, King George V visited the Normandy assault area, the same day that Admiral King decided to transfer Admiral Moon from *Operation Overlord* and send him to the Mediterranean to join the Eighth Fleet to participate in *Operation Dragon*. On the 5 August 1944, Admiral Moon committed suicide. The reason he took his own life is open to speculation, including the failure experienced in Exercise Tiger and the losses suffered from the E boat attack in Lyme Bay. In a recent American biography of Rear Admiral Don Moon there is a three-page scenario implying that he was assassinated by a British agent.[40]

Kapitan Rudolf Petersen, the leader of the 5th Schnellboot flotilla that was responsible for the devastating attack on convoy T4.during the early hours of the morning of 28 April 1944.

---

1. http://www.history,army.mil/documents/ ww11/beaches/ bchs-7.htm. paragraph 254.
2. Eisenhower, General Dwight. *Desk Diary, 27 April 1944*, Eisenhower Library, USA.
3. Hoyt, Edwin. *The Invasion Before Normandy, The Secret Battle of Slapton Sands*, 1987. Robert Hale. p.93.
4. Yung, Christopher. *Gators of Neptune Naval Amphibious planning for the Normandy Invasion*. National Institute Press, Maryland , USA. p.164.
5. Yung Christopher. p.161.
6. Campbell, Christopher and Lewis, Nigel. *Sunday Telegraph*. 20 July 1997 p.5
7. Bass, Richard. *Exercise Tiger*. p.49.
8. Ambrose, Stephen. *Band of Brothers*, 2001. Pocket Books. P.59.
9. Hoyt, Edwin. *The Invasion Before Normandy. The Secret Battlle of Slapton Sands*, 1987 Robert Hayle. p126.
10. Summersby, Kay. *Eisenhower was my Boss*, 1949. Prentice Hall, New York p.141.
11. Eisenhower, General Dwight. *Desk Diary, 27 April 1944*. Eisenhower Library. USA
12. Love, Robert and John, Major (eds) *The Year of D-Day; the 1944 Diary of Admiral Sir Bertram Ramsay*, 1994. University of Hull, p.60.
13. Butcher, Harry. *Three Years with Eisenhower*, 1946. p.452.
14. Krien, Bernhardt. *Once Around the Block*, 2011. Author House, USA. p.11.
15. Francois, Dominique. *Normandy: Breaching the Atlantic Wall*. Zenith Press. 2008 p.77.
16. Fenton, Ben. *Secret Papers detailing RAF raid on Royal Navy*. Daily Telegraph 29th August 1994.
17. Hinsley, F.H. (.ed). *British Intelligence in the Second World War, its influence on strategy and operations*. 1988. Vol 3, part 1 HMSO p.543.
18. Hoyt, Edwin. *The Invasion Before Normandy, The Secret Battle of Slapton Sands*, 1987. Robert Hale. p103,
19. Harding, John. *A Child's War in Cornwall*, 2010. Ryelands ,Somerset. p.88.
20. Lewis ,Nigel. *Exercise Tiger. The dramatic true story of a hidden tragedy of World War 2*, 1990. Prentice Hall Press. New York, p 87-88.
21. Bass, Richard. *Precious Cargo 133*. Lee Publishing, Exeter. p.104
22. Love, Robert and John, Major (eds.), *The Year of D- Day, The 1944 Diary of Admiral Sir Bertram Ramsay*. 1994. University of Hull Press. p.65.
23. Love and Major (eds.), p.p 65-66.
24. Yung, Christopher. *Gators of Neptune Naval Amphibious planning for the Normandy Invasion*. National Institute Press, Maryland , USA. p.167.
25. Yung, Christopher, p.119.
26. Bass, Richard.*Exercise Tiger, The D-Day practice landing tragedies uncovered*. 2007. Tommies Guides. p.254-255.
27. Yung, Christopher. p .167.
28. Harding, John. *A Child's War in Cornwall*, 2010. Ryelands, Somerset. p.88.
29. Legg, Rodney. *Dorset at War*, 2010. Halsgrove. p.125.
30. PC, Mrs Gladys Inder to Gerald Wasley.
31. Mackay, Ron. *The Last Blitz , Operation Steinbock, Luftwaffe operations over Britain January to June 1944*, 2011. Red Kite, UK p.360-2.
32. Hoyt, Edwin. *The Invasion before Normandy, The Secret Battle of Slapton Sands*, 1987 Robert Hale. p.102.
33. Hocking, Charles. *Dictionary of Disasters at Sea during the age of Steam, 1824-1962*. Volume 1. 1969. Lloyds Register of Shipping.
34. Bass, Richard. *Exercise Tiger*, p.146.
35. Bernage, Georges. *Normandy 1944, First US Army*, 2004. Heimdal, France. p.145.
36. Butcher, Captain Harry. *Three Years with Eisenhower, The Personal Diary of Captain Harry C, Butcher*. Naval Aid to General Eisenhower, 1942-1945. P.455.
37. Small, Ken. *The Forgotten Dead, Why 946 American servicemen died off the coast of Devon in 1944, and the man who discovered their true story*, 1988. Bloomsbury. p.133.
38. Small, Ken. *The Forgotten Dead* p.5.
39. Macdonald, Charles, *Army, The Magazine of Landpower*, June 1988. USA pp.66-67.
40. Crouch, Daniel and Alter, Jonathan (eds). *'My Dear Moon' Rear Admiral Don Pardee Moon*, 2005. Book Surge, USA. chapter 10 npn.

9 Departure for D-Day

THE MONTHS OF exercises and rehearsals had come to an end with the completion of Exercise Fabious. Whatever the consequences of the disastrous Tiger Exercise may have been, the Allies were confident that their invasion plans had not been compromised. At the end of May 1944 General Eisenhower moved from Widewing, his headquarters at Bushy Park, Teddington, to Southwick Park, near Portsmouth, to prepare for the departure of the greatest armada that was ever to sail. The massive allied air raids were an indication to the enemy that the expected invasion by the Allies was not far off. However the German High Command was still unsure as to when and where exactly the main Allied landings would take place.

After exercise Tiger and Fabius the troops did not return to their base camps but went to their marshalling areas, there to wait for almost a month before they departed for Normandy. For many of these men Devon would be their 'last home'. How the soldiers felt after all their training is open to speculation; the 4th Infantry had never experienced combat before. However the troops were not briefed about *Operation Overlord* until the last week in May. What had been a cause of concern to the commanding officers was the troops that had completed their invasion exercises had sufficient vital information, that if it became known to enemy agents it would jeopardize the invasion operation. For this reason all the troops in the marshalling areas were sealed behind barbed wire and for Force 'U' this meant 2000 Counter Intelligence Corps men were used to closely guard them. In addition all the American army camps were isolated from all contact with civilians. If a civilian was found talking to a soldier they were immediately arrested.[1]

Camouflage was severely enforced during the week prior to their departure to Normandy. Briefing of all field officers began at once. The strict security measures imposed

Troops of the US 29th Infantry Division waiting by the Torpoint ferry slip to be taken across the River Tamar to a departure point in Plymouth

Troops boarding three landing craft on the Torpoint ferry slip.

at the marshalling areas would have suggested to the men that was about to happen was no exercise, but military combat against the enemy. One indication was the sudden improvement in the food served to the troops. Fried chicken, white bread and butter and fruit cocktail being among the delicacies.

Bragging stopped among the troops, replaced by a silence that pervaded the camps as the men contemplated their fate. Whatever feeling the GI's had after their training on damp and cold Dartmoor, the Spring of 1944 had transformed the dreary moorland landscape into a beautiful pattern of green and gold that they had heard about but never seen before. For the troops who would soon be departing for Normandy, this glory of nature would be the way some GI's would remember England.

It was believed that the Luftwaffe, although weakened by the Allied air forces, was capable of damaging air raids against troop concentrations. This in fact occurred at the end of May when an ordnance battalion camp near Falmouth was bombed and suffered casualties. Loading Force 'U' began on 30 May–1 June 1944 at Dartmouth, Plymouth, Torquay, Salcombe Brixham and Poole. All troops were aboard their ships by 3 June. Force 'U' craft, comprising some 865 vessels was organised into 12 separate convoys.[2]

On 3 June Admiral Moon received a signal from the Admiralty informing him of the date of D-day and H-Hour (the specific hour that the military operation will commence).

Below left: A column of troops waiting at Torpoint to board a landing craft.

Below right: The 87th Chemical Mortar Battalion of V11 Corps loading up on the hard by the Royal Albert Bridge for their journey to one of the Normandy beaches. Saltash in Cornwall is seen across the River Tamar.

Above left: Four LSTs being loaded at the Barn Pool hard situated below Mount Edgcumbe east Cornwall.

Above right: Troops of the 29th Infantry Division entering Trebah Farm field, Cornwall, to march down to Trebah hard to embark on a Landing Craft Ship (LST).

Right: A column of troops having marched across Trebah Farm reach the Trebah hard where they will embark on a LST.

Below: LST's anchored in Plymouth Sound preparing for D-Day.

DEPARTURE FOR D-DAY

Above left: Ships assembled at Salcombe, Devon ready to sail for D-Day. An amphibious force of 66 ships of the US Navy departed from Salcombe on 4 June for the Normandy beaches.

Above right: An advanced party of men of the 7th Beach Battalion embarking at Salcombe for Normandy.

Left: Loading LST 47 at the hard by the higher ferry, Dartmouth, in preparing for D-Day. All vehicles are loaded in reverse to enable them to be directly driven out of the ship to prevention congestion on the Normandy beaches. There were also hards up the River Dart that were used for loading.

An interesting open-bow view of a landing craft being loaded on the Dartmouth hard.

PRELUDE TO D-DAY

Loading for D-Day also took place on Dartmouth embankment. This picture shows troops of the US 4th Division embarking from the embankment on to one of three Landing Craft Infantry (LCI).

An embroidery of Philips & Co., shipyard (now the Dartmouth Marina) showing rows of tented camps set up in the fields around the Royal Naval College. There were also tented camps in the fields around Dartmouth in the areas of Above Town and Townstal. When the order came for these troops to report at Dartmouth, masses of men swarmed over the fields and marched down to the town.

Preparing for D-Day. Loading a tank and other military vehicles on to an LST alongside Dartmouth embankment. The gantry crane, since dismantled, was part of Dartmouth gas works.

A picture of a fully-loaded LST at Dartmouth bound for Normandy. The scene conveys the remarkable amount of military activity that had taken place in this small riverside port.

The same day 485 ships and landing craft departed from the River Dart to join up with the rest of Force 'U'.[3] On the morning of 4 June at 9.30am, Admiral Moon, together with Major General Collins (Commanding General, V11 Corps), and Major General Barton (Commanding General 4th Infantry Division), embarked on the USS *Bayfield* and sailed from Plymouth to rendezvous with the sections of the Force 'U' convoy that had entered the open waters of the English Channel. There was an important change of plans as on 4 June General Eisenhower postponed D-Day for twenty-four hours to 6 June because of the poor weather forecast.[4] The Force 'U' convoys were all able to be recalled, except one. A USS destroyer was dispatched post-haste to catch up with it and bring it back to port.

On recommencing its journey across the English Channel, Force 'U' followed the swept paths through the German minefields and anchored off Utah beach. It was an amazing oper-

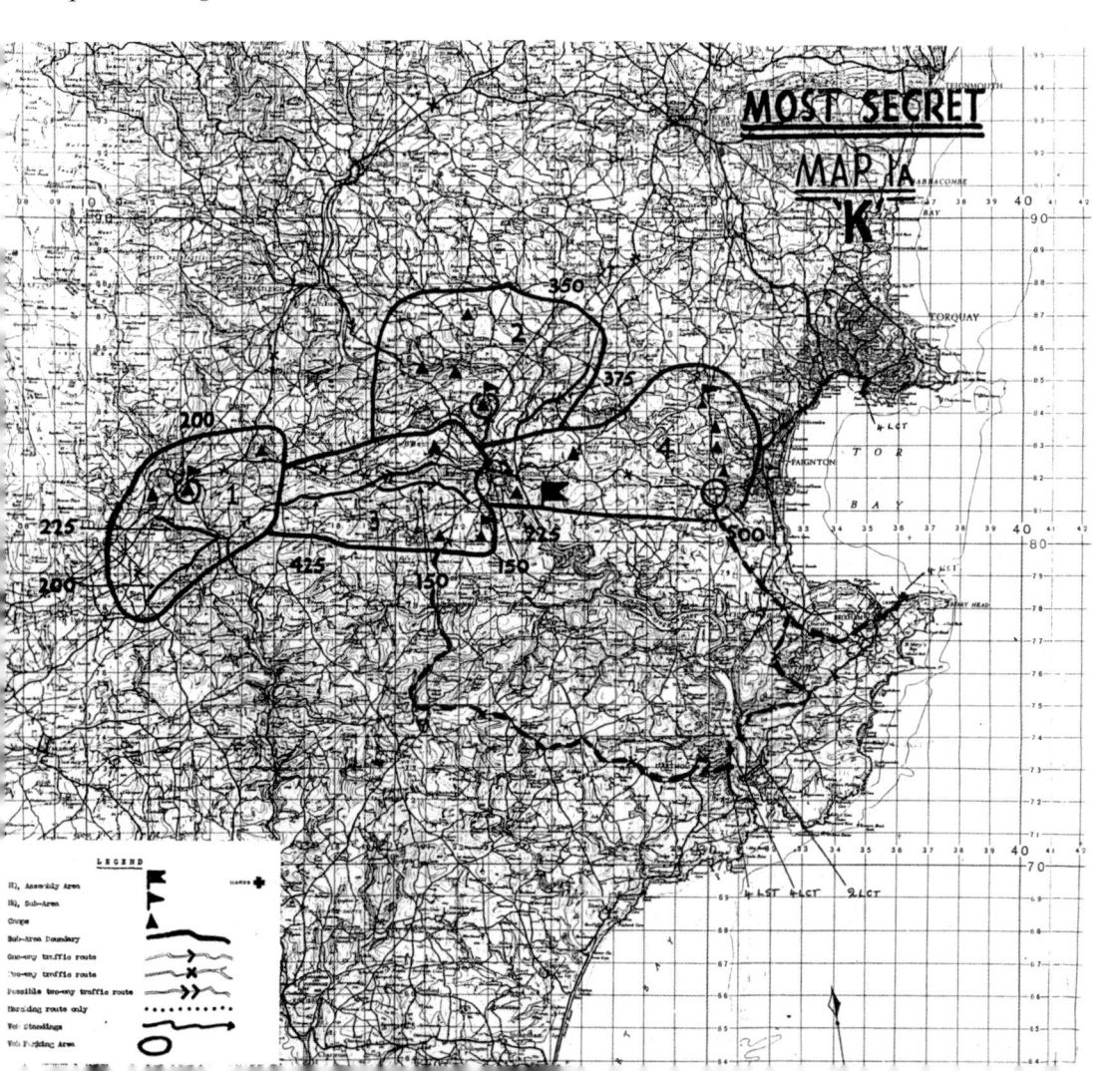

A 'Most Secret' map of the assembly area and camps used by the 4th Infantry Division prior to their departure across the English Channel for D-Day. The map indicates the routes that were taken by the troops and road convoys to the departure points.

A column of troops of the 4th US Infantry Division passing public air raid shelters as they approach a control post at Torquay, before arriving at the two hards in the harbour.

The classic picture of four LSTs at Brixham harbour in the process of being loaded with troops of the US 4th Infantry Division and equipment that would land on Utah beach.

Above left: The point of no return. Such notices were placed close to the embarkation points to advise departing troops to give up all identifying items except their dog tags.

Above right: Pilots of the 439th Troop Carrier Group assemble at Upottery airfield, East Devon, for their D-Day mission.

ation so far, as every one of Admiral Moon's forces of 800 warships, transports and landing craft took to their offshore position as assigned and according to the plan. Combat troops landed on Utah beach on 6 June, the easiest landing undertaken at Normandy by the Allied forces on D-Day. A strong tidal current had swept the amphibious force 2000 yards south from where it was planned to land, resulting in it meeting minimal enemy opposition. The troops responsible for leading the 4th Division ashore on Utah beach were from four companies of the 8th Infantry Regiment that had been camped in east Devon. The success of the Americans landing on Utah Beach without sustaining a high casualty rate was not without hazards as throughout D-Day the troops were exposed to accurate and heavy enemy artillery fire that came from batteries placed on high ground some 1–2 miles behind the coast.

An Officer of Force 'U' records how over-burdened the troops of the 4th Division in the assault wave were. They were issued with so much equipment in their combat packs that they were unable to climb the accommodation ladders to embark; they had to be pushed up the ladders.[5] A British naval officer who was attached to the American Assault Engineers records: "we were loaded with tanks and went into Utah about twenty minutes after H-Hour. There were lots of mines on the beaches and obstructions that had to be got through, but we had a team of underwater divers who disposed of most of them."[6] By the end of D-Day 23 000 men of the American 4th Division had landed.

The 29th American Division encountered severe problems at Omaha Beach while bringing their DD Sherman tanks ashore, where 29 of the 34 of their tanks foundered and sank. At Utah Beach 28 of the 32 DD Sherman tanks made it to the shore and went on to help destroy the German's defensive positions.

If the 4th Infantry had been fortunate in their early encounters with the enemy on D-Day their good fortune would change for in the next eleven months the 4th Division would suffer 23 000 battle casualties. No Allied army division would lose more men.[7]

An evening picture taken at RAF Exeter of troops of the 506th Parachute Infantry Regiment approaching the C-47 troop carriers. The men included Easy Company, known to many as the 'Band of Brothers' who had trained at Slapton Sands.

1. Balkoski, Joseph. *Utah Beach*, 2005. Stackpole Books p.69.
2. Balkoski, Joseph. *Utah Beach*, 2005. p.70-71.
3. Freeman, Ray. *We remember D-Day*, 1994. Dartmouth History Research Group.
4. Penrose, Jane (ed). *The D-Day Companion*, 2009. Osprey. p.105.
5. Balkoski, Joseph. *Utah Beach*, 2005. p.186.
6. Bailey Roderick, *Forgotten voices of D-Day,* 2009. Ebury Press. p.286.
7. Balkoski, Joseph. *Utah Beach*, 2005. p,186.

Memorials

THE SLAPTON SANDS evacuation monument and the Torcross tank memorial are commemorative artefacts. They act as memorials of historic events despite differences of opinion about their meaning and existence. Whatever the cause of remembrance and dedication the memorials unfortunately have a history associated with error and omission.[1]

Both memorials have in the past been defaced by graffiti. The evacuation monument and tank memorial serve respectively to commemorate the sacrifices made by civilians in the nearby villages of South Hams and the loss of American troops on exercise in the English Channel during the Second World War. The two events commemorated occurred at different times and places. No consensus was taken from local people as to the design, inscription or the location of the two memorials. For local people the memorials commemorate events associated with personal and family history.

The evacuation monument is located on Slapton Beach, just off the A379 road on what was the site of the Royal Sands Hotel before it was completely destroyed during the Second World War. The obelisk memorial built of Dartmoor granite is flanked by two flagpoles. It was first erected in 1945 by the US armed forces to commemorate the evacuation of those civilians who were expelled from their homes in the South Hams in December 1943, to allow the area to be used as a battle training area. A second ceremony took place in 1954. Due to storm damage the monument was rebuilt in 2001 (giving an opportunity to add the name of the village Sherford to the inscription which had been omitted on the original monument) and to relocate it closer to Slapton Ley.

The Torcross tank memorial stands on a plinth close to Slapton Ley and is flanked by two flagpoles. It was established by the late Ken Small who had retrieved the Sherman tank from Slapton Bay in 1984, which he then dedicated as a memorial to those American troops who had lost their lives in the Exercise Tiger disaster on the 28th April 1944 in Lyme Bay off the Dorset Coast. The Sherman tank had not seen service at Normandy and was not directly concerned with the Tiger disaster. It is a retrieved object that is only meaningful in the landscape in which it was found. Walls and Williams in their detailed study of both memorials state that tanks are rarely employed in Britain as war monuments given their aggressive connotations.[2] Despite this, local people, visitors and war veterans continue to visit the site to pay homage to the dead and missing American servicemen by laying wreaths and flowers on or near the tank or to attend memorial services. Unlike the Exercise Tiger monument in the USA that is painted in military colours, the Torcross memorial is shrouded in a black preservative that has over the years has been applied annually. The late Ken Small saw himself as the sole custodian of the tank, and arguably because of his absence the tank is now beginning to look fatigued.

---

1. Walls, Samuel and Williams, Howard, 'Death and Memory on the Home Front: Second World War Commemoration in the South Hams, Devon'. 2010 *Cambridge Archaeological Journal* 20:1, 49-66
2. Walls and Williams, p.61.

Bibliography

Alter, Jonathan and Crouch, Daniel. " *My Dear Moon'. Rear Admiral Don Pardee Moon"*, 2005. Book Surge, USA.

Ambrose, Stephen. *D-Day, June 6, The Battle for the Normandy Beaches,* 2002. Simon & Schuster. USA.

Ambrose, Stephen. *Band of Brothers,* 2001. Pocket Books UK.

Andrade, Allan. *Leopoldville, Remembrance for Valor,* 2007. Private publication. USA.

Bailey, Roderick. *Forgotten voices of D-Day,* 2009. Ebury Press.

Balkoski, Joseph. *UTAH Beach, The Amphibious Landings and Airborne Operations on D-Day,* 2005. Stackpole Books. USA.

Barnett, Correlli. *Engage the Enemy More Closely: The Royal Navy in the Second World War,* 1991. Hodder and Stoughton.

Bass, Richard, *Spirits of the Sand: The History of the US Army Assault Training Centre, Woolacombe,* 1991. Lee Publishing,

Bass, Richard, *Precious Cargo: The History of the US Army 146th Quartermaster Truck Company,* 1993. Lee Publishing.

Bass, Richard, *Exercise Tiger: The D-Day practice landings tragedies uncovered,* 2008. Tommie's Guides: Eastbourne.

Bass, Richard, *Spirits of the Sand, Field Edition* 2005 no publisher cited.

Beesley, Patrick. *Very Special Intelligence. The Story of the Admiralty's Operational Intelligence Centre 1939-1945,* 2000. Chatham Publishing. London.

Beevor, Antony. *D-Day, the Battle for Normandy,* 2009. Viking.

Bennett, G. *An American Infantry Regiment in Devon. The US Army 116th Infantry Regiment, Omaha Beach and the Photography of Olin Dows,* 2003. Flash and Thunder Press. USA.

Bennet, James. *The Rohna Disaster: World War 11's Secret Tragedy,* 1999. Private publication

Berberrich, C. *The Image of the English Gentlemen in Twentieth Century Literature, Englishness and Nostalgia,* 2007. Ashgate Publishing.

Bernage, Georges, *Normandy 1944. First US Army,* 2004. Heimdal, France.

Black, Col. Robert. *The Battalion, The Dramatic Story of the 2nd Ranger Battalion in World War 11,* 2006. Stackpole Books. USA.

Bott, Lloyd. *The Secret War from the River Dart 1942- 1945. The Story of the Royal Navy's 15th Motor Gunboat Flotilla,* 1997. The Dartmouth History Research Group: Dartmouth, Devon.

Bradbeer, Grace. *The Land Changed It's Face, The Evacuation of Devon's South Hams 1943-44,* 1973. David & Charles, Newton Abbot.

Bruce, Colin, *Invaders: British and American experiences of seaborne landings 1939-1945,* 1999. Chatham Publishing: London.

Bucton, Henry. *Friendly Invasion, Memories of Operation Bolero. The American Occupation of Britain 1942-1945,* 2006. Phillimore

Butcher, Harry. *My Three Years With Eisenhower: The Personal Diary of Captain Harry C Butcher, USNR, Naval Aide to General Eisenhower, 1942- 1945,* 1946 Simon & Schuster, New York.

Chapman, T. *Outbreak 1939, The World goes to War,* 2009. Virgin Books.

Chickerin Roger, Forster, Stig and Griener, Bernd (eds). *A World at Total War. Global conflict and the politics of destruction, 1937-1945,* 2005. Cambridge University Press: Cambridge.

Clamp, Arthur. *United States Naval Base Plymouth 1943-1945,* 1994. Private Publication.

Clamp, Arthur. *Dartmouth and Kingswear during the Second World War 1935-45,* 1994. Private Publication.

Clayton, Aileen. *The enemy is Listening. The story of the Y Service,* 1980. Hutchinson & Co.

Collier, Basil, *The Defence of the United Kingdom,* 1957. HMSO.

Cook, Arthur. *Exmouth at War, Life on the Home Front in Devon during World War 2,* 2010. Halsgrove: Wellington, Somerset.

Crouch Daniel and Alter Jonathan (eds) *"My Dear Moon" Rear Admiral Don Pardo Moon.* 2005 Book Surge, USA.

Davies, E. and Grove, E. *The Royal Naval College, Dartmouth,* 1980. Gieves and Hawkes.

Devon and Cornwall, A Preliminary Survey. Report by University of The South West, Exeter, 1947. Wheaton, Exeter.

Dobinson, Colin. *AA Command. Britain's anti-aircraft defences of the Second World War,* 2001. Methuen: London.

Ellis, L.F. *Victory in the West, Volume 1, The Battle of Normandy.* The Naval and Military Press. History of the Second World War. 2004 United Kingdom Military Series.

Fenby, John. *The Sinking of the Lancastria, Britain's greatest disaster and Churchill's Cover-up,* 2005. Simon & Schuster.

Fowler, Will. *The Commandos at Dieppe: Rehearsal for D-Day. Operation Cauldron No 4 Commando attacks on the Hess Battery 19 August 1942*, 2002. Harper Collins: London.

Francois, Dominique. *Normandy. Breaching the Atlantic Wall*, 2008. Zenith Press. USA.

Freeman, Ray. *We Remember D-Day, British and American Eyewitness Accounts from the Dart Area and Normandy*, 1994. Dartmouth History Research Group: Dartmouth Museum.

Freeman, Ray. *Memories of War. By local people at home and abroad 1939-1946.* 1995. Dartmouth History Research Group

Gardiner, Juliet. *The GI's in Wartime Britain*, 1992. Collins and Brown.

Gaydon, Tina. *Braunton*, 1989. Badger Books: Devon.

Glenton, Robert. *The Royal Oak Affair. The Saga of Admiral Collard and Bandmaster Barnacle*, 1991. Leo Cooper: London.

Godson, Susan. *Viking of Assault: Admiral John Leslie Hall, jr., and Amphibious Warfare*, 1982. University Press of America: Washington.

Gray, Todd. *Exeter Remembers the War. Life on the Home Front*, 2005. The Mint Press: Exeter.

Harding, John. *A Child's War in Cornwall. The Voice of a Schoolboy*, 2010. Ryelands, Wellington, Somerset.

Harris, Len. *A Two Hundred Year History of Appledore Shipyards*, 1992. Hargill Partners: Devon.

Hart, Liddell, L.H. *Thoughts on War 1944*. Faber & Faber. London.

Hinsley, F.H. (ed) *British Intelligence in the Second World War, its influence on strategy and operations*, 1988. vol 3 part1 HMSO.

Hinton, James.*Women, Social Leadership and the Second World War,* 2002. Oxford University Press

Hocking, Charles. *Dictionary of Disasters at Sea During the age of Steam, Volume 1*, 1969. Lloyds Register of Shipping.

Hoyt, Edwin. *The Invasion Before Normandy: The Secret Battle of Slapton Sands*, 1987. Robert Hale, London.

Hummelchen, G. *German Schnelleboote (E boats). Profile Warship no 32*. Profile Publications Ltd: Windsor.

Isaac, Walter. *The Way Twas, A County Boy's Memories.* nd : private publication.

Jones, Lt. Clifford. *Neptune Training, The Administrative and Logistical History of the European Theatre of Operations,* 1946 US Army Centre of Military History.

Krein, Benhardt. *Once around the Block*, 2011. Authorhouse. USA.

Lavery, Brian. *Assault Landing Craft. Design, Construction and Operation*, 2009. Pen & Sword, Barnsley.

Lawrence, Wendy. *Exercise Tiger, The forgotten Sacrifice of the Silent Few*, 2013. Fonthill.

Legg, Rodney. *Dorset at War*, 2010. Halsgrove.

Levine, Joshua. *Operation Fortitude The story of the spy operation that saved D-Day,* 2011. Harper Collins: London.

Lewis, Nigel. *Exercise Tiger: The Dramatic True Story of a Hidden Tragedy of World War 2*, 1990. Prentice Hall. New York.

Longmate, Norman. *The G.I's The Americans in Britain 1942-1945*, 1975. Hutchinson: London.

Love, Robert and Major, John (eds), *The Year of D-Day, The 1944 Diary of Admiral Sir Bertram Ramsay*, 1994. The University of Hull Press.

Mackay, Robert. *Half the Battle: Britain in during the Second World War,* 2002. Manchester University Press.

Mackay, Roy and Parry, Simon, *The Last Blitz, Operation Steinbock: Luftwaffe operations over Britain January to June 1944,* 2011. Red Kite: Walton on Thames.

Montgomery of Alamein. *A History of Warfare*, 1968. Collins: London.

Morison, Samuel. *The Invasion of France and Germany 1944-1945,* 2011. Navy Institute Press. Maryland, USA

Murch, Muriel and Murch, David, *American and British Naval Forces at Salcombe and Slapton 1943-1945*, 1994. Phantom Publishing, Salcombe.

O'Brien, Terence. *Civil Defence*, 1955. HMSO.

Pack, Captain S.W. *Britannia at Dartmouth*, 1966. Alvin Redman.

Penrose, Jane (ed). *The D-Day Companion*, 2004. Osprey.

Piper, Lilian. *Report of the Evacuation which followed the heavy raids of April on Plymouth, 1941.* Friends of War Victims Relief Committee.

Price-Rose, Robin and Parnell, Jean. *The Land we left behind: A pictorial history and memories of the war years in the South Hams*, 2004. Orchard Publication, Chudleigh, Devon.

Reynolds, David, *Rich Relations. The American occupation of Britain 1942-1945*, 1995. Harper Collins: London.

Rottman, Gordon. *Landing Ship, Tank (LST) 1942-2002*, 2005. Osprey, Oxford.

Rottman, Gordon, *Landing Craft, Infantry and Fire Support*, 2009. Osprey, Oxford,

Saunders, Anthony. *Hitler's Atlantic Wall*, 2001. Sutton: Stroud.

Slaughter, John. *Omaha Beach and Beyond, The long march of Sgt Bob Slaughter*, 2009. Zenith Press: USA.

Small, Ken. *The Forgotten Dead*, 1998. Bloomsbury: London.

Smith, Peter. *Naval Warfare in the English Channel, 1939-1945*, 2007. Pen & Sword: Barnsley.

Smith, Sydney Clare. *The Golden Reign, The Story of My Friendship with Lawrence of Arabia*. 1940 Cassell.

Stranack, David, *Strete: Tales and Pictures of the Past*, 2009, Blackawton and Strete History Group, Kingsbridge: Devon.

Summersby Kay, *Eisenhower Was My Boss*, 1948. Prentice-Hall: New York.

Summersby, Kay. *Past Forgetting, My Love Affair with Dwight D. Eisenhower*, 1977. Collins: London.

Talty, Stephan. *Agent Garbo the Brilliant, Eccentric Secret Agent who Tricked Hitler and Saved D-Day*, 2012. Houghton Mifflin Harcourt: New York.

Thomas, David and Holmes, Patrick. *Queen Mary and the Cruiser. The Curacoa Disaster*, 1997. Leo Cooper.

Titmuss, Richard. *Problems of Social Policy*, 1950. HMSO: London.

Turner, E.S. *The Phoney War on the Home Front*, 1961. Michael Joseph.

Wakefield, Kenneth. *The Fighting Grasshoppers, US Liaison Aircraft operations in Europe, 1942-1945: United States Liaison Aircraft*, 1990. Midland Publishing.

Walling, R. *The story of Plymouth*, 1950. Westaway Books.

Walls, Samuel and Williams, Howard. *Death and Memory on the Home Front: Second World War Commemoration in the South Hams, Devon*.
  Cambridge Archaeological Journal 2010 20:1.

Wasley, Gerald. *Devon in the Thirties. The way We Were*, 1998. Halsgrove: Tiverton.

Wasley, Gerald. *Devon at War 1939-1945*, 2011. Halsgrove: Wellington.

Weigley, Russell. *Eisenhower's Lieutenants; The Campaign of France and Germany, 1939- 1941*, 1981. John Wiley.

Williams, David, *Kingswear at War*, 2011. Kingswear Historians, Devon.

Winser. John de S. *The D-Day Ships, and Neptune: the Greatest Amphibious Operation in History*, 1994. World Ship Society: Kendal.

Wright, Patrick. *The Village that Died for England*, 2002. Faber & Faber.

Young, J. *Britain's Sea War, A Diary of Ship Losses 1939- 1949*, 1969. Patrick Stephens.

Yung, Christopher. *Gators of Neptune: Naval Amphibious Planning for the Normandy Invasion*, 2006 National Institute Press, Annapolis, Maryland. USA.

The Slapton Memorial was presented by the US Government in recognition of those who gave up their homes for the military training area used in the prelude to D-Day.